"In *Religion and Film: The Basics*, Dr. Solano offers the student of religion and film an invaluable resource for navigating contemporary life: a tool for understanding ourselves and the (religious, political, racial) other in and through the cinema. The book is equal parts accessible and irenic, drawing on the best of religion and film scholarship while also being eminently readable. I highly recommend it."

Kutter Callaway, Associate Professor of Theology and Culture, Fuller Theological Seminary, USA

RELIGION AND FILM

THE BASICS

Religion and Film: The Basics is an accessible and engaging introduction to the history, diverse approaches, and ideas associated within the study of religion and film. Referencing films from around the world from the early 20th century to the present day, this unique introduction includes the following topics:

- the history and dynamics of religion and film
- various methods to approach religion and film
- the evolution of religion and film scholarship
- film genre and theory
- world religions and film
- unique themes—from race and gender roles to karma and redemption.

A fascinating range of films are discussed, from early silent films such as *Hypocrites* to recent releases such as *Minari*. Five genres are explored, including horror in *The Wicker Man* (UK) and *Let the Right One In* (Sweden), and world religions are analyzed in films such as *OMG*, *The Big Lebowski*, and *Malcolm X*. Tropes examined include gender in *Water*, karma in *It's a Wonderful Life*, death in *Biutiful*, redemption in *Magnolia*, and evil in *Get Out*.

With helpful features including recommendations for further study and key films to view, this book is an ideal starting point for students approaching religion and film for the first time as well as those interested in learning more about the field while broadening their methods, knowledge of film, and their film canon.

Jeanette Reedy Solano is Associate Professor at California State University, Fullerton, USA. She is Co-chair of the Religion, Film, and Visual Culture Unit in the American Academy of Religion and serves on the Editorial Board for the *Journal of Religion and Film* for which she has served as a film critic for Sundance and other film festivals.

The Basics

JUDAISM
JACOB NEUSNER

RELIGION (second edition)
MALORY NYE

BUDDHISM
CATHY CANTWELL

ISLAM (second edition)
COLIN TURNER

CHRISTIANITY
BRUCE CHILTON

CHRISTIAN THEOLOGY
MURRAY RAE

ROMAN CATHOLICISM (second edition)
MICHAEL WALSH

THE QUR'AN (second edition)
MASSIMO CAMPANINI

RELIGION IN AMERICA
MICHAEL PASQUIER

MORMONISM
DAVID J. HOWLETT AND
JOHN-CHARLES DUFFY

RELIGION AND SCIENCE (second edition)
PHILIP CLAYTON

THE BIBLE (second edition)
JOHN BARTON

QUEER THEOLOGIES
CHRIS GREENOUGH

CHRISTIAN ETHICS
ROBIN GILL

BAHA'I FAITH
CHRISTOPHER BUCK

QUAKERISM
MARGERY POST ABBOTT AND
CARL ABBOTT

THOMAS AQUINAS
FRANKLIN T. HARKINS

BIBLE AND FILM
MATTHEW S. RINDGE

RELIGION AND FILM
JEANETTE REEDY SOLANO

For more information about this series, please visit: https://www.routledge.com/The-Basics/book-series/B

RELIGION AND FILM
THE BASICS

Jeanette Reedy Solano

LONDON AND NEW YORK

First published 2022
by Routledge
2 Park Square, Milton Park, Abingdon, Oxon OX14 4RN

and by Routledge
605 Third Avenue, New York, NY 10158

Routledge is an imprint of the Taylor & Francis Group, an informa business

© 2022 Jeanette Reedy Solano

The right of Jeanette Reedy Solano to be identified as author of this work has been asserted by him/her/them in accordance with sections 77 and 78 of the Copyright, Designs and Patents Act 1988.

All rights reserved. No part of this book may be reprinted or reproduced or utilised in any form or by any electronic, mechanical, or other means, now known or hereafter invented, including photocopying and recording, or in any information storage or retrieval system, without permission in writing from the publishers.

Trademark notice: Product or corporate names may be trademarks or registered trademarks, and are used only for identification and explanation without intent to infringe.

British Library Cataloguing-in-Publication Data
A catalogue record for this book is available from the British Library

Library of Congress Cataloging-in-Publication Data
Names: Solano, Jeanette Reedy, author.
Title: Religion and film: the basics / Jeanette Reedy Solano.
Description: Abingdon, Oxon; New York, NY: Routledge, 2022. |
Series: The basics | Includes bibliographical references and index. |
Identifiers: LCCN 2021023200
Subjects: LCSH: Motion pictures—Religious aspects. |
Religion in motion pictures.
Classification: LCC PN1995.5 .S65 2022 | DDC 791.43/682—dc23
LC record available at https://lccn.loc.gov/2021023200

ISBN: 978-0-367-13519-5 (hbk)
ISBN: 978-0-367-13520-1 (pbk)
ISBN: 978-0-429-02882-3 (ebk)

DOI: 10.4324/9780429028823

Typeset in Bembo
by codeMantra

I dedicate this book to two fearless women, Nancy Marguerite and Lillian "Mimi" Kuhns (my grandmother and great grandmother) who, in 1919, packed their bags in Missouri and headed west to Hollywood, California to be in the movies.

I dedicate this book to my mother, Dorothy, who took me to see *The Little Prince* at the Cinerama Dome on Sunset Blvd in Hollywood in 1974 where I had my first experience of what Nathaniel Dorksy calls "devotional cinema."

Finally, I dedicate this book to my family, Narciso, Dante, and Aurora for the countless films you have watched with me and your support.

CONTENTS

List of figures xiv
Acknowledgements xvii

1 **Discovering the divine in the dark: an introduction to religion and film** 1
   Religion and film dynamics: a unique coupling 2
   The history of religion *in* film 6
   The evolution of Religion and Film Studies 11
   Structure of *Religion and Film: The Basics* 15
   Criteria for the selection of films analyzed in this volume 18
   A note for instructors 19
   For further viewing 19
   For further reading 20

2 **Dimensions and bricolage: methodological approaches to religion and film** 21
   Theological-biblical lenses 22
   Religious studies approaches to film 28
   Cultural studies and reception studies approaches 32

Film studies approaches 39
  For further reading 52
3 **Flickering faith: exploring world religions through film** **53**
  Hinduism 54
  Judaism 60
  Buddhism 69
  Christianity 78
  Islam 83
  Inter-religious relations in film 88
  For further viewing 94
  For further reading 95
4 **Shaking with fear or laughter: exploring religion and film through film genres** **96**
  Films analyzed in this chapter 96
  Science-fiction 97
  Comedy 103
  Horror 109
  Drama 114
  Pilgrimage/Quest/Road Trip 120
  Documentary Film 126
  For future viewing 134
  For further reading 134
5 **Demons, redeemers, ghosts and more: recurrent tropes in religion and film** **135**
  Films and tropes analyzed in this chapter 135
  Evil and suffering 136
  Sex, gender roles, and religion 143
  Religion and race 149
  Redemption and Healing 156
  Karma and Reincarnation 163

	Death and the afterlife	169
	For further viewing	175
	For further reading	176
6	**Before the credits roll: a conclusion**	**177**
	That's a wrap!	177
	The present and future of religion and film	179
	Commissioning of the reader	192

Appendix A: films analyzed in *Religion and Film: The Basics* — 193
Bibliography — 195
Index — 203

FIGURES

1.1	The unveiling of Naked Truth in *Hypocrites* (Lois Weber, 1915)	9
1.2	The Naked Truth revealing hypocrisy with her mirror in *Hypocrites* (Lois Weber, 1915)	10
3.1	Kanji and Krishna, now friends, let go of religion at end of *OMG* (Umesh Shukla, 2012)	56
3.2	Satyavati, Jai Santoshi Maa and her perspective of devotion in *Jai Santoshi Maa* (Vijay Sharma, 1974)	60
3.3	Zvia and Abed smoke together while gazing at Temple Mount/Al Aqsa mosque (Yaelle Kayam, *Ha'har (Mountain)*, 2015)	68
3.4	Moon scene with Lillian Gish and Richard Barthelmess in *Broken Blossoms* (D.W. Griffith, 1919)	70
3.5	Daigo prepares the body of his recently-deceased father while pregnant wife watches in *Departures* (Yojiro Takita, 2008)	74
3.6	Abe attempts to exorcise Benny in *Free in Deed* (Jake Mahaffy, 2015)	82
3.7	Malcolm X during Hajj in *Malcolm X* (Spike Lee, 1992)	88

4.1	Dr. Banks makes contact with the heptapods in *Arrival* (Denis Villeneuve, 2015)	102
4.2	David and Goliath sermon in *The Pilgrim* (Charles Chaplin, 1923)	105
4.3	Reza the Lizard is besieged by eager townsfolk in *The Lizard* (Kamal Tabrizi, 2004)	108
4.4	Lord Summerisle leads a ritual before burning Sergeant Howie alive in *The Wicker Man* (Robin Hardy, 1973)	111
4.5	Aquiano explains to Wilberforce how shackles are used on slaves in *Amazing Grace* (Michael Apted, 2007)	119
4.6	Learning compassion as a family in *Little Miss Sunshine* (Jonathan Dayton, Valerie Faris, 2006)	124
4.7	The Hoovers sit together, touching, and look with one accord as they are sentenced by security guard in *Little Miss Sunshine* (Jonathan Dayton, Valerie Faris, 2006)	125
4.8	Gibreel surveys the disputed border between Israel and Palestine in *5 Broken Cameras* (Emad Burnat, 2005)	129
5.1	Chris is trapped in the Sunken Place in *Get Out* (Jordan Peele, 2017)	142
5.2	Shakuntala learns the truth about the treatment of widows from her guru Sadananda in *Water* (Deepa Mehta, 2007)	146
5.3	The public torture of Topiltzin by Capitán Cristobal with Maria and Fray Diego looking on in *The Other Conquest* (Salvador Carrasco, 2000)	151
5.4	Fray Diego realizes Topiltzin's conversion to Christianity is mixed with indigenous beliefs in *The Other Conquest* (Salvador Carrasco, 2000)	152
5.5	Josué comforts Dora after her collapse in the House of Miracles, an inverted pietà in *Central Station* (Walter Salles, 1998)	158
5.6	(a and b) Frank Mackey confronts his father Earl on his death bed in *Magnolia* (P.T. Anderson, 1999)	161

5.7 The ghost of Huay manifests as Tong and Auntie Jen look on in *Uncle Boonmee Who Can Recall His Past Lives* (Apichatpong Weerasethakul, 2010)   167

5.8 Uxbal looks towards his deceased father in the snowy wood and crosses over at the end of *Biutiful* (Alejandro González Iñárritu, 2010)   175

ACKNOWLEDGEMENTS

My exploration of religion and film has always been a communal one. From my religion and literature class at the University of Chicago Divinity School to screenings with my colleagues in Pasadena sponsored by Fuller Seminary's Reel Spirituality Institute. For almost two decades, post-screening conversations and collegial challenges have shaped me and made this book possible. I would like to thank my California cohorts: Rob Johnston, Craig Detweiler, Amir Hussain, Cathy Barsotti, and Kutter Callaway for sharing their passion for film and scintillating conversation. I am grateful for the deep friendships forged working with my academic colleagues in the American Academy of Religion's Religion, Film, and Visual Culture Group which I joined as a steering committee member in 2008, later serving as Co-chair. These AAR colleagues include John C. Lyden, Rachel Wagner, Stephanie Knauss, Daniel White Hodge, Jenny Caplan, Ken Derry, Adnan Hussain, S. Brent Plate, Rebecca Moody, Antonio Sison, Joel Mayward, and my favorite New York cinephile Joe Kickasola. I will always treasure our dinners, from Nova Scotia to San Diego, discussing film late into the night.

I am indebted to my students at California State University, Fullerton who have helped me become a better teacher of religion and film and for indulging my love of independent and classic film.

Thanks as well to colleagues and friends who read and offered feedback on drafts of chapters, including, Lina Verchery, Clair Morrisey, Dorothy Reedy, and Mugdha Yeolekar. A special thanks to Patty Yoho who allowed me to escape to her mountain cabin for a month to finally start writing this book and Sue and Steve Hogren for their support.

I especially want to thank John Lyden for inviting me to the Sundance Film Festival for several years to review films for *The Journal of Religion and Film* and for reading drafts of some chapters. My Park City film adventures were shared with the wonderful Bill Blizek and his wife Monica whose mentorship I cherish. The Windrider Forum at Sundance deepened my knowledge of the intersection of religion and film as well.

I am grateful for Amy Doffegnies, editorial assistant at Routledge, for her quick responses and enduring patience through this process, especially during the Covid-19 pandemic and the many delays this engendered as I wrote. I would also like to thank Rebecca Shillabeer, publisher of Routledge Religion for inviting me to write this book and providing encouraging feedback when I most needed it. I also want to thank the anonymous readers who reviewed the proposal and manuscript for Routledge with care and provided incisive feedback.

I want to acknowledge the independent filmmakers from Nigeria to New Zealand who toil without studio support to create amazing films. Your work fills these pages. For all the directors, actors, writers, producers, musicians, and sound engineers who have shared their thoughts with me I am so grateful.

Finally, I want to thank my husband, Narciso, who cooked delicious food, kept the household going, and allowed me to escape in order to write. To my daughter Aurora, my love, I needed your notes and hugs more than you know. Dante, my son who loves film as much as I do, I treasure our countless hours during lockdown watching *The Story of Film* and Criterion classic films until 2 a.m., may you and all film lovers, enjoy these pages.

DISCOVERING THE DIVINE IN THE DARK
AN INTRODUCTION TO RELIGION AND FILM

When I tell people my niche within the academic study of religion is "Religion and Film," three general reactions ensue: incredulity: what could something as serious as religion possibly have to do with movies, a relatively shallow pedestrian pop art form?; analogical excitement: "do you talk about Buddhism in the *Matrix* and *Star Wars*?"; or cinematic devotion: those who believe a certain director is a divine genius or a certain film is transcendent. Ask yourself, where would you place yourself today, the purist skeptic, the enthusiastic analogist looking for connections, or the devotee? To those in the first category, I explain the value of analyzing both religious and secular films as a fecund and serious source for discussion of religious or spiritual ideas. The second group, the analogists, can list dozens of films where they discovered religious themes, but they tend to stop at analogy, for instance: Neo in *The Matrix* serving as a Christ-like figure. Few in the second or third groups consider how the medium of film itself is a uniquely rich art form for religious studies. Those in the third group are perhaps the most open, as they have already experienced the powerful connection between film and religion. *Religion and Film: The Basics* is written for all these groups.

Why learn about religion and film? First, visual media has supplanted texts in late-modern culture as a site in which social and existential questions are grappled with. Today, people are more likely to reference *The Hunger Games* as a study of political power than Machiavelli's *The Prince* or watch a filmic version of a beloved text, like *Lord of the Rings* or *Pride and Prejudice* rather than tackle hefty tomes. Another reason is the sheer influence of the billion-dollar film industry and its global popularity: China and India each boast more tickets sold per capita in 2020 than the USA. Beyond box office, films often pull off the scab of festering social wounds, from racial injustice to sexual abuse to ideological divides and discussing them often connects back to religion, or religious themes. Discussing religion and film together engenders important and sometimes difficult conversations we should be having. Who should consider examining religion and film in conjunction? Anyone who is fascinated with exploring humanity itself, 85% of whom self-identify as religious.

RELIGION AND FILM DYNAMICS: A UNIQUE COUPLING

Let us consider the innate connection film and religion might have. Human beings are visual creatures and whether we are speaking of Paleolithic French cave paintings (Lascaux, c. 17,000–c. 15,000 BCE) or the latest work of Terrence Malick, we use images to capture history and human life and to create beauty and meaning. In *The Republic* (375 BCE) Plato confessed: "I strain after images" (488a). Most 21st-century film lovers concur with Plato, we long for images and filmic stories to help make sense of our world and our place within in it. Films are more than images, they are *moving* images, flickering frames of light. So how is film a unique art form and how might it evoke spiritual insight or even religious experiences in viewers? Beginning with several French film theorists, then moving on to arguments fromreligious studies scholars and filmmakers, I argue for a natural affinity between religion and film.

The relationship between cinema and religion/spirituality has drawn the interest of film theorists since the early days of cinema. For example, in 1924 Jean Epstein (1897–1953) a French impressionist filmmaker, novelist, and early film theorist found film to be animistic, polytheistic, and theogonic. By this he meant that filmed objects are dramatized, animated, and take on a life of their own. The world depicted on film is not our everyday reality, these "lives are like the lives in charms and amulets, the ominous tabooed subjects of certain primitive religions." Understanding the power of these animated images and the cinematic world they inhabit can help us better understand the power of animistic religion. The personality of the director also determines whether a film is theogonic and soulful or plebian. Epstein called cinema "poetry's most powerful medium" upon which early 20th-century artists had entrusted their highest hopes.[1] Fellow Frenchman Antonin Artaud, actor, playwright, and author, also noted the sorcery-like effect film had on viewers: "raw cinema (*le cinéma bruit*) emits something of the atmosphere of a trance, conducive to certain revelations" noting the "physical intoxication" one feels when watching film. Like Epstein, Artaud felt that cinema uniquely moved the human spirit, that it had the power to rummage the depths of the mind, to point viewers to the really real. In a 1928 essay entitled "Sorcery and Cinema," Artaud called this the "occult," the reality beyond the mundane. Filmmakers are modern shamans, artistic "Illuminati" according to Artaud who wrote a short story that inspired the first surrealist film *The Seashell and the Clergyman* (Germaine Dulac, France, 1928). Although the melting images of this film confounded many viewers, it displays Artaud's conceit that cinema, above all "should express things of the mind, the inner life of consciousness" for this is film's most profound purpose, not narrative storytelling.[2] The only way to understand this surrealistic film, he instructed viewers, is to look deep within themselves to the hidden life. In an exhausted post-World War I Europe, many artists hoped film would offer them a new window into reality, reveal the hidden life, and allow them to dream again.

French film critic and theorist Andre Bazín began his 1951 essay "Cinema and Theology" by declaring: "The cinema has always been interested in God" by which he meant not only have religious stories inspired much of early cinema but also the idea that film captures reality and all reality is full of the immanence of God. He spoke of films as "a kind of miracle" and referred to film as a phenomenon of "salvation and grace" (Bazin, 1997, 61). Bazin was a Catholic dissident, a Personalist, part of the Novelle Théologie movement, and the spiritual father of the French New Wave (Francois Truffaut, Jean-Luc Godard, Agnes Varda, et al.). In a post-World War II utilitarian world, he hoped cinema could lead to spiritual self-interrogation by pointing us to truths beyond the mundane. Bazin believed photographic images could catapult us through reality to the truth. This trust in the photographic image explains why Bazin championed naturalistic filmmaking and detested montage. He is yet another thinker who argued for the fundamental connection between religion and film.

Nathanial Dorsky, an experimental filmmaker whose ideas are more fully developed in the next chapter, builds on Bazin's affective theory with his theory of "devotional cinema." By this he does not mean film is traditionally religious, but rather that it sparks an opening or interruption that allows us to experience what is hidden and accept with our hearts our given situation. As an editor and photographer, Dorsky is keenly attuned to how film affects our unique human metabolism, i.e., how our brains process information, emotion, and knowledge. Dorsky turns to the technical features of film: intermittent light/vision, time, and editing and explains how they affect us. The intermittent quality of film is close to how we see all reality, i.e., in bits and pieces. Thus, when we watch a film that handles this intermittence deftly, our minds are stimulated in a unique way. Time is one of the most powerful ways film affects the viewer and Dorsky delineates two types: (1) relative time in which we see actions have effects and help the narrative advance and (2) absolute time, in which the viewer is propelled into nowness and reality opens up. Devotional cinema, and not all films qualify as such, incorporates both types of time. Editing is the final influential factor in devotional cinema. Editors control both the narrative and the effect by using shots and cuts. Shots and cuts are cinema's primal handmaidens as the former establishes the visual connection and evokes emotion, and the cut brings clarity and awakens our view. For cinema to be truly transformative, according to Dorsky, luminous shots must engage our being and then are "popped like soap bubbles by the cut" (Dorsky, in Mitchell and Plate, 2007, 413). All filmic elements: intermittence of light and image, use of relative and absolute time, and shots and cuts, must be crafted with artistic intention to produce devotional cinema that can be spiritually transformative.

Another understanding of the unique dynamics of film as they relate to religion is provided by S. Brent Plate, a religious studies scholar and one of the pioneers in the field of Religion and Film. He takes a functionalist approach arguing that religion and film are naturally coupled because they are *like* each other in that both re-create a world and invite your participation in that world. In *Cinema and the Re-Creation of the World* (2008), Plate analyzes the similarities in structure between religion and film. He clearly distinguishes his approach from the "film-as-text" literary approaches, theological "spot-the Christ-figure" approaches, or discovery of theological tropes typical of early Religion and Film Studies. Films function, according to Plate, by recreating the known world and then presenting the alternative version of the world to their viewers/worshippers. He echoes Dorsky by asserting that religions and films each create alternate worlds by using the raw materials of space, time, and filmic elements (camera angles and movements, framing devices, lighting, costume, acting, editing, and other aspects of production). Religions "edit" reality by setting objects and time and calling them sacred. A more detailed explanation of Plate's theory in which he applies Etianne Sourniau's film theory to anthropologist Cifford Geertz's religion theory is found in Chapter 2.

Film and religion should be studied together. Films are our new myths, stories that grapple with the most fundamental of human dilemmas and attempt to answer big existential questions such as where did we come from?, how ought we live?, how did the world begin?, and what happens after we die? Various religious studies scholars have pursued the idea that films have become our new religious myths, including John C. Lyden who offers us another functionalist answer to the skeptics in the first group who question why we should study religion and film. Lyden, editor of *The Journal of Religion and Film* and author of *Film as Religion: Myths, Morals, and Rituals* (2003, updated in 2019), fully developed the thesis that film functions like a religion in modern society. Lyden detailed how films create new myths, how film watching is similar to religious ritual, and finally, how these worlds, characters, and stories can create ethical codes and inspire moral codes. He also proposed that religious studies and film studies engage in a new dynamic of equals, an "inter-religious dialogue." Lyden's thesis is detailed in the next chapter as well as his idea of how moral codes found in films can influence viewers' ethics. Some dramatic examples of film fandoms engendering religiosity are Jedism (inspired by *Star Wars* films), which now boasts over 50,000 adherents around the world and has developed rituals (including marriage ceremonies) and Dudeism, inspired by *The Big Lebowski* which ordains Dudeist priests in

The Church of the Latter-Day Dude and has produced Daoist and Buddhist-like scriptures related to the film. Even if you don't formally become a Dudeist or a Trekkie or a Jedi, you may have your own rites and rituals around film: you may prepare ritual foods before you dim the lights either at your home altar (TV) or in a theater, you may watch a certain film ritualistically like *It's a Wonderful Life* every December, there may be certain films that are sacred to you and not to be interrupted, or you may even engage in fun interactive ritual actions like throwing rice during the *Rocky Horror Picture Show* (1975) or spoons during *The Room* (2003).

THE HISTORY OF RELIGION *IN* FILM

The relationship between religion *and* film can be traced back to the dawn of cinema itself as religious stories and figures (especially Jesus and Hebrew prophets) were often the fodder for some of the earliest films made by the Lumiere brothers, Thomas Edison, D.W. Griffith, and Cecil B. De Mille, who created many early biblical epics. The passion story of Jesus inspired films from 1898 (*The Passion Play of Oberammergau*) to *The Passion of the Christ* (2004). Some of the first Jewish films in Yiddish were "Purimspeils" which dramatically portrayed the Book of Esther. Religion and sex inspired early films such as Ferdinand Zecca's *Samson and Delilah* (1902). The first biblically inspired murder story appeared in 1905 in George Melies' Cain-and-Abel-inspired *Justice and Vengeance Pursuing Crime.*

Most of the early creators of film were religious themselves or at least influenced by organized religion. Rather than list the many early filmmakers such as Cecil B. DeMille, D.W. Griffith, et al., who were influenced by religion and highlight how religion was depicted in their work, I would like to focus on one representative film auteur: Lois Weber (1879–1939). Why Weber? She was one of the three great directors of early Hollywood, the other two being D.W. Griffith and Cecil B. DeMille, however few know of her work. In a career that spanned a quarter of a century, Weber wrote, directed, produced, and performed in more than 200 films. Though most of Weber's films are now lost, a handful survive and serve as testimony to her mastery of cinema. She was not only a gifted screenwriter and actor, but she directed, worked with lighting and cameras, marketed, and cut her films. Lois Weber was raised in a devout Anglican Protestant Christian home and wanted to be a missionary as a young girl, but her heart lay in writing stories. Her talent ultimately led her to the stage as a musician and actress in New York City while still a teen. In 1910, she had to return from her dramatic pursuits in New York City in order to support her family in Philadelphia as her father fell ill and died. One hurtful incident during this time proved pivotal for Weber's development as filmmaker and person of faith: the deacons of her church refused to allow her to sing in the church choir because she had morally sullied herself by appearing on stage. Her grandmother counseled her not to be a hypocrite: "If you have chosen a worldly career, don't pretend to be religious." This deeply hurt the devout Lois and ultimately forced her to seek to live out her faith in other ways. To atone for her disdained artistic work, she began to work with her Episcopal church Army in the red light and tenement district of Philadelphia. There she saw immigrant and urban struggles with poverty up close, and they left a perduring impression on her. She was often frustrated with her limited ability to communicate with the immigrants she sought to serve. Although she was banned from artistic expression within the church, she retained this heart of a missionary and social justice pioneer throughout her life. She translated this concern into a series of socially concerned films such as *Shoes* (1916) which deals with the plight of the working poor. By the time, 35-year-old Lois Weber and her husband Phillips Smalley arrived in Hollywood in 1914, she had come to understand cinema as a "voiceless language" that allowed her the creative freedom to "preach to my heart's content."[3] This does not mean that she produced "Christian films," she wrote and directed everything from Shakespeare's *Merchant of Venice* to operas to romances. Her religious commitments informed her work, whether it featured explicitly religious characters (*Hypocrites*, 1915) or centered on social issues like birth control (*The Hand that Rocks the Cradle*, 1917), abortion (*Where Are My Children?* 1916), domestic violence, a critique of gender roles, or consumerism (*Idle Wives*, 1916).

ANALYSIS OF LOIS WEBER'S *HYPOCRITES*

Hypocrites (1915) was the first feature-length film over which Weber exerted complete creative control. This silent film, her first at Bosworth Studios, is an example of faith-informed filmmaking and demonstrates the power of a film to denounce religious hypocrisy while portraying the societal prophetic possibilities of religious figures. As with most of her films Weber wrote and directed the film. She declares her authorship with an opening slide with her photo and the words "Yours Sincerely, Lois Weber" signed across the bottom.

Hypocrites creatively juxtaposes two parallel stories, one set in medieval times and one in 1914 Los Angeles. Weber's interweaving of the timelines and characters was masterful, using dissolves, actors cast in dual roles and parallel *mis en scène* to visually reinforce the connection. Courtney Foote stars as both the weary contemporary minister of a wealthy church in Los Angeles and the ascetic medieval monk, Father Gabriel. The film opens with the modern Rev. Gabriel preaching a sermon on hypocrisy (based on Matt 23;28 to a congregation that is disinterested at best and perturbed at the length of the service). The congregants take their leave and congratulate him on a wonderful sermon and then plot outside the church to ask for his resignation. The Reverend falls asleep, and Weber has his image dissolve into that of an ascetic medieval monk, Father Gabriel, however he is still in modern times and tries to lead the congregants up a steep hill to see the truth, but they all fail the climb. He ends up in a wood and encounters a nymph, the Naked Truth and implores her to come down to his people. Cut to medieval times and medieval Gabriel is laboring on a marble statue in private. When complete, a large crowd of guild members, royalty, fellow monastics, and the community gather anxiously to see the work of art. It is unveiled revealing the figure of a naked woman holding a mirror on a pedestal inscribed with the words "Truth." Of course, the figure scandalizes those gathered, and they turn into an angry mob and kill the artistic monk (Figure 1.1).

Cut back to Father Gabriel as a monk that escorts the Naked Truth to visit his congregation in contemporary times. His congregation is more concerned with social networking and money than spiritual affairs. She brings her mirror to reveal the hidden truths of several different situations. She first visits a political rally where she reveals the politicians are secretly taking bribes despite running on a "platform of honesty." He then escorts her to a high society party where a socialite offers her shawl to cover Truth's nakedness

Figure 1.1 The unveiling of Naked Truth in *Hypocrites* (Lois Weber, 1915).
Source: screenshot by author.

and says she is welcome "if clothed in our ideas." The Naked Truth next visits a home and reveals the indulgence of the children and the moral laxity of the parents. Her mirror next reveals the true character of the suitor as we see him engaged in smoking, drinking, kissing another woman, gambling, and brawling. His seemingly innocent target is also a hypocrite as the mirror reveals she dismissed another ardent young man as life with him would bring her domestic drudgery and she wants the life of luxury that the wealthy suitor promises (Figure 1.2).

There are many ways to interpret the figure of the Naked Truth: is she scripture or morality found within religion? Is she the writer? Is she an ideal in human form? Or most enticing for our purposes, is she a metaphor for cinema? Perhaps Weber wanted viewers to start understanding film as a mirror of culture. We do know that Weber wanted her films to expose the truth and induce moral reform and action. Father Gabriel desperately wants those who gaze in the mirror to recognize their error, whether it be indulgence or adultery or greed. Weber admitted as much: "I hoped the picture would act as a moral force." (Stamp, 2015, 60).

Figure 1.2 The Naked Truth revealing hypocrisy with her mirror in *Hypocrites* (Lois Weber, 1915).
Source: screenshot by author.

Not only did *Hypocrites* establish Lois Weber as a true auteur, but it was recognized as one of the first films to be considered a true work of art. It moved beyond 'photoplay' with her complex story, shots, use of light, framing, and editing. By today's standards *Hypocrites* was a blockbuster. Although, due to the full nudity of the faint figure of Truth it took over a year to be approved by the National Board of Censorship, it ultimately played nationwide to sold-out audiences. It was also the first film to play in grand theater halls as well as nickelodeons. Screenings were accompanied by full orchestras and, in some locations, full choruses and tableaus. It was made for approximately $18,000 and earned $133,000 domestically and abroad. In sum, the work of near-forgotten Lois Weber, one of the most important, prolific, and fiercely independent writer-directors of early Hollywood, is an apt starting point for our examination of religion and film, a study that prefers to focus on independent filmmakers who produce original stories that make you examine yourself, your society, systems, mores, and more.

THE EVOLUTION OF RELIGION AND FILM STUDIES

Critical thought about religion and the power of film goes back to the turn of the 20th century with Herbert Jump enthusiastically outlining "The Religious Possibilities of the Motion Picture" in 1910 and American poet Vachel Lindsey, in 1915, calling cinema a new form of art that the church should embrace if it was placed into skilled hands of "prophet-wizards." Beyond religious insiders advocating for the connection between religion and film, by the 1920s French film theorists such as Jean Epstein and Louis Delluc were reflecting on the cinematic transformation of reality (*photogenie*) and religious parallels. Each decade in the first half of the 20th century brought more theories about religion and film, such as Andre Bazin in the 1940s–1950s, but it was not until the 1980s that a cohort of theorists began to emerge in what we now refer to as Religion and Film Studies as a nascent field.

THE FIELD BEGINS TO EMERGE: 1960s–1980s

By the mid-20th century, the first in-depth studies in religion and film began to be published. This era primarily produced Christian theological treatments of film that focused on religious symbols and themes found in both religious and secular films (Butler, 1969). The 1970s brought more nuanced approaches by film scholars and writers such as Paul Schraeder whose 1972 master's thesis *Transcendental Style in Film* focused on the films of Ozu, Bresson, and Dreyer. Schrader was raised in a strict Christian Reformed Church in the Midwest and attended Calvin College. He went on to cinematic success after writing *Taxi Driver* (1976), *Raging Bull* (1980), and more recently, *First Reformed* (2017). His thesis was important for several reasons: he was one of the first to focus on how a film's style could lead to transcendence rather than its content. "Transcendental style" creates an unease the viewer must resolve, an unexpected act or image leads to stasis which can lead to hierophanies (inbreaking of the sacred). The transcendental director "seeks to escort the viewer to another level of consciousness, a Wholly Other [echoes of Rudolph Otto] world."[4] Schraeder called such directors "spirit guides." The year 1982 brought one of first edited collections of those working in the field, *Religion in Film,* edited by John R. May and Michael Bird. It is worth noting that May and Bird were already reflective about methodology, urged respect for the visual structure of film, and included ideas that would be deepened later such as "religion and popular culture," how film evokes a religious experience, film as hierophany, auteur theory, genre theory, etc.

THE 1990S: METHODOLOGICAL MATURATION AND EXPANSION

Up until this point, most religion and film scholarship discussed religious figures and themes from a distinctly religious perspective and focused on serious arthouse filmmakers like Bresson, Ozu, Tarkovsky, and Dreyer. The 1990s represents an important shift moving beyond arthouse and religious films to analyzing more secular popular films. In addition, important broadening of methodological approaches is evident. An example of this shift is Margaret Miles' 1993 work, *Seeing and Believing: Religion and Values in the Movies* in which she uses lenses of race, gender, and class in her cultural studies approach to film. She is still only considering religion *in* films and limits her focus to Christianity, Islam, and Judaism in popular Hollywood-produced films from 1983 to 1993; however she was asking new questions. She was not interested in finding religious tropes in films, Miles asked what cultural values are exhibited by these filmic narratives? Miles was one of the first to turn from studying films as texts or works of auteurs and consider them as products of a particular historical moment, attending to the film's production, distribution, marketing, funding, box office, critical reception, as well as narrative and directorial intent. She chose films that portrayed pressing social anxieties and offered possible resolutions. Second, Miles was one of the first to examine how a film affects a viewer and how they use a film: merely for entertainment or is meaning negotiated by the viewer as they grapple with their own values? She argued movies fulfill the role the theater played in ancient Greek society where audience members expected the story to force them to ask the question: "how shall we live?"

Method, theory, and pedagogy were also being critically addressed in conferences and publications in the 1990s. One indication of the seriousness of scholarship in this nascent sub-specialty within religious studies was the creation of the Religion, Film, and Visual Culture Group in 1997 which was created after five years as a special topic consultation within the American Academy of Religion (the AAR is the pre-eminent international organization of more than 12,000 religion scholars). This group continues today, and I was honored to serve as co-chair from 2014 to 2020. Much of the publishing in the field was first presented at the AAR Annual Meeting in sessions organized by this group. Original members of this group, William L. Blizek and Ronald Burke (University of Nebraska at Omaha), launched *The Journal of Religion and Film* in 1997 as the first academic, peer-reviewed online journal in the field. Today this publication remains a leader in the field and is under the editorial guidance of John C. Lyden (former co-chair of the AAR group). Readers will find hundreds of movie reviews, special reports from film festivals such as Sundance, TIFF, SXSW as well as thought-provoking peer-reviewed articles in this journal. Another peer-reviewed open-access scholarly journal is the European interdisciplinary *Journal for Religion, Film, and Media* which was founded in 2015.

THE FIRST DECADE OF THE 21ST CENTURY: SELF-CRITIQUE AND METHODOLOGICAL INNOVATION

The first decade of the 21st century brought self-critique and new depth to Religion and Film Studies. Melanie J. Wright's *Religion and Film: An Introduction* (2006) castigated the majority of religion and film scholars for neglecting to study film itself in favor of a narrative, thematic treatment. Significant collections of scholarship were being published including Jolyon Mitchell and S. Brent Plate, eds. *The Religion and Film Reader* (2007), the first major academic reader of the new century followed closely by John C. Lyden's 500-page edited *Routledge Companion to Religion and Film* (2009). Religious presses were also producing much more scholarly, yet still faith-oriented works, such as Robert K. Johnston's *Reel Spirituality* (2000) and *Useless Beauty: Ecclesiastes through the Lens of Contemporary Film* (2004) and Craig Detweiler's *Into the Dark: Seeing the Sacred in the Top Films of the 21st Century* (2008). During this era, scholars were beginning to develop a more nuanced critical methodology for approaching religion and film from a decidedly non-theological religious studies perspective (Lyden, 2003; Plate, 2008).

Theological approaches to film were maturing as well, for example, an eclectic international group of scholars, church leaders, and filmmakers in the field gathered for a three-year consultation (2005–2007) to discuss the present and future of the field. Supported by the Luce Foundation, this consortium was sponsored by the Reel Spirituality Institute at Fuller Theological Seminary. The fruit of this consortium was *Reframing Theology and Film: New Focus for an Emerging Discipline* (2007) edited by Robert K. Johnston. By 2005, it was clear that the field needed to spend some time being self-reflective and honest about is lacunae. The study encouraged people working in the field to move beyond a literary paradigm, to include film theory, sound design, and music in their analysis. There was also an injunction to move beyond European and American films, to not be afraid of subtitles and include world cinema. The group also advocated extending one's conversation partners to include historians, sociologists, and viewers (reception studies) and be attuned to ethnic and cultural difference in reception. Finally, since this was a theologically grounded study, the volume ends with suggestions for broadening the film canon of theological engagement, penetrating under the narrative surface and incorporating a more diverse array of theologians into the dialogue: from C.S. Lewis to Roberto S. Goizueta to Miroslav Volf.

By this time, many universities and seminaries were teaching religion and film courses. The American Academy of Religion also recognized the Religion and Film Studies were here to stay and published the first collection of essays about *Teaching Religion and Film* in effort to increase pedagogical rigor. This was significant as it recognized that educators had moved on from merely augmenting their courses with films to teaching film in a more informed and critical manner. Gregory Watkins, both a religion scholar and a filmmaker with a master's degree in film production, edited the 2008 volume. The text examined the state of the nascent field; has several chapters on particular religious traditions and film; and explored theological, ethical, and religious studies approaches to teaching religion and film. More than a decade later, *Religion and Film: The Basics* is also designed to aid in the teaching of religion and film. I will end this overview of the development of the field until 2010 here. The present and future of the field of religion and film will be discussed in the concluding Chapter 6. Let us now turn to the structure of this text.

STRUCTURE OF *RELIGION AND FILM: THE BASICS*

This text was carefully designed to ground the reader in the first two chapters; however after this, you may jump to whichever of the final three chapters most strikes your fancy: if you have a favorite genre of films, horror, for example, you may want to jump to Chapter 4 on genres; if you have always been curious about Buddhism and wonder how film might reveal more of its teachings to you, please turn to Chapter 3: Flickering Faith: exploring world religions through film; if the Covid-19 pandemic has forced you to ponder life and death anew and you are curious about how films have addressed the reality of death, please turn to the final chapter on tropes and learn how two very different directors (Iñárritu and Kahiu), from two very different contexts (Spain and Nigeria) have grappled with death in dramatic, yet hopeful films.

The first chapter in *Religion and Film: The Basics* begins by examining the unique dynamics between religion and film. A historical survey of religion in film from the dawn of cinema to today follows. A survey of the development of religion and film scholarship from the 1920s to 2010 is offered to provide an overview of the history and development of the field. The field's evolution and lacunae are highlighted.

Before analyzing almost 40 films in-depth in Chapters 3–5, the next chapter offers the reader some avenues to approach religion and film. In Chapter 2, *Dimensions and bricolage: methodological approaches to religion and film*, you will be introduced to four approaches: (1) theological/biblical, (2) religious studies theories, (3) cultural studies/reception studies, and (4) film studies. I describe the basics of each approach, offer examples from select scholars who employ these methods, and highlight what each can contribute to the study of religion and film. In practice, I advocate methodological bricolage when approaching films, meaning using several of these approaches to craft a deeper filmic analysis and appreciation. Different approaches will naturally appeal to different viewers based on their background and context; for example, those of you with a film background will naturally gravitate to auteur analysis and note the influence of sound, editing, and cinematography, while those readers with theological training will naturally see theological themes.

I encourage you to familiarize yourself with each of these approaches and feel comfortable using all of them as you delve deeper in your appreciation of religion and film. Be bold, try a new approach, such as cultural studies or feminist film analysis! I demonstrate methodological bricolage as I analyze films in Chapters 3–5.

How might you learn about world religions through film? This is the main query behind Chapter 3: *Flickering faith: exploring world religions through film*. The five traditions examined are Hinduism, Judaism, Buddhism, Christianity, and Islam. Please refer to a world religions textbook for a tradition's basic beliefs and history. My intent is not to ground you in The Five Pillars of Islam or explain the Christian Trinity's inner dynamics, but rather allow elements of a religion to come alive through filmic characters and stories. Many religion and film books have sections dedicated to exploring world religions in film; however, most of these are devoted to simply chronicling the depiction of that religion throughout the history of film or they focus on films produced by religious insiders. *Religion and Film: The Basics* takes a different approach. Rather than painting in broad strokes, Chapter 3 has three approaches: (1) global diversity within a religious tradition; (2) lived religion: examples of how a practitioner of that religion would face the world and live out their faith; (3) exploring how key ideas unique to that religion are put into practice, grappled with, or exemplified.

Chapter 4: *Shaking with fear or laughter: exploring religion and film through film genres* explores religion and film through six film genres: sci-fi, comedy, horror, drama, pilgrimage/quest/road trip, and documentary. Each genre has its own conventions that influence everything from character types and narrative arcs to filmic elements that include iconic scenes, stock characters, shots, cuts, music, color, and pace. Each genre selected for this chapter grapples with a different theme or concern of religion. A wide variety of films and topics are analyzed in this chapter: from a Palestinian documentary to demon possession to pagan folk horror. You will laugh with Charlie Chaplin and the Hoover family in *Little Miss Sunshine* and ponder art and freedom with Andrei Rublev and William Wilberforce. I selected genres that have not been extensively explored in other Religion and Film Studies. Each genre's general filmic conventions are briefly elucidated and then two films from that genre are analyzed highlighting specific religious ideas. Perhaps you are a huge sci-fi film buff, but never considered the religious ramifications of a road trip film. Or maybe you only watch serious dramas and need to laugh a little! I hope this chapter reveals new angles for appreciating your favorite genre and encourages you to explore other genres with new eyes.

Chapter 5 explores recurring motifs and themes in religion and film. These tropes are a mixture of religious mainstays and important current topics. External evil, demonic possession, and the systemic moral evil of racism are examined in *The Exorcism of Emily Rose* (USA, 2005) & *Get Out* (USA, 2017). Sex and gender in Hinduism, patriarchy, and women's roles in India are examined in Deepa Mehta's lyrical *Water* (2007), and the role religion can play in influencing normative sexuality is featured in the dramatic documentary about homosexuality and politics: *God Loves Uganda*. Protests against racism have proliferated around the globe in recent years. Church-sponsored Iberian Hispanic Colonial racism and indigenous religion in Mexico are front and center in *The Other Conquest* (Mexico, 2000). How Christianity can be used to both justify and dismantle racism in the Southern USA is the story of *Burden* (USA, 2020) based on the true-life story of a leader in the KKK and his conversion. Interpersonal human redemption and generational healing are the foci of two films that demonstrate redemption, reconciliation, and healing: Walter Salles' *Central Station* (Brazil, 1998) and Paul Thomas Anderson's *Magnolia* (1999). You are sure to be intrigued by the choices for two key tenets in both Buddhism and Hinduism: karma and reincarnation: *It's a Wonderful Life,* and the experimental Thai film *Uncle Boonmee Who Can Recall His Past Lives.* The final trope in the chapter is death. The terrorist bombing of the U.S. Embassy in Nairobi inspired Wanuri Kahiu to create a film that unpacks how we prepare for and recover from death. This chapter fittingly concludes with Alejandro Iñárritu's filmic study of fear and coming to terms with death and the afterlife in his haunting masterpiece *Biutiful* (2010) starring Javier Bardem. Some of the films, such as *Water*, are clearly religious; however, most of films are popular fare, like *Get Out* or *Magnolia,* that have profound things to say on the topic.

Religion is concerned with more than the transcendent realm, it is intimately concerned with human life, therefore cinematic portrayals of human life in all its messiness are the perfect place to find religious themes and concerns.

This text concludes with Chapter 6, a brief conclusion offering up a summary of the book as well as a snapshot of the present state of the field of Religion and Film Studies. I suggest some avenues to pursue for maturation and diversification moving forward as well as a charge to readers.

CRITERIA FOR THE SELECTION OF FILMS ANALYZED IN THIS VOLUME

In conclusion, I would like to comment on the selection of films for this volume. *The Basics* series is dedicated to providing expert introductions to a wide variety of topics by considering past developments as well as elucidating the present state of the field. The 39 films analyzed in this volume are historically and geographically diverse and include Hollywood hits and many "art house" independent films as well. In this survey of religion and film, I have purposively selected films for in-depth analysis from 1915 to 2020; however, the majority of the films are from the 21st century. In addition to this historical breadth, I wanted to make this volume one with a truly global variety of films. The geographic breakdown of films is as follows: Africa: 2, Asia: 8, Europe: 7, Latin America: 2, USA: 16, and West Asia/Middle East: 4. Several of the films produced in the USA were the work of Latinx or Black filmmakers. All the films discussed in this volume are readily available either as a DVD or via streaming platforms. Most religions, genres, and topics are explored in two films chosen to reveal different aspects of that topic; for example, we explore Buddhism in *Departures* (Japan, 2009) and *The Big Lebowski* (USA, 1998), and the genre of comedy is explored in a Charlie Chaplin film, *The Pilgrim* (USA, 1923), which was later remade in the wildly popular and controversial Iranian film *The Lizard* in 2004. Films were carefully selected to offer provocative comparative dyads which lend themselves for lively weekly classroom discussions. My hope is you will get a taste for international independent cinema as well as re-view some popular favorites like *It's a Wonderful Life* (1947) or *Little Miss Sunshine* (2006) from a new angle.

A NOTE FOR INSTRUCTORS

Although *Religion and Film: The Basics* is designed as an introduction to the topic for the general reader, I have designed the book to work well as a semester-long text. Additional films and readings are recommended at the end of each chapter to augment the content. Depending on your context, I suggest the following: if you are teaching a course on religion and film, I recommend spending the first week on Chapter 1, the next two weeks on methods and approaches in Chapter 2, and the remainder of the term divided equally (four weeks each) on the final three thematic chapters. If you are teaching a world religions course and using this as a supplemental text, you could focus on Chapter 3 and supplement your teaching of the fundamentals of the five major world religions with one to two films related to that religion to make it come alive. If you are in a seminary setting, I would recommend grounding students in Chapters 1 and 2, then jumping to Chapter 5 and spending 6–12 weeks considering the films and themes therein.

FOR FURTHER VIEWING

Intolerance (D.W. Griffith, USA, 1916)
Quo Vadis (Mervyn LeRoy, USA, 1951)
The Passion of Joan of Arc (Carl Dreyer, France, 1928)
The Seashell and the Clergyman (Germaine Dulac, France, 1928)
The Story of Film: An Odyssey (Mark Cousins, UK, 2011)
Triste (Nathaniel Dorsky, USA, 1996) & *The Visitation* (Nathaniel Dorsky, USA, 2002)

NOTES

1 Jean Epstein, "De quelques conditions de la photogénie," *Cinéa-Ciné-por-tous* 19 (August 15, 1924), 6–8. Translated by Tom Milne in *Afterimage* 10 (Autumn 1981), 20–23.
2 Antonin Artaud, "Sorcery and Cinema," 1928 Jolyon Mitchel and S. Brent Plate, eds. *The Religion and Film Reader*. New York: Routledge, 2007, 54–56.
3 "High Standards of Pictures Is Urged," *Exhibitor's Times*, August 9, 1913, 20; Cited in Shelly Stamp's excellent biography *Lois Weber in Early Hollywood*. Oakland: University of California Press, 2015, 13.
4 Paul Schader, "Rethinking Transcendental Style," new introduction in *Transcendental Style in Film: Ozu, Bresson, Dreyer*. Berkeley: University of California Press, 2018, 1–39, 26–27.

FOR FURTHER READING

Lindvall, Terry. *Sanctuary Cinema: Origins of the Christian Film Industry*. New York: New York University Press, 2007.

Lyden, John C. *Film as Religion: Myths, Morals, and Rituals*, second edition. New York: New York University Press, 2019. First edition, 2003.

Lyden, John, ed. *The Routledge Companion to Religion and Film*. London: Routledge, 2009.

Mitchell, Jolyon and S. Brent Plate. *The Religion and Film Reader*. London: Routledge, 2007.

Plate, Brent S. *Religion and Film: Cinema and the Re-creation of the World*. London: Wallflower Press, 2008.

DIMENSIONS AND BRICOLAGE
METHODOLOGICAL APPROACHES TO RELIGION AND FILM

- Theological-Biblical Lenses
- Religious Studies Theories
- Cultural Studies and Reception Studies
- Film Studies Approaches

This chapter is the methodological heart of this introductory text. It outlines four of the most prominent and fruitful approaches to religion and film. I will describe the basic ideas of each approach, offer examples from select scholars who employ these methods, and highlight what each can contribute to the study of religion and film. In practice, I advocate what I term methodological bricolage when approaching films, this means using several of these approaches at once for deeper filmic analysis and appreciation. Different approaches will naturally appeal to different viewers based on their background and context; for example, those of you with a film background will naturally gravitate to auteur analysis and note sound and cinematography, while those with theological training will naturally see theological tropes. I encourage you to familiarize yourself with each of these approaches and feel comfortable using all of them as you delve deeper in your appreciation of religion and film. Be open and fearless when it comes to learning a new method! Methodological bricolage encourages interdisciplinarity and questions whether any one approach should be normative when approaching a film. My analysis of almost 40 films in the following chapters will demonstrate this interdisciplinary approach.

THEOLOGICAL-BIBLICAL LENSES

As mentioned in the evolution of religion and film traced in Chapter 1, Christian theologians pioneered religion and film analysis. Their early theological approaches borrowed heavily from influential Protestant theologians of the 20th century, for example, Clive Marsh and Kaye Ortiz's *Explorations in Theology and Film* (1997) applied Niebuhr's incarnational and dialectical model of "Christ engaging culture" to film analysis. They argued film can have a constructive role to play as it engages theology, but theology needs to maintain its critical edge. That same year, John May used theologian Paul Tillich's cultural-engagement categories to approach film in his book *Theology and Film*. Christian English professor Roy M. Anker's *Catching Light: Looking for God in the Movies* (2004) is another good example of applying Judeo-Christian theological themes to popular film. Anker builds on Frederick Buechner's theological tropes and traces the theological idea of grace in historical dramas, explores the problem of evil in Vietnamese war films and the sorrows of an alcoholic singer, and ruminates on human alienation in the loneliness of an endearing extraterrestrial. Women theologians working in the area include Catherine Barsotti, Sister Rose Pacette, pioneer Margaret Miles, and biblical scholar Adel Reinhartz.

One of the most prominent theological scholars working in the field for over 25 years is Robert K. Johnston, a professor of Theology and Culture at Fuller Theological Seminary in California. He is the author or editor of over 12 books including *Reel Spirituality* (2000 and 2006), *Useless Beauty: Ecclesiastes through the Lens of Contemporary Film* (2004), and *Finding God in the Movies* (2019 co-authored with Barsotti). A past president of the American Theological Society and the recipient of two major research grants from the Luce Foundation, Johnston is an ordained minister in the Evangelical Covenant Church. Johnston's book, *Reel Spirituality*, advocated using both Tillich and Niebuhr and their typologies of culture to understand the different possible dynamics between theology and film. Johnston used Niebuhr's five approaches to Theology and Culture: Avoidance, Caution, Dialogue, Appropriation, and Divine

Encounter. His method has evolved as more recent work (see *Deep Focus: Film and Theology in Dialogue* co-authored with Callaway and Detweiler, 2019) downplays preconstructed theological categories and advocates beginning with the film's effect on the viewer. Johnston now advocates a more dialogical approach between theologians and film and teaches all "theologizing should follow, not precede, the aesthetic experience" (Johnston et al., 2019, 120). Asking how God "shows up" in the film-watching experience is being attuned to many possibilities: is it a trace, an echo of grace, or the impetus for moral action? Johnston speaks of the idea of "general revelation": the notion that all truth is God's truth and thus all artistic creations can be places to discover God's message, even films that seem to subvert Judeo-Christian ideas:

> Christians need not claim that non-Christian filmmakers are covert Christians or simply appropriate from their movies what is congenial or congruent with their understanding of the Christian faith. Rather, if viewers will join in community with a film's storyteller, letting the movie's images speak in their full integrity, they might be surprised to discover they are hearing God as well. If we allow ourselves to be open to others, the Other might also prove to be present. If this sounds surprising, it is no more so than Assyria once being God's spokesperson to Israel.
>
> (Johnston et al., 2019, 149)

The allusion to a prophetic Assyria is found in the Hebrew scriptural book of Isaiah, Chapter 10: 5–6 and refers to God using the Assyrians' lack of faith to be a "rod of anger" to club to the godless Israel. In other words, no film is "off-limits," all stories can be used to teach moral lessons or push us to question the good, the true, the beautiful. Using Johnston's Assyrian model, let's consider an independent film some religionists might find morally disturbing: *Concussion* (2013). It is a story about Abby, a 42-year-old bored housewife raising two kids in the suburbs who suffers a concussion when her son accidentally hits her in the head with a baseball. This inciting incident leads her down a path of sexual self-discovery and she seeks passion outside her marriage eventually becoming a lesbian prostitute/ "escort." Some may be disturbed by her deceit (the protagonist lies to everyone: her clients, her children, her partner, herself) as well as the business of sex for money. If we apply general revelation to this tale, however, like the Assyrians' lack of faith, the protagonist's lack of love, fidelity, and emotional depth does force viewers to answer difficult questions such as: what is the core of a marriage bond?; what role does honesty play in parenting?; what is it, deep within us, that longs for sexual interpersonal connection? Several of these questions are theological in nature. Johnston's general revelation approach to such a film would find God shows up in these moral and relational questions, not necessarily in the narrative.

Many Catholic theologians approach religion and film using a sacramental approach; basically this means considering film to be a place to encounter God and God's grace. Many Roman Catholic scholars in religion and film start with the film itself and discover theology within it. Richard A. Blake, in his book: *After Image: The Indelible Catholic Imagination of Six American Filmmakers* (2000) took an auteur approach by focusing on seven Catholic filmmakers from Scorsese to Ford to Coppola and traced how their Catholic faith and worldview shaped their imagination and narratives. Blake traces Catholic ideas such a sacramentality (the scared being present in profane things), mediation (God works through our lives in people), and communion (salvation is found in community) in a variety of their films: from *The Searchers* to *Apocalypse Now*. Consider how George Baily is saved by community—and an imperfect angel—in *It's a Wonderful Life* directed by Frank Capra. Blake illustrates how films can mediate the presence of God (the purpose of a sacrament) in unexpected ways, for example, by making you question what a world would look like without God, for example, at the end of Coppola's *Apocalypse Now*.

Another example of an in-depth auteur study is found in Lauren Hubner's 2007 work *The Films of Ingmar Bergman: Illusions of Light and Darkness* which delves into everything from religion, truth, and symbolism in the *Seventh Seal* to dreams, ghosts, and death in *Cries and Whispers.*

Another subset of theological approaches to religion and film are the plethora of practical theology guides which explore specific films with the explicit goal of teasing out theological issues and to spark discussion among the faithful. For over 20 years, Sister Rose Pacette and Peter Malone have published Roman Catholic guides to contemporary films entitled *Lights Camera, Faith* which focus on discussion and supply questions to apply. Catherine Barsotti and Robert K. Johnston have also excelled in providing such discussion-based film reviews designed to be used as small group viewing and discussion, see *Finding God at the Movies* (2019) for their most recent edited collaboration.

In his book *Into the Dark: Seeing the Sacred in the Top Films of the 21st Century* Craig Detweiler, who has a Master's from USC's School of Cinema/TV as well as an MDiv and a PhD in theology and culture from Fuller Theological Seminary, mines the 45 top popular films produced from 2000 to 2006 according to the IMDb list of top 250 films of all time. He reverses the hermeneutical flow of theology approaching film and starts with the film as the place to discover God's general revelation, revealing God's grace and the theological lessons in everyday life. Utilizing Hans Urs von Balthasar's method, Detweiler proclaims that the Bible itself is like an ensemble drama according, calling God "the ultimate screenwriter"! We are part of the cast: "Our job is to support the director's vision rather than impose our own notions of what might make a better script." (Detweiler, 2008, 131). He explores the idea of community in *Little Miss Sunshine* as the perfect example of an ensemble comedy: (1) a clearly defined group; (2) united in a particular place or particular time; and (3) who share a common goal. "Ensemble stories make us wince, but they ultimately renew our commitment to each other" Detweiler explains, "this film makes us ask ourselves: Can we remain committed to each other despite our significant flaws and differences? Genuine disagreements could be the beginning of wisdom" (Detweiler, 2008, 129).

SAMPLE THEOLOGICAL READING OF A FILM

To demonstrate this method, I will explore the theological idea of redemption in the Lar Von Trier's 1996 film *Breaking the Waves,* a story of a deeply religious young Scottish woman, Bess, who falls in love with Jan, an outsider from the oil rig off the coast. After a short period of wedded and sexual bliss, Jan returns to life at sea. The forlorn Bess beseeches God to return her love. Jan then has a terrible accident and returns home paralyzed and ill. Whether due to his love, his illness, or drugs, he pleads with Bess to take other lovers and tell him of her exploits in order to help him live and heal.

The rest of the tale is Bess' response to his request, which she understands as proving her love for Jan to God and securing his healing. Bess believes in the power of bodily redemption as she uses her flesh to broker salvation and healing for her paralyzed husband, Jan. She ultimately loses her life and Jan is miraculously healed.

A theological reading of this film would start with exploring the nature of the theological tenet (redemption) anchoring the analysis by exploring the following questions: What lies at the heart of Judeo-Christian notions of redemption? From whom or what do we need to be re-deemed? Does redemption necessarily involve bodily sacrifice? How does this postmodern film offer us both new theories of redemption and a critique of Christian understanding of redemption?

Hebrew temple sacrifice to Yahweh believed atonement is received through the sacrifice of the life embodied in the blood (Lev. 17:11). Christian theologian Bradley Hanson outlines four distinct metaphors associated with Christian redemption: sacrifice, victory over evil, doing justice, and revealing love (Hanson, 1997, 162). Jesus's confounding of demons, healing of the sick, and his death on the cross are understood as triumphs over evil. Explaining how Jesus' person and death satisfy God's sense of justice is more complicated. Theological explanations from Pauline substitutionary atonement theory to Anselm's compensatory satisfaction theory to Calvin's classic substitutionary punishment explanation fall short in satisfying both our contemporary notions of a loving God and a just system. Retribution schemes do not work for many late moderns. Recently some theologians have interpreted the heart of Jesus' work of redemption as setting people free and working an inner transformation.

Breaking the Waves, despite the rather heavy-handed representation of Bess (Emily Watson) as a Christ figure, offers us a complicated portrait of sacrifice and redemption. Bess chooses to prostitute herself in order to heal and free her husband Jan (Stellan Skarsgard). Many feminist critics have discarded any possibility of Bess's autonomy, seeing her as a figure sacrificed on the altar of patriarchy by a sadistic husband and a cruel God. Bess's actions, however, could be read as depicting her growing autonomy. The story chronicles Bess' transformation from "feeble lass" to an assertive protagonist. Even after being stoned, shunned by her mother, and knifed by sailors, Bess has enough inner strength to instruct her friend Dodo to assume her place petitioning God for Jan's healing. Bess is very calm and explicit in her instructions to her friend Dodo: "I'd like for you to pray for Jan to be cured and rise from his bed and walk." Dodo obeys and follows her instructions to the letter. In fact, Dodo is down on her knees at the hospital as Bess is being beaten to death on the ship. Bess had all her bases covered. Dodo was plan B if her bodily sacrifice to God did not work. Bess' last words, as she lays dying on the gurney, are: "I've freed Jan." They are eerily reminiscent of another battered and broken figure: Jesus, whose last words were: "It is done." Von Trier is no fan of a Christian notion of Jesus as redeemer, yet he produces a tale in which bodily sacrifice mysteriously brings redemption and healing. Early in the film Jan insisted he wanted to free Bess from her life of regimented conservative Reformed Christianity. Ironically, in the end, it is a healed Jan that is freed. The female savior has turned the tables, broken the rules, and turned our expectations on their head. Bess's broken body brings healing, and while this may raise feminist suspicion, it also ultimately affirms a feminist theological vision of this-worldly redemption, rather than an eschatological disembodied reunion with God in the heavenly realms. It certainly provides us with intriguing narrative fodder to discuss what we believe redemption to be about.[1]

BIBLICAL APPROACHES TO FILM

The first wave of religion and film scholarship spawned many studies of the Bible depicted in film, as well as biblical themes and characters in film. Adele Reinhartz, a professor of Classics and Religious Studies, was the president of the Canadian Society of Biblical Studies (1997–1998) and is the editor of *The Journal of Biblical Literature*. Her *Scripture on the Silver Screen* (2003) is one significant example of biblical approaches to film. In this text, she examines how contemporary films make use of the Bible. A different, more dialogical approach is found in Robert K. Johnston's *Useless Beauty: Ecclesiastes through the Lens of Contemporary Film* (2004). He engages both film and scripture with respect. The "dangerous book" of Ecclesiastes comes alive in dialogue with contemporary films like *American Beauty, Signs, Magnolia, and Run Lola Run*. Johnston uses gritty films like *Magnolia* (Anderson, 1999) to better understand what

Ecclesiastes could teach us about this useless, short, meaningless life and conversely, he uses Ecclesiastes as a cipher to unlock meaning in these postmodern, seemingly cynical films. He considers both scripture and film "edgy sources of wisdom" and offers up this book as a corrective of past biblical approaches to film that assume they held the "truth" and films were texts to support these *a priori* assumptions. Both Ecclesiastes and these films are brutally honest and depict the difficulties of life; yet, as his chapter on *American Beauty* reveals, they also affirm life's fragile, if fleeting beauty. Johnston's interpretation of Qoheleth's (author of Ecclesiastes) wisdom sees life's preciousness in the face of death and enjoins us to respond with wonder as we acknowledge life's paradoxes, vanity, and futility (Johnston, 2004, 72). This filmic-biblical exegesis concludes with three helpful appendices that trace Ecclesiastes' history of interpretation (from Martin Luther to Jacques Ellul), Christian Film Criticism, and Biblical Criticism (from pre-critical to historical criticism to reader-response to post-modern approaches).

RELIGIOUS STUDIES APPROACHES TO FILM

FUNCTIONALISM AND RITUAL THEORY: FILM *AS* RELIGION

The idea that film could serve a religious function has been around for more than a century. The Rev. Dr. Percy Sticky Grant, writing in a 1920 edition of *Photoplay Magazine,* argued that films could vivify and cleanse a person's mind and soul more powerfully than a sermon:

> Pictures are the supreme thing that a mind can see. …The movies clear out the cobwebs of the mind, putting in carefully prepared facts. They are a tonic, a regulator, a clarifier of the inner life, of the imagination. We must think of the movies as that wonderful clean sweep that is clearing out the unhealthful fantasies of the brain.
> (Grant, in Lindvall, 2001)

By the mid-20th century, atheist experimental filmmakers such as Nathaniel Dorsky, wanted to formally replace organized religion with film. "We all thought of cinema as a shrine, and Jonas Mekas was often trying to acquire an abandoned church or synagogue on the Lower East Side. We were interested in the possibility of a cinema Mass."[2] While most people do not formally replace their religion with film and their places of worship with theaters as Dorsky and his 1970s cohorts advocated, film watching has come to perform a religious function in contemporary culture. John C. Lyden in *Film as Religion: Myths, Morals, and Rituals* (2003, 2nd edition 2019) argues as much. Lyden details how films create new myths, how film watching is similar to religious ritual, and finally, how these worlds, characters, and stories can create ethical codes and inspirational morals. He further proposes that Religious studies and Film studies can enter into "inter-religious dialogue" as equals.

Lyden was one of the first to rigorously apply religious studies methods and theory to film, consider how we use it, and how film affects us. He builds on anthropologist Clifford Geertz' 1966 famous essay "Religion as a Cultural System" which provides a five-part definition of religion as:

> 1) a set of symbols which acts to 2) establish powerful, powerful, persuasive, and long-lasting moods and motivations in men [sic] by 3) formulating conceptions of a general order of existence and 4) clothing these conceptions with such an aura of factuality that 5) the moods and motivations seem uniquely realistic.
>
> (Geertz, 1973, 90)

Geertz was also fond of explaining that religious symbols helped believers keep the chaos of the world at bay. Lyden demonstrates how films can function in ways similar to Geertz' five aspects: they can provide a set of visual and narrative symbols that they can inspire hope or action in viewers who appreciate the packaged world presented in the film. Lyden rejects the media studies theories that look at consumers of popular culture as empty vessels injected with the intentions of the filmmaker, arguing instead that the aura of factuality may be convincing, but viewers are fully capable of distinguishing what is real and often grapple with the content of films after viewing them. Finally, Lyden highlights that films, especially those experienced in a theater, "take on a dimension of reality within the context of their viewing" (Lyden, 2019, 24–28). Filmgoers know films are not "real," but they can convey truths about our reality. Lyden suggests cinema offers myths and rituals that take us out of our everyday lives.

WORLD BUILDING

S. Brent Plate takes a decidedly non-theological approach to religion and film arguing that filmmaking and religion-making are *like* each other in that both recreate a world and invite you to participate in that world. In *Cinema and the Re-Creation of the World* (2008), he states his goal is nothing less than a "critical religious film theory" giving equal space to film theory and religion theory. His is a purely functionalist approach that analyzes the similarities between religion and film. He clearly distinguishes this approach from "film-as-text" literary approaches and "spot-the Christ-figure" of pioneers in the field. He situates his method within a "third wave" of Religion and Film Studies that incorporates Cultural Studies, Reception Studies, and application of ritual and myth theory to film analysis.

Can you think of a filmic world you happily lost yourself in? Perhaps wondering the halls of Hogwarts in Harry Potter or traipsing alongside Bilbo and Sam through the shire in *Lord of the Rings*? Or perhaps you have found yourself in a cinematic world that was frightening: swimming at night in the ocean (*Jaws*) or lost in the woods (*Blair Witch Trail*)? Plate argues that

> Religion and film are akin. They both function by recreating the known world and then presenting the alternative version of the world to their viewers/worshippers. Religions and films each create alternate worlds using the raw materials of space and time and elements, bending each of them in new ways and forcing them to fit particular standards and desires. Film does this through camera angles and movements, framing devices, lighting costume, acting, editing and other aspects of production. Religions achieve this through setting apart particular objects and periods of time and deeming them "sacred...."
>
> (Plate, 2008, 2–3)

This world-making analogy is forced at times, but his equal deference to religious studies approaches and film theory was long overdue. Like Freud, Plate sees religious worlds and analogically, cinematic worlds, as places we willingly escape to survive our mundane lives. Religionists would obviously disagree with this thesis, understanding their religiously grounded world as the real world. Plate sees filmmakers as manipulators of space and time as they craft their cinematic new worlds. His approach further provides an example of how film theory and film aesthetics can deepen our appreciation of religion and film by teasing out the similarities between Etianne Sourniau's levels of film realties: afilmic, profilmic, filmographic, screening, diegetic, spectatorial, creational (filmmaker's intended reality), and cultural anthropologist Clifford Geertz's five-point definition of religion. For example, he compares profilmic reality with Geertz's understanding that religion uses symbols to establish "powerful, persuasive and long-lasting moods," filmic reality seems really real, like a religious worldview, to believers, so real, in fact that they are "clothed with an aura of factuality." The inclusion of film mechanics and theory in his critical religious film theory was new and an early 21st-century demonstration of the maturation of Religion and Film Studies. Plate was also one of the first to promote the idea mutual edification between Religious Studies and Film Studies.

FILMS ARE TODAY'S MYTHS

Lyden considers films to be today's new myths and therefore utilizes myth theory and applies it to film. He begins with early notions about myth by Edward Tyler and James Frazer and works his way through psychological theories of myth by Carl Jung and Joseph Campbell, critiquing their reductionism and pointing out that the unique variety of cinematic myths extend beyond concepts like Campbell's "monomyth" of the hero's quest. He finds fecund fodder in the work on myth by historian of religion, Mircea Eliade who taught that there is a strong division between sacred and profane time and space. All myths, according to Eliade's Myth of the Eternal Return, come back to creation. Myths were not created to help us deal with chaos as Geertz proclaims, but to help us tap into the generative power of original creation. Although a bit skeptical about the centrality of the creation narrative in Eliade's mythic theory, Lyden does adopt his notion of myths "providing us with a pattern for living." Films are mythological in the sense that they create an alternative, non-profane world. Johnathan Z. Smith, religion scholar, reminded us that any story is not *sui generis,* that all myths contain something of their context. Wendy Doniger, another historian of religion and a student of Mircea Eliade, rejected notions of a monomyth and resisted Eliade's insistence on finding patterns between myths. Doniger believed the perdurance of myths in human life is related to their tendency to grapple with the big ontological questions and human struggles with life, death, sexuality, and pain. Myths can be understood as "true stories," according to Doniger, that grapple with these questions and help us find meaning in them. Lyden points out that this is what most films do as well, and they function as modern myths that help us find meaning.

Myth and ritual are the bread and butter of academic Religious Studies. John Lyden and S. Brent Plate focus on films as modern myths and fan devotion and interaction as popular ritual. Historians of religion like Wendy Doniger and Mircea Eliade describe myths as stories that answer big existential and ontological questions such as: where did we come from?; how ought we live?; how did the world begin?; and what happens after we die? Myths are meaningful stories that inspire us and are passed down to remind us of a larger story. They are often populated with heroes who go on a journey and overcome obstacles. I agree with Lyden that films are our new myths, but they are not *sui generis*, they arise from and reflect our stories, hopes, and fears as well as our historical context. This relationship between film and culture is a topic to which we now turn.

CULTURAL STUDIES AND RECEPTION STUDIES APPROACHES

Over the past 30 years, the study of religion and film has matured and has become increasingly more comfortable utilizing multiple methodological tools. Incorporation of social scientific and empirical methods began in the 1990s and is common in the 2020s. This section outlines the basics of these approaches. The academic roots of Cultural Studies can be traced back to The Centre for Contemporary Cultural Studies at the University of Birmingham in the mid-1960s. One of the most notable ideas to emerge from this center was their theory that popular culture (including film) was not low-brow and worthless, but rather was a site for alternative cultures and ideas to resist and challenge hegemony and dominant culture. In the 1970s, these academics began to study reggae, mod, and punk music scenes in a sociological, empirical way and later added racial and gender studies to their methodological approach. Staples of social scientific research such as archival work, surveys, group and individual interviews, and participant-observation are standard in Cultural Studies. Cultural Theory is a broader category and seeks to explain culture through epistemological, linguistic, psychological, gendered, or political lenses. Some examples of cultural theories include feminism, Marxism, poststructuralism, postmodernism, queer theory, and post-colonial theory. Approaching film as a cultural phenomenon using questions from both Cultural Studies and Cultural Theory benefits Religion and Film Studies. It is often one of the most popular approaches with my students as they are adept at accessing film reception data (boxofficemojo.com) and reviews (mrqe.com), are excited to explore how culture influences a director and production, as well as to apply lenses such as feminism or race or gender studies to a film.

Margaret R. Miles was one of the first religious studies scholars to approach films asking what they revealed about the cultures that produced them rather than using a theological lens. Her 1995 book *Seeing and Believing: Religion and Values in the Movies* used a Cultural Studies approach to religion and film. She adjured scholars of religion to climb down from their ivory tower and engage the anxieties and problems of contemporary cultures. The best index of these anxieties and concerns, according to Miles, is popular film. Miles approached religion and film as a religious historian using a Cultural Studies lens. She was compelled to turn to movie theaters as the site of new congregations due to the historical shift away from organized religion in the late 20th century arguing that cinemas are the new site where Americans ponder the moral quandaries of life and negotiate values. Miles was one of the first to advocate that religious studies scholars must engage with popular culture if they wanted their quest of critical religious discourse on culture to be relevant. Finally, she understood religion to be fundamentally concerned with human relationships, emphasizing that analyses of race, sex, gender, class, and sexual orientation are central to religious values and filmic stories that explore these relationships are a valid source for critical reflection.

If this engagement is critical, how does one go about doing it? Miles described the interdisciplinary field of Cultural Studies as one which begins by analyzing the social, political, and cultural matrix of the film's production and distribution. Films represent private and public confrontations of values and tend to be successful at the box office when they accurately identify and explore a current area of societal discomfort and anxiety and visualize a possible resolution. Films capture and narratively present the struggles of the moment by the questions they raise and the cultural tensions they dramatize. Elucidating these cultural tensions is always an important task. Miles therefore intentionally limits her analysis to popular films successful at the box office (as opposed to art-house, independent films) hypothesizing that these films "identify currently pressing social anxieties and examine possible resolution" (Miles, 1996, 18). Incorporating Richard Johnson's Cultural Studies method, Miles analyzes the cultural life cycle of a film from creation to production to distribution and reception. Issues such as the origin of the story, funding struggles, pre-production are considered as well as the mechanics of the film's production and location decisions. She prompted students to begin by posing the following questions: Was the film a commercial success? How was it funded, written, produced, distributed, and received? How are religious characters and institutions depicted? How are race, sexual orientation, and class depicted? Does the story refer to or avoid a contemporary social issue or anxiety? What is valued by the characters? Film spectators are given special attention in this approach and are considered active interpreters of the film, not passive receivers of media. Accordingly, religion and film scholars who use this approach will give special attention to indices of reception: from film reviews (both professional and popular) to box-office receipts. We will examine Reception Studies in more detail below.

Miles was a trailblazer in recognizing the value of approaching film using a Cultural Studies lens, although it took more than a decade before this method became common. In 2009, Gordon Lynch, a professor of Sociology and Director for the Centre for Religion and Contemporary Society at the University of London, urged viewers to consider the wider cultural processes of power, ideology, and oppression. Lynch advocated that scholars of religion take empirical research seriously in their study of culture and film. One template for this approach is founded on Richard Johnson's work which laid out a four-step "Circuit of Culture" approach to understanding any cultural product: (1) study the context, structures, and processes of cultural productions, (2) examine the artifacts produced; (3) consider the ways in which people read or use or experience these artifacts in the real world; and finally (4) study how these processes of specific cultural productions are situated in and influenced by broader societal structures and relationships. I concur with Lynch that Cultural Studies approaches can broaden our appreciation of film, grounding thematic or theological analyses in the real world. Using data from popular sources such as boxofficemojo, imdb.com, interviews with filmmakers, movie reviews, etc., exemplifies a more dialogical engagement with society and may be a means for academic scholarship to lead to constructive social transformation (Lynch, in Lyden, ed., 2009, 281). Academics are very territorial and infamously suspicious of those outside their field of study. Lynch dares to suggest that one of the lacunae in Cultural Studies and Film Studies has been their lack of nuanced understanding of lived religion and suggests that as religion and film learns to incorporate data from Cultural Studies, so too should the former disciplines open themselves up to insights from theological and religious studies scholars (Lynch, in Lyden, ed. 2009, 287–288). There is deep suspicion of religious studies scholars, as Malory Nye admits: "… the majority of those working in cultural studies have yet to be convinced that religious studies scholars are not closet theologians" (Nye, 2003, 17). Lamentably many in the social sciences harbor the same suspicion to this day, and this ignorance of methodological diversity in religious studies and theological studies precludes cross-pollination.

One of the ways a Cultural Studies approach augments our appreciation of religion and film is by pushing the discussion beyond theoretical or theological analyses. We begin to understand that finished film is much more complicated than an original story idea being translated into a screenplay and ultimately produced. Looking into the circuit of culture and discovering the powerful effect profit, commercialization, and distribution have in today's film industry force us to think beyond a film as mere text. In other words, a film's message is often profoundly influenced by market forces. Cultural Studies also focus on the variables of film consumption: where and when do we watch these films and with whom? How might age, class, sexuality, religious commitments, or family status affect one's access to certain types of films? By considering films as productions within the circuit of culture we notice how politics, the economy, and society are powers that influence a film as much, if not more than, an auteur.

EXAMPLE OF APPLYING CULTURAL STUDIES TO FILM

The cultural studies approach in religion and film has evolved from Miles' early work or a methodological chapter within anthologies to more nuanced studies such as Matthew P. John's *Film as Cultural Artifact: Religious Criticism of World Cinema* (2017). With academic training in film production and anthropology as well as advanced degrees in theology and intercultural studies, he was well-equipped to produce an in-depth study of religion and film grounded in social scientific method. Focusing on world cinema, John's method incorporates theological critique and cultural exegesis which employs virtual participant observation, auteur commentary and critique, and context criticism. Films are cultural documents, using Clifford Geertz' language, they are "thick descriptions" or interpreted reflections on cultural meaning. Films as ethnography are creative, serious fictions that do more than describe, using sound, and image, they also help us experience a culture which is why they are a perfect avenue to learn about world religions and cultures. By entering into the world of a film we are like ethnographers entering into the world of the other.

John anchors his ambitious methodological agenda with analysis of Deepa Mehta's Elements trilogy: *Fire* (1996), *Earth* (1999), and *Water* (2005) and fieldwork in Varanasi, India. The films are very interesting, well-made stories set in India, and well received on the international film festival circuit. The first film won the People's Choice Award at the Toronto Film Festival in 1996 however its controversial content that includes an illicit lesbian love affair was not well received in India—in fact, protestors stormed and burned down theaters in protest and called for the film to be banned. This made Mehta a *persona non grata* in the land of her birth and caused problems for her when she tried to film her third film in the trilogy in the holy city of Varanasi years later. *Earth*, the second film in the trilogy, put a dramatic spin on the painful and bloody separation of India and Pakistan and the forced migration of millions based on religion. The religious diversity of India is represented by the main protagonists who are Zoroastrian, Muslim, Hindu, and Sikh. The third film, *Water*, explores Hindu widows' fate in 1948. Mehta explains "The Trilogy is about politics—*Fire* is about the politics of sexuality, *Earth* is about the politics of nationalism and *Water* is about the politics of religion." (John, 2017, 80).

Unlike many religion and film scholars, John conducted extensive field research in the world depicted in the film: he visited Varanasi, the holiest city in India for three months, spent time in a Hindu widows' ashram as well as conducted screenings of *Water*, surveyed viewers post-screening in focus groups, interviewed local anthropologists and the filmmaker herself, Deepa Mehta. Data culled from the focus groups was intriguing, for instance, male participants tended to collectively condemn Mehta's feminist ideas, while the women focused on the widows' suffering. Christians tended to comment on the physical suffering of the widows, whereas Hindus focused on the psychological suffering and mental affliction. Good anthropologists are always self-reflective and John, an Indo-Canadian like the director Mehta, felt this helped him better understand Mehta's double-consciousness, her emic-etic tensions. Many Indians criticize Mehta as someone who "disgusted them" by exploiting certain controversies in India to sell a film. Although born in India, many local Indians consider Mehta an outsider now that she has entered into the diasporic land of Canada, in other words, her India-based films are suspect (John, 2017, 91). They also felt the film *Water*, which was set in the 1930s and closed with the statement: "There are 21 million Indian widows in 2001 who still live under the ancient Laws of Manu," was "an attempt to project an India in a frozen time warp." In sum, John found many who viewed the film emerged defensive of Indian culture regarding Mehta's perceived attack on religious and gendered norms. John, speaking as an on-location observer, believes the depravation of widows still prevails in India, however the root cause is not attributable to religion, but economics (widows are seen as an economic burden on the family). In sum, John offers a new method that deepens our approach to religion and film, not by jettisoning all theological readings, but by demonstrating how to incorporate the cultural exegesis interlacing film analysis and auteur criticism with context criticism and participant observation, creating a "trialogue" between film, culture, and theology (John, 2017, 119).

John's approach exemplifies my bricolage approach as it is intentionally methodologically hybrid: he instructs a religious critic of film to wear "spectacles with a theological lens on one eye and a cultural lens on the other" seeing transcendent meanings as well as cultural perceptions of religion from within the world of the film itself. Both the substantive and the functional aspects of religion are highlighted in a continual oscillatory loop. The cultural lens is shaped by the culture and the human spirit as it searches for meaning and includes the realm of myths, rituals, folklore, while the theological lens is seeking to discern divine revelation through the filmic story, is more intellectual, and acknowledges that film can become a religious experience. His spectacle metaphor may be a bit much, but it offers a model for employing two methodological lenses simultaneously.

RECEPTION STUDIES

Reception Studies is a sub-field of Media Studies. It is concerned with the reception, transmission, production, and consumption of cultural products. Reception Studies applied to film focus on how a viewer experiences, responds to, and makes meaning while watching a film. It teaches a film has no inherent meaning, rather meaning is created in the interaction between the film and the viewer. Factors such as the viewer's sense of identity, mood, education, ethnicity, preconceptions, gender, biases, genre assumptions, as well as the location (home or public theater viewed with others versus on as phone or laptop viewed alone), and historical socio-political context are critical and influence how the film is received and processed. This is also an approach that brings film analysis down to earth, there are no fancy French terms or semiotic deconstruction going on, it simply focuses on how film affects the individual. Reception Studies is interested in how all moviegoers experience the film, not merely academics and professional film critics. Swedish media scholar Cecelia von Freilitzen suggests there are four ways we relate to media: (i) the education model in which we are an empty vessel filled with knowledge; (ii) the reinforcement model in which one's culture, myths, values, and worldview are bolstered, implicitly or explicitly, by the film; (iii) the more dynamic mediation model in which the individual chooses the media, interacts with it mentally and bodily; and finally (iv) the power relation model which refers to being enveloped and mesmerized by the experience of film watching (Staiger, 2005, 18–19).

Why might you consider Reception Studies as an approach to religion and film? One reason is it grounds other more subjective theological or philosophical readings of a film in a more objective, social-scientifically interpreted world. So, how might you discover what is going on inside a viewer and consider her or his context? Box office proceeds of a film (boxofficemojo.com) is one place to start as it will reveal much about its cultural impact and marketing success. Professional film critic reviews can be found in film industry outlets and major newspapers, as well as their own sites; however culling through various review sites (Movie Review Query Engine-mrqe.com, rottentomatoes.com, metacritic.com, or imdb.com) will give you a fuller picture of the third model (mediation). Reading these reviews, as well as viewers' comments on social media, will reveal how the film affected people, moved them, angered them, and enthralled them. Adding some data from a film's reception includes the public in your analysis of a film.

When it comes to Reception Studies, theologian Clive Marsh suggests that theologians and religion scholars attend to the following: (i) theology/religious studies must be interested in where meaning-making is happening; (ii) religious and non-religious viewers are not different from each other in kind; (iii) theology, religion, and audience reception of film all require attention to be given to multiple intelligences; (iv) as a discursive discipline, theology must adapt itself to a dialogical understanding of audience reception of film (Marsh, in Lyden, 2009, 270–271). Many are heeding this inclusion of reception data as they analyze films.

FILM STUDIES APPROACHES

Film Studies and Religious Studies have long held each other at an arm's distance, suspicious of the other's methods. In 2007, Melanie J. Wright leveled an incisive critique of religion and film scholarship to date that has haunted the field ever since. In her work, *Religion and Film: An Introduction*, she took special aim at those who read films as a text and simply inductively teased out religious themes and focused on the narrative: "Could it be that – despite the growing bibliography and plethora of courses – *film* is not really being studied at all?" (Wright, 2007, 22). Wright issued a clarion call to study "film *qua* film" in Religion and Film Studies. Unfortunately, in the 2020s, there are still many, many scholars who assume they can simply apply their literary or theological exegetical skills and "read the film." This section will take Wright's challenge seriously and demonstrate how the interdisciplinary tides are slowly changing.

Of course, this appreciation of the other disciplinary methods should go both ways. Religion and theology are not areas most secular film theorists are comfortable addressing, even if they recognize their illiteracy. Film Studies have distinct Marxist and psychological foundations and those within the discipline tend to be militantly secular, in general, and averse to exploring religious ideas. Nevertheless, let us now turn to how film studies and insights should be a vital part of approaching religion and film.

The lack of attention of "film *qua* film" by religion scholars and theologians is slowly changing. As we have seen in this chapter, religion and film appreciation began with theological and biblical lenses to which social scientific methods and religious studies theories were gradually added. Several who work in the field have earned Master's degrees in film production, screenwriting, direction, and producing. In addition to this small, but productive cohort, are those of us trained in religious studies and theology who have taken Wright's charge to heart and have independently studied film history and theory in order to make religion and film a truly balanced interdisciplinary field. Several religion and film scholars have also become filmmakers (Detweiler, Solano, Kickasola, Sison, Tucker, to name a few).

Cinema/Film Studies focus on film forms: editing, cinematography, mis-en-scéne, sound, and music as well as situating the film within cinematic history, the auteur's influence, and genres. Before demonstrating how one might approach a film by honing in on some of these distinct cinematic elements, let us begin by reflecting on how film form and its effect on us can be similar to religious experience.

EDITING

Experimental filmmaker and film editor Nathaniel Dorsky has been making films since 1963. Steve Polta describes his experimental films as follows:

> The films of Nathaniel Dorsky blend a beauteous celebration of the sensual world with a deep sense of introspection and solitude. They are occasions for reflection and meditation, on light, landscape, time and the motions of consciousness. Their luminous photography

emphasizes the elemental frisson between solidity and luminosity, between spirit and matter, while his uniquely developed montage permits a fluid and flowing experience of time. Dorsky's films reveal the mystery behind everyday existence, providing intimations of eternity.

(Polta, San Francisco Cinematheque)

In 2001, Dorsky gave a lecture at Princeton University which he later published as short book entitled *Devotional Cinema*. I often use this book at the start of my religion and film course to begin to help students think about how *the very nature* of film may be connected to spirituality and religion. He begins by describing exiting a movie theater film as a young boy and feeling as if he were in another dimension, a different reality. Have you ever left a film feeling something akin to this? Can you remember leaving a screening with a sense of awe, quiet, feeling deeply aware, awakened, or disturbed? Dorsky posits that visionary film has such a powerful effect on us because it affects our unique human metabolism. Editing is the final influential factor in devotional cinema. Editors control both the narrative and the effect by using "shots and cuts." Shots establish the visual connection and evoke emotion whereas the cut brings clarity and awakens our view. For cinema to be truly transformative, luminous shots must engage our being and then be "popped like soap bubbles by the cut" (Dorsky et al., 2007, 413). A wonderful example of the power of shots, angles, and cuts can be found in *The Passion of Joan of Arc* by Carl Theodor Dreyer.

Cinematography is increasingly being given its due by religion and film scholars. S. Brent Plate, for example, interprets how camera angles, shots, and framed space affects the viewer in the 1999 film *Chocolat*. The hierarchical world of the church is captured and expressed by extreme vertical shots either from the congregation looking up at the priest or the priest looking down on the congregants. The upright and uptight Comte Reynaud (Alfred Molina) is also shot often from below to emphasize his authority over the small French town. These upshots are juxtaposed against straight-on medium shots of the chocolate shop opened by Vivien (Juliette Binoche). The film depicts a war between these two spaces and ultimately, the puritanical Comte breaks into the chocolate shop, indulges in the forbidden sweets (it is Lent), and falls asleep (horizontally) in the shop's window—captured with a medium shot (Plate, 2008, 44–46). As you watch films, make note of how shots communicate power, perspective, as well as how they make you feel. Angles, shots, and cuts powerfully influence your experience of a movie, however there is another, equally powerful element we have yet to touch upon: sound.

SOUND AND SCORE

Sound deeply affects viewers, imagine a *Star Wars* light saber duel without the saber's hum or any disaster movie without the all-enveloping rumble, crumbling buildings, breaking glass. Dolby Surround Sound and THX have only heightened the powerful effect of sound in a theater. Sound is captured during filming, but much of the magic occurs in postproduction after a film is "locked" meaning the images are set. It is during postproduction that dialogue gets corrected (ADR), extraneous sounds are deleted (helicopters, barking dogs, wind), and/or augmented with Foley sound effects. This is also when artistry of sound mixing occurs as well as the musical score is added. Sound affects your experience of the images: it can soothe you, immerse you, trigger emotions. If the sound is off or the music intuitively does not fit the scene, the viewer's experience is negatively impacted. If the sound is good, we hardly notice because we are aurally and emotionally enveloped.

The 2017 film depicting the battle of Dunkirk won many film awards for its sound editing, mixing, and score. The movie, based on a true story, is about the evacuation of thousands of British and Allied soldiers during World War II from the French coast across the English Channel as the Germans are closing in on them on the beach. While the cinematography and story were riveting, it is the masterful sound mixing and editing by Gregg Landaker (who was urged by the director and Prince William to mix one last film before retirement), Richard King, and Gary Rizzo that brings you there and gets your heart racing. Shockingly the only sound that was usable after the film was locked was the dialogue because the noisy IMAX cameras, rain, and wind ruined the other sounds so they had to recreate most of the sounds and layer in Hans Zimmer's majestic score. King and Rizzo, who have both worked on most of Christopher Nolan's films, agree that Nolan's approach is unique.

"Chris uses sound in a way that many others try, but few achieve," says Rizzo. "He almost hijacks your cardiovascular system. It's about pulse, pace and purpose." For example, when a bomb falls in most battle films, the sound gets fainter before impact. "But when you think about it," says King, "the noise should increase in pitch as it gets closer. We reversed all incoming shell sounds so they rose in pitch" (Gray, 2017). Good sound changes everything.

I interviewed sound editor/ADR engineer David Bach who has worked on over 140 popular feature films including *Dunkirk, Pacific Rim, Argo, Tenet*, etc. When asked about balancing sound, score, and mood he explained there is a

> continual hand-off between dialogue, music, and sound effects (SFX) – usually they can't all be the main thing at any moment, so when done craftily, they each do their thing and step back when letting another take over. It's the tension and release of soft/loud, busy/open, bright/dull, etc. that makes a moving soundtrack.

When I asked for an example of a masterful soundtrack Bach responded:

> *No Country for Old Men* (2007) was a sound masterpiece in my opinion. With only six minutes of score [the film runs 122 minutes], the ambiance and sound effects did it all, built the incredible tension and provided such an interesting soundscape. Supervising sound editor and mixer Skip Lievsay would often have things be "too loud" for a moment (I'm remembering the coin flips for example) and this serves as a reminder to not smooth every cut and to not "split the difference" all the time, sometimes you must be bold. The genius is knowing when.
>
> (Bach, 2020)

USING SOUND THEORY IN RELIGION AND FILM

Joseph Kickasola is a theologically trained scholar who consistently incorporates cinematic theories of sound in his analysis of films. Kickasola has been steeped in the world of film and cinema studies in New York City for over 20 years. Incorporating the ideas of avant-garde composer John Cage, legendary Russian filmmaker

Sergei Eisenstein, and French film theorist and experimental composer Michel Chion, Kickasola considers sound in the films of Polish filmmaker Krzystof Kieslowski, especially *The Double Life of Veronique* (1991) and *Blue* (1993). John Cage spoke of allowing "sounds to be themselves rather than vehicles for man-made theories or expressions of human sentiments," reminding us that there is always something to hear, "try as we may to make a silence, we cannot." (Kickasola, 2012, 62). Kickasola traces the stylistic parallels between the composer and filmmaker and emphasizes both knew the soundscape of daily life, their art explored human curiosity about spiritual dimensions of reality, and both used *musique concrète* techniques. Eisenstein privileged the image and is famous for his silent film tableaus. When he was forced to use sound, he valued it only for its dialectical tension with the image, whereas Kieslowski used *musique concrète* to de-familiarize the viewer, daring to displace the image's prominence with sound. Kieslowski, who began as a documentary filmmaker, had always considered sound and image to be equals. This is uncommon. As he evolved from a documentarian to more experimental formalist filmmaker, he played with sound in attempt to "de-familiarize" the viewer. He would use sounds, for example, a scream off camera, to fool and disorient the viewer—but with a purpose: to push the audience to consider that the universe was larger and more connected than any image would allow us to know. He often added sounds during editing that had no referent or that were diegetically impossible, but emotionally appropriate. Kickasola explains how Kieslowski's sound editing directly relates to religion: "…[it] challenges the viewer search for meaning in the moment, to extend his or her conception beyond the local referential plot point, and to consider larger, metaphysical issues" (Kickasola, 2012, 67–68). Kieslowski used sound to convey the idea that larger, transcendent forces were at work independent of characters' full apprehension of them. In the film *The Double Life of Veronique* sound is the bridge between the Veronique and her doppelganger, especially through a tape with sounds from a train station. In sum, Kieslowski's sonic aesthetic was crafted not only to evoke emotions but also to deepen possible meanings and challenge our epistemology. As Veronika/Veronique sings on stage just before her heart gives out, we are transported, Kieslowski used sound not only to break us with the beauty of life, but to point us to something more wonderous too. Kickasola's reflection on sound in Kieslowski's films is a masterful example of how considering sound can deepen a spiritual reading of a film.

MUSICAL SCORE

Music moves us and we intuit its power. My four-year-old son won a kids' essay contest at a Cal Philharmonic concert when he wrote the following simple response: "Music makes me glad and sad." He knew the emotive power of music. Music has the ability to delight or revive us, to bring us to tears or make our hair stand on end. When the violins start in a horror film, we know it is a cue that death or danger is around the corner. While there are moments when silence is artfully used to extend time or allow the viewer to focus on an image, for most of the films we are considering, sound and music are integral components. When we watch a film without music today, we feel something missing. In class I often play a scene from Carl Dreyer's 1928 silent film *The Passion of Joan of Arc* with and without the musical score to exemplify the difference. There was a reason silent films were accompanied by a live orchestra: it dramatically affected how the audience received the film. Not only are religion and film scholars now including musical analysis in their written exegesis of films, they are also playing live movie music and sound clips during academic presentations instead of merely reading their papers. This incorporation was taken even further at the 2013 American Academy of Religion Annual Meeting when John Lyden and his son Karl led a live jazz quartet playing Michael Giancchino's leitmotiv while screening the opening montage of Pixar's film *UP!* By the time the music stopped, the room full of staid academics were visibly moved, most of us were in tears…such is the power of music accompanying images! Kutter Callaway's *Scoring Transcendence: Contemporary Film Music as Religious Experience* (2013) explores God's presence and voice in the music of Pixar films and is another example of the increasing incorporation of film elements. He refers to the empathetic relationship between the music and the film's images and traces how the leitmotiv is connected to a sense of adventure and life while it points to something beyond (Callaway, 2013, 39–41).

AUTEUR THEORY

What is auteur theory? It simply means "author" and professes we can best understand the nuances and intentions of a film by knowing its creator well. Not every filmmaker qualifies as an auteur. The term is reserved for those directors who maintain decisive influence, who have developed a body a work, and have exercised extensive creative control their films. This usually means they come up with the idea of the story, write the screenplay, direct the film, and are intimately involved in the editing process, usually reserving final cut authority.

One filmmaker who has emerged as an auteur with a distinctive style known for ontological angst and meditations is Terrence Malick (born 1943). Early religious experiences shaped his consciousness and his style. His grandfather was an Assyrian Orthodox Christian immigrant, he was raised in a Protestant (Lutheran) home in Texas, and he attended an Episcopal boarding high school. Attracted by both theology and philosophy, Malick graduated *Summa cum laude* from Harvard University with a degree in Philosophy and studied European philosopher Martin Heidegger at Oxford as a graduate student. He turned his back on the academic world and decided to pursue film instead. Malick was part of the inaugural class (1969) of budding filmmakers at the American Film Institute in Los Angeles.

Students of religion and film have found much fodder in the works of Malick. He is an auteur with a philosopher's soul and theologian's mind. According to film critic Roger Ebert, a unifying common theme of his films is the diminishing of human lives beneath the overarching majesty of the world. Most of his films touch upon spiritual themes, from the problem of evil and the importance of faith in 2019s *A Hidden Life* to *The Thin Red Line* (1998). Peter Leithart wrote an entire book about the biblical and theological motifs and musings in his epic film *Tree of Life*. This text, entitled *Shining Glory: Theological Reflections on Terrence Malick's Tree of Life,* is a marvelous and concise example of using two of the approaches in this chapter: a theological lens coupled with auteur theory. This is an excellent example of applying these two approaches to one filmmaker and a single film.

THE AUTEUR APPROACH: ANDREI TARKOVSKY

I will demonstrate how you might apply auteur theory by focusing on one of my favorite filmmakers: Andrei Tarkovsky. He only made seven films and three of them are in *Sight and Sound*'s poll of the 50 Greatest Films of all time. The first step to understanding an auteur is to study their biography, familial history, education, and cultural context as all of these will inform their filmmaking. Andrei Tarkovsky was born in 1932 in Russia and died too young (lung cancer) at the age of 54 in Paris, France. He was the son of an influential modern Russian poet, Arseny Tarkovsky, who was once imprisoned for his anti-Lenin poetry. This political edge was inherited by his son who never allowed his artistic presentation of truth to be suppressed by political considerations, which cost him dearly.

Tarkovsky's first film, *Ivan's Childhood* (1962) was based on a short story of boy orphaned during World War II and was his film thesis. You can see his nascent artistry and attention to detail in the austere shots. The film's box office success allowed Tarkovsky the time and funds to create his second film in 1966, the historic epic following the spiritual quest of the famous 13th-century Russian icon painter, *Andrei Rublev*. This film established Tarkovsky as a unique talent, albeit one who pushed the political envelope. The film, which during the Brezhnev era in Russia, was considered controversial, played only one time in Moscow before being banned for over five years as it was deemed to be too dangerous. Tarkovsky directed and produced three more films: *Solaris* (1972), *Mirror* (1975), and *Stalker* (1979) in Russia before leaving his homeland forever in order to freely create. In exile in the early 1980s, he completed his final two films: the autobiographical film *Nostalgia* (1983) which was shot in Italy and centers on artist stricken with nostalgia for his homeland and the difficulties of translating art, culture, and meaning, and finally, *The Sacrifice* (1986) which was shot in Sweden and deals with nuclear war. One of the reasons Tarkovsky is an excellent candidate for an auteur approach is he not only produced complex and compelling films but he also published a self-reflective book elucidating his method, aesthetic theory, and thoughts on his films entitled *Sculpting in Time* (1986). Having an entire text that articulates a director's thought process is a rarity; usually an auteur's intention, method and theory must be teased out from interviews and articles.

After discovering something about the filmmaker's life history, one should turn to their aesthetic theory and discern their driving motives. Tarkovsky was quite clear about the purpose of art: "Art should force the observer to strive with the crucial questions of his existence. ...The aim of art is to prepare a person for death, to plough and harrow his soul, rendering it capable of turning to good" (Tarkovsky, 1986, 43). The Orthodox Christian filmmaker always understood his role as a divinely appointed one, speaking of the artist as a servant perpetually trying to pay for the gift that has been given to him miraculously. All art is a spiritual endeavor according to Tarkovsky and arises as an answer to a spiritual need. Like poetry, theology, and literature, Tarkovsky hoped his films would provoke intellectual and spiritual questioning:

> I see it as my duty to stimulate reflection on what is essentially human and eternal in each individual soul...My function is to make whoever sees my films aware of his need to love and to give his love, and aware that beauty is summoning him.
>
> (Tarkovsky, 1986, 200)

Auteur theory also focuses on the director's unique filmic style which one can trace through their many films. For Tarkovsky these cinematic hallmarks include long panning shots, texture (sticky mud, murky water, etc.), dramatic contrasts and frames, a slow pace (slow cinema), opaque plot points, and unanswered questions. Although he understood film as capturing reality and "sculpting in time," he is not concerned with realism, preferring to capture dreams, thought, memory over objective, logical shots. He believed the best a filmmaker can do is offer up images that evoke the transcendent. He explained "We cannot comprehend the totality of the universe, but the poetic image is able to express that totality...The great function of the artistic image is to be a kind of detector of infinity" (Tarkovsky, 1986, 106). Raised in the Russian Orthodox Church, Tarkovsky's films are not overtly theological (with the exception of *Andrei Rublev*) yet he was always existentially curious, spiritually earnest, and despite living in a Soviet era hostile to organized religion, he was haunted by the idea of God. For Tarkovsky *imago dei* is found in human creativity: "Perhaps the meaning of all human activity lies in artistic consciousness, in the pointless and selfless creative act. Perhaps our capacity to create is evidence that we ourselves were created in the image and likeness of God?" (Tarkovsky, 1986, 241).

To conclude, auteur theory originates in Film Studies and is one, among many, helpful ways to approach developing a richer understanding of a film or body of films by a specific filmmaker. Of course, films can stand alone, and their narrative power does not depend on the viewer's knowledge of the director's background or artistic commitments; however I would argue that such knowledge deepens one's appreciation of the images on the screen. One last word of advice when it comes to applying auteur theory to your analysis of any film: do not become overwhelmed, you do not have to have watched *every* film by a certain director to utilize this approach. Begin by watching a few of their films from different epochs of their work, research their background and training, if possible, watch some post-screening Q and A's and read some articles and interviews. Auteur theory reminds us that films are subjective human creations made by unique authors who create works of art which are influenced by their unique life experiences, obsessions, and demons.

PHILOSOPHICAL AND GENRE APPROACHES

Using the entrée of genres to explore religion and film is fully developed in Chapter 4 of this volume. In this chapter, the following genres are examined as they relate to religion: horror, sci fi, drama, comedy, pilgrimage/quest/road trip, and documentary. One of the first film theorists to philosophize about film form was Paul Schrader. Unlike most film theorists, Schrader is also a filmmaker himself and thus naturally focuses on camera angles, cinematography, dialogue, and editing. His *Transcendental Style in Film: Ozu, Bresson, Dreyer* (1972) argues that these three auteurs craft films that capture a spiritual state by means of austere camerawork, acting devoid of self-consciousness, and editing that avoids editorial comment. Schrader defines the transcendent as "beyond normal sense experience" and expressive of the Holy, it transforms experience into a repeatable ritual and points toward the ineffable (Schrader, 1972, 11). Schrader points out how these auteurs use off-screen space and sound, narrative ellipses, and low-key acting and allow room for mystery and human spirituality. In his 2018 revised Introduction, Schrader reflects on how transcendent slow cinema exhibits a different attitude toward time which becomes the central component of the story instead of merely servicing it, he also considers how time affects the images and then the viewer. Action is replaced with little or no action. Schrader observes, "expectations are turned in on themselves, no music to guide the emotions, no close-ups to indicate importance, no acting to affect feelings, no fast motion to distract the eye" (Schrader, "Rethinking Transcendental Style," 2018, 32). In other words, slow cinema forces us to become self-reflective. His 2018 edition of the book adds transcendental-styled auteurs Andrei Tarkovsky (Russia), Béla Tarr (Hungary), Theo Angelopoulos (Greece), and Nuri Bilge Ceylan (Turkey). Schrader utilizes the tenets of transcendental style: stasis and the fundamental spiritual unity it suggests, in his recent film *First Reformed* (2018).

GENDERED, RACIAL, POLITICAL APPROACHES

As with many realms of knowledge and production, Film Studies have been dominated by white males, from Bazín to Schrader; however since the late 20th century, perspectives and critiques of women, people of color and those of minority sexual and political orientations are being increasingly included. These critiques and angles deepen religion and film analysis, whether we are discussing neocolonial politics and religion in *Black Panther* or the sexist treatment of Hindu widows in *Water*. Several pioneering studies of film from a feminist perspective were published in the 1970s including Molly Haskell's *From Reverence to Rape: The Treatment of Women in the Movies* or the influential 1974 psychoanalytic study by Laura Mulvey, Oxford professor of Film and Media studies, on male voyeurism and the "male gaze" of directors entitled *Visual Pleasure and Narrative Cinema*. These works, and others, by female filmmakers, critics, and academics altered not only the field of Film Studies but also gave us a new way to critique films. Attention was paid to how women were personified in films and manipulated to very specific patriarchal ends. Bracha Lichtenberg Ettiger, an Israeli artist and philosopher, advanced the field of feminist film studies by moving on from the phallic male gaze to the "matrixinal gaze" of women. Although it is still an appalling minority, more and more women are writing, producing, and directing films and replacing the traditional male gaze and sexual objectification of women on screen. According to the Celluloid Ceiling annual report by California State University San Diego, in 2019 only 14% of directors working on the top 100 movies were women, which is down 1 percentage point from 2018. Recognizing women working as directors is still stunningly absent. For example, in the more than 93-year history of the Academy Awards only six (yes, six) women have been nominated for Best Director and only two women have won (Katheryn Bigelow in 2010 for *The Hurt Locker* and Cholé Zhao for *Nomadland* in 2021). Film Studies at the intersection of religion and race are emerging, for example, Judith Weisenfeld's *Hollywood Be Thy Name: African American Religion in American Film 1929–1949* (2007). Sexual orientation and religion are central to many academic journal articles in the field and several manuscripts including Daniel S. Cutrara's *Wicked Cinema: Sex and Religion on Screen* (2014). Postcolonial critique and film theory are a critical part of Antonio D. Sison's work in world cinema. Although LGBTQ and race-oriented film theories are found in religion and film analyses, this is clearly an area that needs to be increasingly included.

In conclusion, respect for and inclusion of Film Studies has come a long way since Wright's challenge in 2007. As this final section has established, film forms (editing, cinematography, mis-en-scéne, sound, music, cinematic history, the auteur's influence, and genre conventions) are increasingly fundamental to religion and film analysis. Film Studies is one of four ways outlined in this chapter to approach religion and film; the other three being Theological-Biblical Lenses, Religious Studies Theories, Cultural Studies and Reception Studies. Each of these is a tool or a lens to look deeper into a film. I encourage you to practice methodological bricolage when approaching films, you need not use them all at once, nor be an expert! By this point you have covered the history of religion and film in Chapter 1 and grounded yourself in various approaches in Chapter 2, it is time for the main attraction: time to discuss films and demonstrate film analysis using methodological bricolage in the following three chapters.

NOTES

1 Certain elements of this theological analysis where previously published in my article "Blessed Broken Bodies: Exploring Redemption in Central Station and Breaking the Waves," *Journal of Religion & Film* 8:2, Article 16 (2004). https://digitalcommons.unomaha.edu/jrf/vol8/iss2/16.
2 Nathaniel Dorksy, interview on artforum.com., February 8, 2019, https://www.artforum.com/interviews/nathaniel-dorsky-on-celebrating-light-and-celluloid-78602.

FOR FURTHER READING

Cultural Studies-Reception Studies Approaches: Two chapters in *The Routledge Companion to Religion and Film*, edited by John C. Lyden: Clive Marsh's "Audience Reception," 255–274 and Gordon Lynch's "Cultural Theory and Cultural Studies," 275–291, 2011 [2009].

Film Studies Approaches: Kickasola, Joseph G. *The Films of Krzysztof Kieslowski: The Liminal Image.* Bloomington: Indiana University Press, 2004.

Religious Studies Approaches: Lyden, John C. *Film as Religion: Myths, Morals, and Rituals*, second edition. New York: New York University Press, 2019.

Theological-Biblical Approaches: Johnston, Robert K. *Ecclesiastes through the Lens of Contemporary Film.* Grand Rapids, MI: Baker Academic, 2004. Rindge, Matthew S. *The Bible and Film: The Basics.* London: Routledge, 2021.

FLICKERING FAITH
EXPLORING WORLD RELIGIONS THROUGH FILM

How have you learnt about world religions? Perhaps your education began in an intro course in college, a textbook, by living in a religiously diverse urban center or in relationships, how about film? Religion is a vital part of human society, in fact 85% of the globe today self-identifies as religious and world cinema reveals this reality. Many religion and film books have sections dedicated to exploring world religions in film, and most of these are devoted to simply chronicling the depiction of that religion throughout the history of film or focus on films produced by religious insiders. *Religion and Film: The Basics* takes a different approach. Rather than painting in broad strokes, we will hone in one of three aspects: (1) diversity within the religious tradition; (2) lived religion: examples of how a practitioner of that religion would face the world and live out their faith; (3) explore how key ideas unique to that religion are put into practice, grappled with, or exemplified. For example, for Buddhism we will juxtapose two diverse films: *Departures* is a dramedy set in Japan that exemplifies Buddhist ideas about death, life, and the importance of rituals, while Zen fundamental tenets are explored in *The Big Lebowski* set in California in the 1990s. This second film spawned a fan-based religion called "Dudeism" which boasts 500,000 adherents world-wide. While there will also be exploration of religious ideas and tropes in Chapter 5, here our focus is on how the key idea reveals the heart of that religious tradition. To conclude this chapter on world religion and film, I consider filmic depictions of inter-religious relations. The order of the religious traditions is based on the founding date rather than the number of adherents.

According to adherents.com's 2020 statistics: Christianity is largest world religion with 2.3 billion followers (29% of the world's population), Islam is second with 1.9 billion (24%), Hinduism is the third largest religion with 1.1 billion (14%), non-religious people make up 14% of the world's population, Buddhists comprise 6% of the world's population with 506 million followers, and there are approximately 1.4 million Jews worldwide (0.2%). This chapter should augment your study of the history and tenets of these five major world religions. These characters and stories, flickering fables of faith, doubt, struggle, and love show us lived religion in powerful ways.

HINDUISM

If we consider scared scriptures and rituals to be the barometer of the origin of a religion, then Hinduism, whose Vedic scriptures preserving rites and rituals date back to 1, 800 BCE, is the world's oldest living religious tradition. As far as number of practitioners, there are approximately 1.1 billion Hindus alive today, and they are concentrated in India, Bangladesh, Sri Lanka with sizable populations in the USA and the UK. Several of our films are set in India, a deeply religious country with sizable communities of the world's major religious traditions, several of which originated there: 94% of the world's Hindus live in India, there are also substantial populations of Muslims, Christians, Sikhs, Buddhists, Jains, and adherents of folk religions. According to the 2011 census, 80% of the population of India practices Hinduism, 14.2% adheres to Islam, 2.3% are Christians, 1.7% adhere to Sikhism, 0.7% adheres to Buddhism, and 0.4% adheres to Jainism. As you can imagine, the Hindu worldview and traditions are a natural and perduring part of Indian cinema. Today the Indian film industry is the largest in the world. The first film entirely shot in India was *Raja Harischandra* (1913) a silent mythological film by D.G. Phalke. There are three main types or genres of Indian films that deal with religion: Mythologicals (which depict stories from the puranas and Vedas, the *Mahabharata* and *Ramayana*, in particular); Devotionals (regional films that are rooted in history and social concerns); Islamicate films (stories related to Islamic experience in India). We will consider one film that is a mix of genres, *Jai Santoshi Maa* (mythological/devotional/social) and *OMG!* a Bollywood comedic satire (devotional). These films were selected to offer windows into lived religious experience and to exemplify theological ideas central to Hinduism.

KEY HINDU IDEA: GOD IS EVERYWHERE

OMG (Oh My God) is an Indian comedic satire written and directed by Umesh Shukla inspired by the 2001 Australian film *The Man Who Sued God* and a Gujarati stage play. The film chronicles the spiritual evolution of Kanji Lalji Mehta (Paresh Rawal), a middle-class shopkeeper and father, who evolves from an atheist who directly profits from exploiting others' faith to a believer with a close relationship with God (in the form of Krishna—played by Bollywood megastar Akshay Kumar). Kanji owns a shop of Hindu statues and antiques in Mumbai. He makes fun of religious activities around him and profits from the faithful, admitting to his employee that "God is a delusion," as he sells "authentic" relics amidst religious kitsch like Holy Ganga water (from the tap). One day, an earthquake hits the city and Kanji's shop is the only building that is destroyed. His family and friends blame this on his atheism. At the insurance office, Kanji learns that the disaster claim does not cover any damage caused by natural calamities classified under "Act of God." Running out of options, he decides to sue God and religious priests are summoned as representatives of God. As the tale unfolds Kanji loses his wife and family, but is befriended by Krishna Vasudev Yadav who claims to be a consultant from Uttar Pradesh, but is actually an incarnation of the Hindu god Krishna. When the court demands *written* proof that the earthquake was an 'Act of God,' Krishna steers Kanji toward holy books like the *Bhagavad Gita*, the *Qur'an*, and the *Bible*. Kanji reads them and finds a passage in each that says the world and all that happens in it, from beginning to end, is a creation of God and everything that occurs is the under the power of God's will alone. The priests agree to this while on the witness stand before they realize this strengthens Kanji's case and increases public support. As the case progresses Kanji evolves from social pariah to folk hero. He goes on TV talk shows and articulates a strong critique of organized religion and especially criticizes the commodification and commercialization of religion in India. He exposes religious leaders' exploitation of the faithful and a grassroots movement begins. Followers start asking questions of their leaders and demanding accountability and transparency. Kanji ultimately prevails in court, but just as the judge is about to rule, he suffers a stroke and is rushed to the hospital. He lies in a coma and is paralyzed for over a month. The religious leaders conspire to have him killed and turned into a saint—whose veneration they will profit from. Krishna appears, heals him, and they have a deep conversation about human-divine relations. In the final scene Kanji and Krishna arrive on his motorcycle and Kanji rejects this religious profiteering and destroys his temple and statue. Krishna's work is done, and he disappears leaving his feather keychain behind. Kanji grabs it and is about to treat it as a religious relic when he hears Krishna's voice commanding him to let go of the talisman—he no longer needs it since he has a direct relationship with God (Figure 3.1).

Figure 3.1 Kanji and Krishna, now friends, let go of religion at end of *OMG* (Umesh Shukla, 2012).
Source: Screenshot by author.

THEOLOGICAL MESSAGE

The post-coma hospital conversation between Krishna and Kanji reveals one Hindu understanding of human and divine relationships. Krishna finally appears in his traditional iconic form to convince Kanji he is who he says he is even though he says that this avatar is dated. He calls Kanji his "friend" and explains that "just as a devotee is incomplete without his God, so God is incomplete without his true devotee." This confession of reciprocal need is a revelation for Kanji who lets go of his understanding of God the divine ruler, replacing it with God as companion. Krishna is relieved, confessing he is very tired of exchange relationships with devotees: "if you grant me this wish I will do this in return" interactions with humans. He does not want pilgrimages or offerings, explaining that he only cares about faith, love, and belief. This puzzles Kanji who has been raised with Hindu devotion based on this transactional relationship with the divine. Krishna counsels him to stop seeking him in temples or trinkets, but to discover him in other human beings and within his own heart—a prophetic message Kanji shares with the crowd in the closing scene. This idea that God is found within is central in many sects of Hinduism. While an outsider to the religion might interpret the many objects and images associated with Hinduism as ends in themselves, Hindus do not, God is indeed, found within.

TAKE YOUR SHOES OFF AT THE DOOR OF THE CINEMA: HINDU FAN DEVOTION

Jai Santoshi Maa (India, 1975) was a low-budget film with unknown actors that became a hit and spawned a socio-religious phenomenon. It is a mixture of the three main types of religious films in Hindi cinema: mythological, devotional, and social. The screenplay itself was based on a story that describes a fast for the goddess Jai Santoshi Maa, the *vrat katha*: a folktale (katha) meant for recitation during the performance of a ritual fast (vrat) honoring a particular deity and undertaken to achieve a stated goal. The Santoshi Ma *vrat* was a simple one and was popular in northern India during the 1960s, spreading among lower-middle-class women by word of mouth and through an inexpensive "how-to" pamphlet and religious poster of the goddess. The film greatly embellishes this devotional story by framing it with heavenly commentary and grounding it in a familial narrative. It tells the tale of a long-suffering housewife who faces numerous trials, including losing her husband, but like Job, is ultimately restored and blessed as a reward for her steadfastness, moral goodness, and devotion to the goddess.

The film begins with a heavenly court scene where we learn that the goddess was created by her father Ganesh, the god of good fortune. The this-world parallel figure, her devotee Satyavati, is first seen offering devotion to Santoshi Maa and requesting that she find her true love. On the way home she bumps into the handsome Birju who quickly becomes her husband. She reveals to him that she promised to visit all the shrines of Santoshi Maa in thanks for the granting of her petition and so the new husband and wife go on a pilgrimage-honeymoon to fulfill her vow. Unfortunately, both human and divine jealous and conniving female figures conspire against her happiness. The three heavenly consorts, Brahimimi, Lakshmi, and Kali become jealous of the depth of devotion this new goddess has inspired and decide to punish her most ardent devotee. On earth Satyavati's cruel sisters-in-law (especially Durga and Maya) are equally intent on making her life miserable. Satyavati's relationship with Santoshi Maa enables her to endure the sufferings inflicted on her by her sisters-in-law and to triumph over them, but it also accomplishes more. It ensures that Satyavati's life consistently departs from the script that patriarchal society writes for a girl of her status: she marries a man of her own choosing, enjoys a companionate relationship (and independent travel) with her husband, and ultimately acquires a prosperous home of her own, beyond her in-laws' reach. While appearing to adhere to the code of a conservative extended family (the systemic abuses of which are dramatically highlighted), Satyavati nevertheless quietly achieves goals that subvert this code. Santoshi Maa's rise as a goddess happens without the intervention, so common in Indian cinema, of a male hero or god and Satyavati emerges as more powerful than her simplistic husband.

RECEPTION OF *JAI SANTOSHI MAA*

Millions of Indian women loved this folksy story about a newer goddess of satisfaction. The film did not create this goddess, but it took a simple religious story and created a film that moved millions.

Her main temple is situated in Lal Sagar, near Mandore, which is about 10 kilometers away from Jodhpur city. The relational and financial success of the heroine inspired many lower-class women to dream of becoming blessed middle-class matrons themselves in the rapidly changing India of the 1970s and 1980s. Much like another B-movie hit of 1975, *The Rocky Horror Picture Show*, interactive film viewing rituals accompanied the screenings. Cinemas became sacred space and attendees left their footwear at the door, pelted the screen with flowers and coins, and bowed reverently whenever the goddess herself appeared on screen. Viewing became worship, it was *darshan* with popcorn.

KEY HINDU CONCEPT: DARSHAN AND THE PATH OF DEVOTION

Using both film studies and religious studies approaches (detailed in Chapter 2), I would like to consider one key Hindu concept: *darshan*. Note should be made of "frontality" in India cinema. Geet Kapur coined this term to signify the direct engagement of viewer with the object as well as their sense of mise-en-scéne. Frontality can involve freezing the image or granting time to allow the spectator to process the meaning. Many forms of visual and performative art have influenced the development of Indian cinematic style, including Parsi theater with its predilection for tableaus, religious art and chromolithography, and photography. What is *darshan*? It is the reciprocal process of seeing a divinity and being seen by the divinity and it lies at the heart of human-divine worship and interaction. Philip Lutgendorf deconstructs *darshan* in the film's opening devotional song scene:

> The camera repeatedly zooms in on Satyavati's face and eyes, then offers a comparable point-of-view-zoom shot of the Goddess as Satyavatai sees her. Finally it offers a shot-reverse-shot from a position just over the goddess' shoulder...closing the *darshanic* loop by showing us Satyavati and the other worshippers more or less as Santoshi Ma sees them. ...Such *darshan* sequences contribute the aesthetic of "frontality" often noted in popular cinema, especially in mythologicals.... The camera's movements invite the viewer to assume both positions in the act of *darshanic* intercourse that ultimately moves (as most Hindu loops do) toward an underlying unity.
> (Lutgendorf, 2007, 26)

Figure 3.2 Satyavati, Jai Santoshi Maa and her perspective of devotion in *Jai Santoshi Maa* (Vijay Sharma, 1974).
Source: Screenshots.

Through its visual treatment of the reciprocal gaze of *darshan* and its use of parallel narratives, the film also suggests that Satyavati and Santoshi Maa are, in fact, one person—a truth finally declared, at the film's end, by Birju's wise and compassionate elder brother Daya Ram. This film inspires all women to find their inner goddess. As Santoshi Maa is available to all women through her *vrat* ritual, she *is*, in fact, all women. This idea is visually reinforced by the goddess' appearances in the film: first as a little girl at the film's beginning, then as a self-confident young woman in her manifestations throughout most of the story, and finally as a grandmotherly crone on the final Friday of Satyavati's fast. In these incarnations, Santoshi Maa makes herself available to viewers as an embodiment of the female life cycle, and as Satyavati explains to her husband: "she is everywhere." (Figure 3.2)

JUDAISM

Films depicting Jewish history date back to Hollywood's first epic biblically based films such as Cecil B. Demille's *The Ten Commandments* (1923) or *Noah's Ark* (1928). Most Hollywood movie studios were founded by visionary Jews: Carl Laemmle, the Yiddish-speaking Warner brothers were from Poland and founded Warner Brothers Studios in 1923, Samuel Goldwyn, the Selznicks, Jesse Lasky, William Fox, Louis B. Mayer are other Jewish founders of major studios. Many comprehensive accounts of Jewish filmmakers and representations of Jews in film exist; therefore, in this section we will focus on how Jewish theodicy, storytelling, and character are presented in the comedic Coen brothers' (Joel and Ethan) film, *A Serious Man* and consider gender roles in present-day Israeli Orthodox families in the independent film, *Mountain (Ha-har)*.

A MODERN-DAY JOB? ANALYSIS OF *A SERIOUS MAN*

This loosely autobiographical film, set in the 1967, has been called a "Jewish masterpiece" and the Coen brothers, whose work spans multiple genres, have long called themselves "Jewish filmmakers"; however, before *A Serious Man,* their films had merely included Jewish characters (Barton Fink, Walter from *The Big Lebowski*, et al.), whereas this film shows us an entire Jewish community: from professors and rabbis to dentists and housewives in a suburb outside of Minneapolis in the in the Midwest of the USA. It is a context they know well as the brothers came of age in the 1960s in the Jewish suburb of St. Cloud, Minnesota and both their parents were professors.

With Hinduism, we focused on the importance of seeing (*darshan*) as a dialectical connection with God using the example of *darshan* in *Jai Santoshi Maa*. In Judaism the emphasis is on hearing the word as a way of connecting to God. The written and aural word is the bridge to G-d ("hasem"). Studying the Torah is the way in which humans can understand Hashem's mind and will and the written commentaries on the law (midrash) are vital as well. Ethan Coen was a philosophy major at Princeton and clearly his dissertation on Wittgenstein manifests itself here in Larry's obsession to interpret language correctly. The film begins with a black screen illuminated by a simple white text, an abridged quote from Rabbi Shlomo Yitzchachaki's ("Rashi"): "Receive with simplicity everything that happens to you." He is commenting on a passage from the Hebrew scriptures, Deuteronomy, Chapter 18:13, which is adjuring the Israelites to avoid trying to figure out the future by consulting mediums, the dead, necromancers, fortunetellers, etc. Rashi promises that those who follow his advice will be with God. This quote dissolves into a vintage prologue set in an 18th-century Polish shtetl with a Yiddish-speaking husband and wife. Velvel, a farmer, comes home full of joy at his good fortune on the road on a snowy night: his cart's wheel fell off and he was befriended by an old friend, Traitle Groshkover, who he has brought home. Dora, his wife, is horrified at this news as she heard a story that Groshkover had died of typhus and concludes he surely must be a "dybbuk" (Yiddish for ghost). After a few obtuse answers and strained moments, she promptly stabs Groshkover with an ice pick. At first, he does not bleed and the audience thinks she is justified in her action; however, he soon starts to bleed and takes his leave. The wife slams the door and bids the "evil" goodbye, while her husband stands aghast at the murder he has just witnessed. The prologue ends and the modern story begins. We are not told if Groshkover was a ghost, but the Coens have cleverly showed us the power of a short story and set up character types: the decisive and active wife versus the passive, bewildered husband.

In short, *A Serious Man* is a story about Larry Gropnik (Michael Stuhlbarg), a sheepish physics professor about to go up for tenure whose life begins to unravel as misfortune upon misfortune beset him. It has been called a modern-day Job story. His wife Judith (Sari Lennick) asks him for a divorce so she can marry Sy Ableman (Fred Melamed) a recently widowed colleague of Larry's who turns out to be thoroughly morally corrupt. From suspicious lung x-rays to car accidents to financial woes, Larry's life unravels, and he ends up living at a sad hotel ironically called "The Jolly Roger" with his odd brother who is constantly draining a sebaceous cyst on the back of his neck and is in trouble with the police for sodomy and gambling. We follow Larry on his quest to understand why all these bad things are happening to him, a simple man, who has "done nothing" to deserve this misfortune.

"WE HAVE A WELL OF TRADITIONS, WE HAVE STORIES": JEWISH HERMENEUTICS

The Jewish tradition is full of stories. In Judaic cosmology all creation was spoken into being. Parables (*mashal*) help us understand the Torah. Wendy Zierler, in her wonderful study, *Movies and Midrash: Popular Film and Jewish Religious Conversation,* compares a parable to a spool of thread that helps you find your way through the labyrinthine palace of the Torah, it is a scythe that allows you to cut your way through the thicket of the midrash and Talmud (Zierler, 2017, 183). The Coen brothers have created a film filled with parables, "it's part of the whole Yiddish-keit," Ethan Coen explains, "part of the whole Jew storytelling thing. Jews are big on stories, you know?" (Coen, *Salon* interview). Bombarding the religious seeker with stories is one Jewish method of leading them to the truth. When Larry confesses his disillusionment with his life and ethical confusion to his friend Mimi, she reminds him the Jews have a special treasury to help in times like these:

MIMI: "It's not always easy deciphering what God is trying to tell you. But it's not something you have to figure out by yourself, *We're Jews*, we have that well of tradition to draw on… handed down from people who had the same problems."

Of course, as a Jew, Larry knows the power of parables and often uses them in the classroom. He uses them, but does not fully trust them. He relays this to Clive, his failing Korean student, explaining that stories can aid you in a general way, but they are not the end point:

LARRY: "You understand the dead cat? (*Clive nods gravely*) But …you…you can't understand the physics without understanding the math. The math tells how it really works. That's the real thing; the stories I give you in class are just illustrative; they are like fables, say, to help give you a picture. An imperfect model."

I am a daughter of a mathematician, so Larry's utter confidence that math holds all the answers and will lead you to a singular truth struck home. This is Larry's struggle throughout the film: narratives can be helpful *only up unto a certain point* and then you must become a rational man, like Telvel, someone who trusts in the science. And therein lies the problem. Uncertainty can be deeply disturbing. Judaism is a religion that specializes in being disturbed and grappling with G-d. It is no accident that Larry is a physics professor teaching Hesienberg's uncertainty principle of indeterminacy of quantum mechanics. Schrodinger's dead (or live) cat paradox is meant to critique Heisenberg's thesis that uncertainty is part of all being. It is a story that leaves us with uncertainty and mystery and more questions than we had in the beginning …just what the filmmakers intended. Larry understands math, it is stories that befuddle him. Throughout the film, from the Yiddish prologue to Rabbi's Warshak's simple words in the penultimate scene, we sense that truly hearing will lead us to the truth.

THE PROBLEM OF EVIL AND INNOCENT SUFFERING: CINEMATIC THEODICY

The Hebrew story of Job (mirrored in this film) is a tale that functions as a theodicy, i.e., it attempts to explain the problem of evil and unmerited human suffering under the auspices of an all-knowing, all-loving God. In the biblical story Job's devotion is tested when God allows the Adversary to test Job's faith by stripping him of everything: his family, his wealth, his home, and eventually his health, besetting him with painful boils. The moral of the story is a bit uncomfortable for cause and effect rational thinkers. Although what was taken from Job is restored, he never gets his neat answers from the voice in the tumult/whirlwind (God), instead he is put in his ontological place and told he will never be privy to the mystery of God's actions and he will never fully understand because he can never share God's perspective. In the end, Job is humbled and apologetic regarding his impertinent hermeneutical quest. Job is a perduring story because it resonates with anyone who has suffered unjustly, who has been angry and hurt by life, and frustrated with God's silence, not because it is comforting and conclusive story. Job is honest: we don't know why a good God allows suffering, it is a mystery. Larry, in his discussion with Rabbi Nachter, is also put in his place much like Job.

RABBI NACHTER: "The answer! Sure! We all want the answer! But *Hashem* doesn't owe us the answer, Larry. *Hashem* doesn't owe us anything. The obligation runs the other way."
LARRY: "Why does he make us feel the questions if he is not going to give us any answers?"
RABBI NACHTER: "He hasn't told me."

This answer from a learned theologian is not one Larry readily accepts, so the Coens have it pop up again in the unlikeliest of places. For example, when the father of the failing Korean student asks Larry to accept a bribe and give his son a passing grade, Larry argues that it does not work that way, that he cannot ethically accept the money and the father calmly advises him to "Please accept the mystery."

Larry the physics professor wants his world to make sense, for his troubles to be the result of his immoral actions. Toward the end of the film the exasperated protagonist confesses to his colleague: "I am not an evil man!" despite watching one illicit movie. If he were an evil man, all his misfortune would make sense. Larry is not a morally serious man, in fact, in the very next scene he cannot bring himself to say: "I am a serious man." Perhaps the Coens are telling us being a "serious man," like Sy Abelman, is not the goal. We see Larry's strength come through in his compassionate response to his brother who is having a nervous breakdown in the drained Jolly Rodger motel pool. As in the story of Job, he cannot tell his brother why his life is full of pain and suffering (the chronic cyst, the police problems, the loneliness) but he can be there for him, he can hug him as he sobs, Larry has found somebody to love....

At the end of Larry's story there is a Jobian restoration, and he has learned his lesson to stop questioning everything and simply enjoy his life. There is a moment at the end of the film at his son Danny's *bar mitzvah*, when his stoned son is finally reciting the Torah and his wife squeezes his arm and smiles. There is so much healing in that moment. This acceptance is made easier with humor. I posit this humorous perspective is like the stabbed "dybbuk" laughing as he stumbles out into the snow overcome by the irony of life. Gabriel Levy suggests that *A Serious Man* is but another example of the Coen brother's using an attitude of "'solemn jest,' a deep humor that suspends and allows us to look wholeheartedly at difficult problems" (Levy, 2016, 231). We will examine one more Coen cinematic tale full of solemn jest when we turn to Buddhism. Judaism has always made room for the comedic. The Coens maintain this solemn jest until the very end of the credits where they proclaim: "No Jews were harmed in the making of this film."

ISRAELI ORTHODOX WALLS AND GENDER ROLES: *MOUNTAIN*

Judaism in the modern world is diverse. There are approximately 15 million Jews in the world today (0.2% of the world's population). The main branches of Judaism are Reform, Conservative, and

Orthodox. Israel, the context for our second film about Judaism, is 75% Jewish and home to approximately 40% of Jews today. The Orthodox and Ultra-Orthodox (Haredi) make up about 20% of the Jewish population in Israel today. There are dozens of films depicting Orthodox Jewish life, from *The Chosen* (1981) to *Ushpizin* (2004) and many more revealing Orthodox gender roles: from *Hester Street* (1976) to *Eyes Wide Open* (2009) to *Fill the Void* (2013). Films that portray the Orthodox women's sexual and emotional frustration are a sub-genre within these Orthodox family dramas, for example, *Price Above Rubies* (1998), *Disobedience* (2017), *Unorthodox* (2020). Israeli filmmaker Yaelle Kayam's first feature film, *Ha'har (Mountain)* is a quiet, slow independent film that provides us with a nuanced portrait of a contemporary Orthodox women's life. What can this film teach us about Judaism? It offers a window to one woman's gender-proscribed religious life amidst the multi-religious world of Jerusalem.

The story is simple, the pace measured and slow, the cast small. Zvia and her husband Reuven are an Orthodox couple who live in a tiny stone house with their four young children in the middle of cemetery on the Mount of Olives in Jerusalem. We follow the lonely daily life of this mother and wife whose conscribed existence is disrupted by the nocturnal visitations of pimps and sex workers who visit the cemetery each night. The Jewish Burial Society decided that they wanted "a Jewish presence" at the cemetery on the sacred mount and Reuven, who makes little money as a Yeshiva instructor (despite being a prodigy), accepted. One day two Jewish women from Tel Aviv encounter Zvia and she jokingly explains they are "the petting zoo." Orthodox communities are very concerned with keeping kosher and maintaining a strong border against the outside world. One of the Tel Aviv women earnestly asks if such a living arrangement is allowed by Jewish law and Zvia explains that it is kosher since there is a wire separating them from the cemetery and she adds she is happy because she can see the Temple Mount from her kitchen window. There is a wonderful *mise-en-scéne* that captures her world: Zvia stands with her back to us smoking in a cool grey kitchen with a sink full of dishes. She gazes out the small window and one can see the Temple Mount and the Al-Aqsa mosque's golden done glistening in the distance.

Jerusalem is a holy city shared by Jews, Muslims, and Christians; however, it is not always a peaceful co-existence. Zvia's unlikely friendship with the Palestinian cemetery caretaker Abed (Hitham Omari) both reveals these tensions and proffers that friendships can offer a model of peaceful religious coexistence. They enjoy smoking together amidst the tombstones. A wary friendship evolves as they share cigarettes and learn more about each other. Her husband Rueven does not approve of her speaking to another man, let alone an Arab Muslim. She shares some poetry with Abed next to the grave of her favorite poet, Zelda Scheenrson Mishkovsky.

"WHAT'S HARD FOR YOU?" DARING TO QUESTION JEWISH GENDER ROLES

Zvia struggles with her eldest daughter, Jeula, 7, as she tries to prepare her for the conscribed domestic role she will inevitably grow into. They argue over taking out the trash, doing the dishes etc. The father dotes on Jeula and quizzes her on theology. One evening, while Zvia is ironing the family's clothes and her husband is studying at his computer, he suggests Zvia should talk to his mentor's wife, a mother of seven, in order to be a better mother and handle the children, especially Jeula, more gracefully.

ZVIA: You're not home enough to know what she is really like, she puts on a show for you.
RUEVEN: She is seven years old.
ZVIA: You don't see it. I am with her most of the day and you are not even here. It is hard for me.
RUEVEN: It's hard for me too.
ZVIA: (with a look of disbelief on her face) What's hard for you?
RUEVEN: It's hard for me.
ZVIA: (gently) what is?
RUEVEN (turning back to his books): Look, I think each of us should do their part, ok?

A look of recognition washes over Zvia's luminous face communicating "It will always be like this." Her role as domestic servant and mother are set in stone, she must shut up and do her part for the sake of the family. They don't need to talk anything over, her gendered role is not up for negotiation (Figure 3.3).

Figure 3.3 Zvia and Abed smoke together while gazing at Temple Mount/Al Aqsa mosque (Yaelle Kayam, *Ha'har (Mountain)*, 2015).
Source: Screenshot by author.

"DO YOU HAVE A CIGARETTE?" JEWISH-MUSLIM FRIENDSHIP IN JERUSALEM

Beyond questioning gendered roles for women within Orthodox Judaism, *Mountain* gives us a glimpse of what quotidian interactions might feel like between Muslims and Jews in Jerusalem. This exchange happens one sunny afternoon while Zvia is smoking with Abed and gazing into Jerusalem.

ZVIA: Ever been to the Temple Mount?
ABED: You mean, Al-Aqsa?
ZVIA: We call it the Temple Mount.
   [Awkward pause, Abed takes a long drag before responding.]
ABED: It's a beautiful place, full of worshippers. You have never been there?
ZVIA: (wistfully) No.
ABED: There are visiting hours for Jews.
ZVIA: They don't let Jews pray there.
ABED: You know what? I have relatives in Ramallah. The Israeli's don't allow them to come here and pray.

Their conversation is then cut short since Abed's permit requires he cross back through the Israeli military checkpoint into Palestine before 5 p.m. This conversation is important because news media and many films often pit Israelis and Palestinians violently against one another. This slow-paced film shows a friendship organically evolve between two figures from different religions stuck in loveless, stale marriages. There is nothing romantic between them, they are friends. In fact, Abed, who once inquires of Avia if she is sad, may be more attuned to the Zvia than her own husband. It is, of course, a forbidden friendship for a strict Orthodox woman. Her interactions with the sex workers and gangster pimps are even more *verboten*.

Mountain is a quiet, moving film that pulls back the curtain on daily life for a fictionalized Orthodox woman. Zvia knows she is stuck. In a surprising and disturbing end, we see her preparing two pots of soup—one for her family and one for the cemetery night visitors who are about to reveal her interactions with them to her husband. Zvia sprinkles deadly rat poison into one pot and gingerly tastes it to make sure it is undetectable. We then see her serving the stew to both her family and later leaving a pot for the nightly cemetery crew. The next morning, she is standing alone amidst the white stone graves. The audience is left to decide which group got the poisoned pot. It is an unexpected plot twist, an effective move for Kayam, one which certainly forces you to discuss the lives and gendered-proscribed roles of Orthodox wives and mothers.

BUDDHISM

Buddhism is a world religion that began with the teachings of Siddhartha Gautama (c. 563 BCE–483 BCE) a prince from a region near Nepal. Buddhists make up approximately 7% of the world's population in 2020 and the number of adherents is decreasing. The majority of practitioners live in East and South Asia. Despite only comprising 1% of the U.S. population, Buddhism has inspired Hollywood films for over 100 years. D.W. Griffith's 1919 film, *Broken Blossoms* was one of the first depictions of a Buddhist monastic on film and established the trope of a mystical, effeminate, peaceful Buddhist monk. The story was based on a short story by Thomas Burke entitled "The Chink and the Child" and follows an idealistic Buddhist named Cheng Huan or "Yellow Man" from China who desires to bring "the message of peace to the warlike Anglo Saxons." The monk is played by Anglo actor Richard Barthelmess in yellowface. His noble intentions are quickly crushed by the harsh realities of life in London's poor Limehouse district where he becomes a shopkeeper and opium addict. He falls in love with a young girl named Lucy (Lillian Gish) who is abused and ultimately killed by her father Battling Burrows (Donald Crisp). The monk's Buddhism is presented as wholly other and one which cannot be assimilated by the West. While he is a sympathetic figure, the xenophobic establishment of his Otherness is hard to miss: he is racially suspect and despite his kindness toward the abused girl, questions about his intentions linger (Figure 3.4).

Another mysterious and slightly suspicious Buddhist monk is found in Frank Capra's 1937 film about Shangri-La, *Lost Horizon*. This is also the first of many films which romanticize Tibet as a prelapsarian Edenic world ruled by wise and mysterious lamas. The peak of filmic dramas related to Tibetan Buddhism came in the 1990s with *Kundun* (1997) by Martin Scorsese and *Seven Years in Tibet* (1997) by Jean Jacques Annaud, both of which focused on the

Figure 3.4 Moon scene with Lillian Gish and Richard Barthelmess in *Broken Blossoms* (D.W. Griffith, 1919).
Source: Publicity still, 1919.

current Dalai Lama, exiled leader of Tibetan Buddhism and favorite guru of the West. Bernardo Bertolucci's *Little Buddha* (1993) relates the quest of a handful of kind monks who go on a worldwide quest to find their reincarnated teacher—a road that leads them to India and Seattle, Washington. This film is an interesting way to explore Buddhism as it intersperses insider and outsider perspectives of Buddhism and weaves in Buddha's origin story (Keanu Reeves portrays Prince Siddhartha). These are just a sampling of the variety of ways Buddhism has inspired film for more than a hundred years. Most of these films offer an exoticized or romanticized portrayal of Buddhism and are far from the lived religious experience of most Buddhists. Our first film considered in-depth, *Departures,* provides us with window in lived Buddhism in Japan.

LIVED RELIGION: BUDDHISM, LIFE, AND DEATH IN JAPAN: *DEPARTURES*

Departures (2008) is Japanese art-house film directed by Yojiro Takita which won an Academy Award for Best Foreign Film as well as more than 40 other awards at various festivals around the world. The screenplay is based on the biographical text by Aoki Shinmom, *Coffinman: The Journal of a Buddhist Mortician.* It stars Masahiro Motoki as Daigo Kobayashi, a mediocre cellist whose orchestra has just been dissolved. This inciting incident forces him to move back to his hometown with his young wife in tow to regroup and start over. Once home, he answers a classified ad entitled "Departures," thinking it is a job at a travel agency, only to discover that the job is actually for a "Nōkanshi" or "en-coffiner," a Buddhist mortician who prepares deceased bodies (most often in front of a grieving family) for burial/cremation and entry into the next life or the Pure Land. Those who work in this position are explicitly avoided as touching the dead is seen as defiling work in this Shinto-influenced culture. Daigo first takes the work in order to survive, but slowly learns the beauty and essential role of his job. He learns not only about grieving families, loss, and death but also the wonder, joy, and meaning of life. Mr. Sasaki mentors young Daigo, training him with humor and patience telling him he was fated to be a *nōkanshi.*

Departures is a humorous, touching film which reveals Buddhist values, ethics, and worldview to viewers. The Buddhist practitioners are not exoticized monks in the Himalayas, but small business owners in a quaint town in northern island of Honshu, Japan. Approximately 35% of Japan is Buddhist, primarily practicing Jodoshinsu (Shin) Pure Land Mayahana Buddhism. This tradition is traced back to the teachings and life of Shinran Shonin (1173–1263). Shinran failed as a monk, however he developed a practice that all people could follow. Unlike Theravada or Tibetan Buddhism which privileges monastic renunciates who make vows to a religious community, Shin Buddhism does not focus on transcendence or require mediation that takes you away from others, monks may marry, for example. Jodoshinsu is Buddhism for everyone, every day. The release of the ego-self and reliance on self-power is also central, and the film's protagonist certainly demonstrates this release as he evolves from elite musician in a Tokyo orchestra to serving as a mortician in a small town. In Shin Buddhism expressions of other-power (*tariki*) displace the monastic ascetic self-power (*jiriki*). Recognizing your interconnectedness and then serving others with humility and compassion is preeminent. The film chronicles Daigo's ability to let go of the past, especially his conflicted feelings for his father who abandoned him, and step into the river of life.

Sharon Suh has written a marvelous book entitled *Silver-Screen Buddha: Buddhism in Asian and Western Film* in which she advances the study of Buddhism and film. She includes, but moves beyond, a critique of the othering and Orientalizing depictions of Buddhism in film and advocates a more inclusive, grounded Buddhism that includes gender, race, and politics as critical lenses and Buddhist interpretations of reality that can be applied to a variety of films. Her reading of *Departures* is nuanced and interweaves religious ideas (especially from Shin teacher Taitetsu Unno) with lived religion. She notes that *Departures* is far from filmic depictions of heroic figures of monastic virtuoso like the Dalai Lama,

> this kind of Buddhism receives little recognition in the West because it is neither exotic, nor heroic. Yet, as *Departures* demonstrates, acceptance of life as it is, with all its defilements and pleasures, is, in fact, profoundly heroic. …the spiritual life comes into play when one humbly accepts one's limitations. …[offering] a more ordinary form of Buddhism that holds this world of suffering to be the place of enlightenment.
>
> (Suh, 2014, 135)

Daigo certainly initially looks at his new job and the ostracization it brings, as suffering, admitting in a voiceover, "this is a trial I have been put through."

KEY BUDDHIST IDEAS: DEATH, LIFE, SEEING

The reality of death is a perduring instigator of religion. Humans tend to fear death and the gnawing sense that human life means nothing in the big scheme of things. Prince Siddhartha's encounter with a corpse was one of the Four Sights that spark his quest to discover the root of all human suffering. After years of asceticism and various forms of religious practice, he becomes enlightened, a fully aware being, a "Buddha." In fact, the central idea of his dharma (teaching) was awareness; furthermore, he taught that awareness is the path to deathlessness while ignorance is the path of death. Baizhang, an ancient Chinese Zen teacher spoke of the "elixir of immortality" being pure, naked awareness. *Departures* is a comedic indie film whose subject is death, but it could also be seen as a tale of Daigo's awakening or growing awareness of the place of death within human life. Perhaps a better title would be *Arrivals* as he himself arrives at awareness through preparing corpses for their next stage of life, in fact he refers to himself as "the gatekeeper" that opens to door for their family and the person to pass on the next stage.

A common trope in Buddhism is seeing. The goal of seeing life clearly is fundamental for a Buddhist. The pioneer Hollywood filmmaker D.W. Griffith shared this goal: "above all, I want you to *see*" he was fond of saying. Films can help us see life in a new way with their flickering intermittent light. This metaphor of seeing as spiritual enlightenment abounds in *Departures* and it is often the direct result of the mortician's craft of *shini-gesho* or death make-up. In one moving scene Mr. Sasaki and Daigo arrive to a funeral five minutes late and are berated by an angry bereaved husband. Daigo watches as Mr. Sasaki gently transforms the pale face of his dead wife to one flush with life resembling her portrait. You see the angry husband transformed as he recognizes his wife Naomi once again, he is then able to grieve her. As they leave the husband rushes out with a heart full of gratitude for his work and saying: "Thank you, she never looked so beautiful." After another preparation of a body a father thanks

Daigo for helping him "see" his son, who was a transvestite, once again. The preparation of the body is so much more than cleaning and make-up, it is about helping the living recognize the dead one last time.

The end of the film offers us one last instance of this dramatic recognition, this time for the protagonist himself, who has been estranged from his father since he was a small boy, in fact he can no longer even recall his father's face—it is a blurry memory. One day a telegram arrives for Daigo's deceased mother notifying her that her estranged husband has died. Miko urges Daigo to go and see his father one last time and he initially refuses, but relents, realizing that this will be the last time he sees his father. This powerful final scene encapsulates a Buddhist approach to life and death. The couple arrive to find his dead father laid out in a fishing shack. Daigo sadly admits he does not recognize him. All his earthly possessions fit in one box and Daigo shrugs and asks: "What was his life for anyway?" The *mis-en-scène* screams the answer: his son is there and behind him sits his wife with a new generation in her belly: his life did matter. Undertakers abruptly arrive and start to hurriedly gather his father's body and shove it in a coffin. Daigo is horrified at their lack of respect and care.

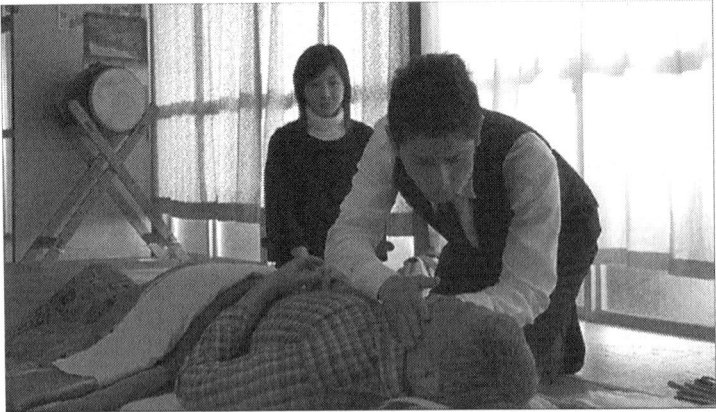

Figure 3.5 Daigo prepares the body of his recently-deceased father while pregnant wife watches in *Departures* (Yojiro Takita, 2008).
Source: Screenshot by author.

Miko intervenes and says "my husband is a professional" with pride, relaying her acceptance of his new calling (Figure 3.5).

Daigo then takes over the preparation of his own father's body and discovers, as he relaxes his fingers, that his father was clutching something, a small white stone, which was foreshadowed in a flashback as being the last gift Daigo gave his father. This discovery changes everything. Daigo realizes his father always loved him and never truly let go of him. He then gently shaves his father and recognizes him, the blurry visage in his memory is restored. The final two minutes of the film show us this recognition, their reconciliation, and his realization that life goes on. Miko tries to return the white stone so it can be buried with his father, but Daigo stops her and wraps her fingers around the stone and pushes it toward her womb signifying this piece of father-son history will be bequeathed to the next generation. Daigo's actions demonstrate his awareness of the interconnectedness of all life, it is a beautiful filmic moment that captures a Buddhist understanding of life and death.

KEY BUDDHIST CONCEPTS: COMPASSIONATE COMMUNITY (SANGHA), LETTING GO OF THE EGO-SELF, AND RECOGNITION OF THE OTHER

Our modern world emphasizes making our own way in life and being independent. Daigo has forged this path, but when it abruptly ends, he returns to his hometown where his mother left him a home. He slowly reconnects with old friends, finding special solace and community in the neighborhood bathhouse run by Tsuyako Yamashita, his boyhood friend's mother. Seeking profit, her son wants her to sell the old bathhouse that she runs to make room for condominiums. She refuses, arguing that the community needs her special hot water. It is clear she is not doing it for the money, but rather for her few faithful clients who find a second home at the bathhouse. Daigo, as a boy, used to escape to the baths and cry to himself while soaking when he thought no one was looking. Tsuyako embodies Shin Buddhist values: she understands we are all connected and must care for one another. When Daigo brings his wife Miko to the bathhouse, Tsuyako, pulls her aside privately and makes her promise to care for the tender-hearted Daigo. Her role as community preserver continues post-mortem; it is while Daigo is preparing her body for the coffin with such grace, love, and skill, that both his wife and his childhood friend who detest his work have a change of heart. They see him and the beauty of his work. Both wife and friend are reconciled with Daigo in this scene. Daigo finds true happiness reinserting himself into a small community, not as a musical star in the big city.

CHILLING WITH THE DUDE: BUDDHIST LESSONS IN *THE BIG LEBOWSKI* (1998)

The f-bomb-laden (292—but it is very un-dude to count them) comedy written and directed by Joel and Ethan Coen begins with a case of mistaken identity which draws a laidback, weed-smoking slacker into a world of millionaires and mayhem. The protagonist, Jeff Lebowski who prefers to go by "the Dude," just wants to bowl with his buddies Walter and Donnie and lie in his bathtub smoking marijuana while listening to whale sounds. The film was originally poorly received, and critics didn't quite know what to do with a comedy that got more outrageous as each new plot twist was introduced and included wild musical dream sequences. *The Big Lebowski* is now treasured by people around the world as part of American film history. It has a cult following much like *Jai Santoshi Maa* and *Star Wars*.

FAN DEVOTION CREATES THE RELIGION OF DUDEISM

Much like *Star Wars* and *Star Trek* devotees, fans have developed a priesthood and rituals and code of ethics based on the film. The film has inspired such a passionate fan base that a new religion has emerged: Dudeism and The Church of the Latter-Day Dude. Taking a Cultural Studies approach, what does this say about our early 21st-century spiritual appetites and predilections? If Zen-ultra lite can inspire 200,000 people to become Dudeist priests, what is the future of traditional organized religion? Dudeism, founded by Oliver Benjamin, is centered in Greenwich Village, New York at the Little Lebowski Bookstore and does not proselytize, but does host Lebowski Festivals attended by thousands and has recently opened an online learning platform in 2018: Abide University and Institute. Here you can learn in various departments from Leisure Science to Abidena Counseling. Benjamin finds the Dude's wisdom more closely aligns with Daoism than Buddhism and wrote *The Dude De Ching*, a translation and reworking of the *Tao Te Ching* using lines from *The Big Lebowski*. Both Daoism and Buddhism developed in Asia in the 6th-century BCE. and some scholars speak of "Buddho-Daosim." Dudeism's worldview is summarized thus:

> Life is short and complicated, and nobody knows what to do about it. So don't do anything about it. Just take it easy, man. Stop worrying so much whether you'll make it into the finals. Kick back with some friends and some oat soda and whether you roll strikes or gutters, do your best to be true to yourself and others – that is to say, abide.
> (Creed from Dudeism.com)

ZEN LESSONS FROM THE DUDE: GO WITH THE FLOW, TAKE IT EASY MAN

The Dude does exhibit some Zen Buddhist fundamental ideas: for example, when he tells his Vietnam veteran friend Walter, who suffers from PTSD: "Don't live in the past, man, life goes on!" Here the Dude exemplifies the Buddhist ideal of going with the flow and fully appreciating, even taking joy in, the fullness of every moment—being fully present. Part of Buddhist enlightenment, as we saw in *Departures*, is discovering the interconnectedness of all life. The Dude, as he investigates the many threads of Bunny Lebowski's kidnapping and the lost money, unravels this interconnectedness. He explains to her husband: "New sh** has come to light, man" and later describes these complex interrelationships to Maude: "There are a lot of strands… a lot of strands in Duder's head." The closing scene has the Dude cheerfully saying farewell to the narrator (Sam Rockwell) with the now infamous phrase: "the Dude abides" as he returns to his bowling game. The film has a life beyond its 1 hour and 58 minutes. Jeff Bridges began a friendship with Zen teacher, Bernie Glassman, when the latter told him at a dinner party: "You know, in some Buddhist circles, The Dude is a Zen Master." Glassman and Bridges wrote a book entitled *The Dude and the Zen Master* in which they discuss central tenets of Zen Buddhism and ways in which the Dude embodies these ideas. Bridges turns to Webster's Dictionary to define "abide" as "to wait patiently for something, or to endure without yielding, accept without objection." In our success-driven, instant gratification-oriented and impatient world, true abiding, confesses Bridges, requires great mastery. In fact, patience (*kshanti*) is a central Buddhist virtue or noble character quality (*paramita*). Glassman sees the Dude as a truly free Zen master: "The Dude is not attached to some self-image, identity, or a life narrative. Since he abides nowhere, he is free to abide everywhere" (Bridges and Glassman, 2012, 75). Despite the lead actor, Jeff Bridges, being a practicing Buddhist and this book unpacking the koans of the Dude, I argue that *The Big Lebowski* and Dudeism falls short of presenting a fully compelling translation of Zen Buddhism for our time. The fandom and resulting religious devotion and books; however, make *The Big Lebowski* a fascinating exemplar of pop culture inspiring a religious response.

CHRISTIANITY

As recounted in Chapter 1, Christianity and biblical stories were the subject matter of films since the dawn of cinema, and Christian theologians were pioneers in Religion and Film Studies. Christian theological themes and figures continue to dominate publications and research in religion and film. Since every chapter in this book features films related to Christianity, from the theological reading of Christian redemption in *Breaking the Waves* in Chapter 2 to analyses of *The Way, Andrei Rublev,* and *Amazing Grace* in Chapter 4 to *God Loves Uganda* in Chapter 5, I will keep this section brief. Christianity is the world's largest religion in 2021 (approximately 2.4 billion adherents), the religion of one third of the globe. Followers believe that Jesus of Nazareth was the Son of God, he incarnated, lived, taught, and ultimately sacrificed his life for their redemption and restoration as children of God. While there are thousands of denominations and significant doctrinal differences between branches, all Christians find their salvation and hope in Jesus' salvific actions. The Holy Spirit and God the Father join Jesus to comprise the Godhead, or Holy Trinity, three-in-one. The two films analyzed below focus on two of the figures in the Trinity: Jesus the Son and the Holy Spirit. Since the demographic center of Christianity in the 21st century is now in Africa (Timbuktu, Mali), I find it fitting to analyze a portrait of Jesus and modern passion story that emerges from the continent. Our second film pulls back the curtain on the fastest-growing segment of Christians today: Pentecostals, which represents approximately 25% of the globe's Christians. By 2060, a plurality of Christians—more than four-in-ten—will call sub-Saharan Africa home and 22% will reside in Latin America.[1] Over the past century, the center of Christianity has shifted from the global north to the global south. The USA and Europe will be home to less than a quarter of all Christians by the mid 21st century.

KEY CHRISTIAN FIGURE: JESUS AS PERSONIFIED IN *SON OF MAN*

Christianity began with the followers of Jesus Christ sharing his story and message around the world. At heart, it is a religion of "Christ followers." Depictions of Jesus have inspired hundreds of films globally, from Cecil B. Demille's 1927 *King of Kings* to Mel Gibson's *The Passion of the Christ* (2004). One way to appreciate the power of Jesus' persona is to compare these various retellings of his life. There are traditional portraits such as *The Jesus of Nazareth* (1977) and more experimental versions such as *Last Days in the Desert* (2016 with Ewan MacGregor as Jesus); however, I have chosen a post-colonial politicized portrait of Jesus set in contemporary South Africa, *Son of Man* (2006). This is one more filmic depiction of Jesus' life adapted for a new context, as was *Jesus of Montreal* (1989) and *Jesus Christ Superstar* (1973). Director Mark Dornford-May sets the Jesus story in an African "Judea" and uses news broadcasts of real socio-political conflicts interspersed with moments of angelic magical realism and Satan lurking to re-tell the story of the birth, life, and death of Jesus. The main scenes from his life are reenacted: from the annunciation with Mary to the Slaughter of the Innocents (with AK 47s) to Jesus overturning the tables in the temple to the calling of his disciples. Jesus is seen as a political threat by representatives of the state and the "Sanhedrin" ask for proof of his "political ambitions." Judas does not betray Jesus with a kiss, but with a video camera that contains footage of Jesus at a rally extolling those gathered to act with "dignity, solidarity and unity." He is still a Jesus of peace, however, and collects weapons from his followers in one moving scene.

Of course, there are many innovations in this contemporary re-telling of Jesus' life and death. For example, the disciples are not simple fishermen, but a motley crew of miners, hustlers, arms dealers, thieves, prostitutes and 3 of the 12 are women. The Garden of Gethsemane is not an idyllic hill of olive trees, but a desolate, abandoned industrial construction site. Jesus is offered more chances to escape his fate in this re-telling: first the angels ask him if he wants to return home to heaven after witnessing the Slaughter of the Innocents by Herod and he responds: "No, this is my world." After he is captured and beaten for sedition, the political mafia ask Jesus to join them and he refuses and is then killed unceremoniously and dumped in a shallow grave in the desert.

There are two striking elements of this Christian passion tale: women are pivotal actors and music is a force for change. From the steely will to live exhibited by Mary in the school massacre opening scene to female disciples to women protesting the disappearance of Jesus, women in this film are strong. Mary ultimately finds Jesus' body and digs it out with her own hands and places him on a cross on a hill. Music is also a powerful force in *Son of Man*. As we learned in Chapter 2, sound is a powerful element in experiencing film, some would argue that it is more powerful than images. The penultimate scene on Calvary hill is an amazingly powerful example of the use of sound and music. Mary, with a redolent alto voice, begins with a solo singing simply "the land is covered in darkness." A chorus of women soon follows singing the refrain and then the men join in and the tune is sung in moving rounds. This chorus is interrupted by sounds and images of a militarized state with their thundering tanks, troops, and helicopters closing in on Calvary hill. An aural battle escalates as St. Peter breaks out stomping and singing "Unite freedom fighters!" The soldiers fire shots at the crowd of mourners and they all hit the dirt, then there is silence. Mary then stands, she looks at her son on the cross and resolutely walks toward the soldiers, using her her voice as her weapon, "the world is covered in darkness" she sings and the soldiers back down, disarmed with the power of music and a collective voice. *Son of Man* is an expression of postcolonial agency, a call to constructive political action, a new interpretation of the Gospel and the passion, and a stunning addition to the Jesus film tradition.

DIVERSITY IN CHRISTIANITY: SOUTHERN BLACK PENTECOSTALS IN THE USA

Free in Deed is an independent film by a New Zealand writer/director/producer Jake Mahaffy. It is a powerful film that never saw wide theatrical release despite strong performances by leads Edwina Findley Dickerson (*Selma, Middle of Nowhere, The Wire*) as Melva and David Harewood (*Blood Diamond, Supergirl*) as the constrained Abe Wilkins. It tells the story of a young mother trying to help her autistic son who is growing increasingly violent. She is poor and the medical system would rather medicate or institutionalize her son than help him. Melva is running out of options and turns to the church and their promises to heal her son.

Mahaffy, who grew up Pentecostal but is now "de-converted," was drawn to a news story of a healing/exorcism gone wrong in which an eight-year-old autistic boy died of asphyxiation in 2003 at the Pentecostal Faith Temple Church of the Apostolic Faith in Milwaukee Wisconsin. Minister Ray A. Hemphill was convicted of felony child abuse and sentenced to 2½ years in prison and 7 years on parole. Whether the boy was asphyxiated or had a bad reaction to his new medication that listed "sudden death" as a possible side effect, is not vital to the film's intention to expose the tension between a spiritual and a scientific worldview.

Free in Deed offers a fascinating glimpse into the world of Pentecostal church services and a select group of Black Christians' experience in the USA. Pentecostal Christians are a sub-group of Evangelical Protestant Christianity and emphasize baptism of the Holy Spirit and exhibition of the gifts of the Spirit, ecstatic worship, and total surrender to God. The 21st century is witnessing significant growth of Pentecostal/Charismatic Christianity. In fact, according to the Pew Forum's research, over 25% of Christians today and 8% of the world's population are Pentecostal/Charismatic. The film takes dramatic license (adding a bit of romance where there was none, having the mom lose her job) but it wonderfully brings viewers into authentic Pentecostal storefront worship services. Mahaffy cast real-life church leader and prophet, Prophetess Libra, and used her church and congregation in the film. The church worship scenes were non-scripted, real, and genuine according to the director. He allowed Prophetess to take charge and then placed his actors into the action, having a background in documentary film surely helped him here. Her real-life congregation is called The Cathedral of God Holy Word Temple. Audiences are enveloped into the fundamentals of a Pentecostal service: passionate bodily singing and dancing, healing stories, personal testimonies, altar calls to dedicate your life to Jesus, laying on of hands and healing prayer, being slain in the spirit, powerful preaching that demands a response, and speaking in tongues (glossolalia) (Figure 3.6).

Pentecostal Christians place an emphasis on the power of the Holy Spirit to defeat Satan and worldly powers of darkness. This world is an arena of spiritual warfare and you must declare whose side you are on. In one scene, the church ladies visit Melva's apartment to "cleanse" it of evil influences that may be contributing to her son's possession by evil spirits. They purge her home of pictures of owls and bats as they represent spirits of darkness in a Pentecostal worldview. A *Star Wars* light saber is also suspect as it represents reliance on a power other than God to combat evil. Abe, who is shown to be a conduit of God's healing power, is enlisted in the spiritual battle to save Benny. Modern medicine is not trusted to save the suffering autistic boy as his torment is believed to be caused by demons. "We don't medicate, we liberate!" Abe explains to Melva,

Figure 3.6 Abe attempts to exorcise Benny in *Free in Deed* (Jake Mahaffy, 2015).
Source: Screenshot by author

"our God is God of love, power, and sound mind." The multiple sessions of healing prayer/exorcism are understood as a battle to free Benny of a demon. To his credit, the final exorcism scene has none of the horror theatrics of *The Exorcist* or the many films in the possession genre. Benny struggles, but cries out only in his voice, his own mother holds down his legs as he writhes, he is not struck, and how he stops breathing is not made clear. What is clear, however, is how fervently Abe believes his prayers for Benny will be answered: "I am gonna deliver you tonight," he whispers in the boy's ear, "in the name of Jesus!"

ISLAM

Islam is the world's second largest religion with approximately 1.9 billion adherents. Islam is a monotheistic Abrahamic-based religion which recognizes Muhammed (570–632 CE) as God's final prophet. Muslims live throughout the globe, the majority (62%) living in Asia, 20% in West Asia or MENA, 16% live in Sub-saharan Africa. Film can provide us with vignettes of Muslim life in these diverse contexts. The first film we will consider dramatizes Muslim life in a Muslim majority region (now Bangladesh—90% Muslim) whereas our second film portrays what is like to be Muslim in a small, ethnic-based Muslim community of the Nation of Islam in a country where Muslims comprise less than 1% of the population (USA). Each tale reveals the enmeshment of Islam with politics; however, the latter complicates the tension by adding the issue of race to religious affiliation. Both films are set in the tumultuous 1960s.

KEY ISLAMIC IDEAS: AUTHORITY AND PEACE

Matir Moina (*The Clay Bird*, 2002) is a Bengali dramatic film directed by Tareque Masud, based on his own childhood and the tumultuous era between 1963 and 1971 in East Pakistan (now Bangladesh). It provides a nuanced portrait of Islam and politics as well as life within a madrassah (religious school) from a child's point of view. Throughout the film, there are references to historical occurrences in agitated political times leading up to the Bangladeshi War of Liberation, and the film portrays these episodes through the eyes of the young protagonist, his family, as well as his teachers and peers at the madrasah. The film's cast includes Nurul Islam Bablu as young Anu, Jayanta Chattopadhyay plays the zealous fundamentalist father Kazi, and Rokeya Prachy portrays the longsuffering and lonely wife Ayesha. *Matir Moina* won a number of awards internationally, but was initially banned in Bangladesh on the grounds that it dealt with sensitive religious issues. The film was a passion project for the husband and wife filmmaking team. Produced by Catherine Masud *Matir Moina* was awarded the FIPRESCI Prize in section Directors' Fortnight competition at the 2002 Cannes Film Festival and became Bangladesh's first film to compete for the Academy Award for Best Foreign Language Film. Catherine Masud, who co-wrote, produced, and edited the film shared that "the biggest obstacle was the subject matter itself: madrasahs and religion." They wanted their portrayal of life in a madrasah to feel authentic and used actual madrasah students and teachers, in place of professional actors. Tareque Masud relayed that the real reward was seeing fellow Bangladeshis find communal healing through watching and participating in the film… "out of that suffering came a new creation [*The Clay Bird*], we weren't alone in our suffering."

LIVED RELIGION: ISLAMIC LIFE IN A MADRASAH

There are two distinct forms of Islam being taught to the boys in the madrasah: a militant, defensive religiosity articulated by their headmaster and a kinder, gentler form inspired by the Sufi tradition taught by Ibrahim, one of the boys' caretakers. The sternness of the headmaster as the authority in the school is established in the very first scene in which Anu is reprimanded for using his shortened name, told it "is not a proper Islamic name" and is re-named "Mohammed Anwar." He teaches the boys that Islam is "a way of life, not just prayer and fasting." The only physical sport allowed is a defensive stick martial art as they are forming religious soldiers to make jihad against the dangerous forces of secularism. He does not allow the boys to ask questions during his lessons and physically punishes those who do. This is the despotic, dire portrait many films paint of life in madrasahs; however, *The Clay Bird* is different. The madrasah is also a place of fun, care for orphans, friendship, and kind adults. Following a particularly fiery sermon, the boys and caretakers discuss the lesson while squatting in the courtyard making clay bricks to use for the toilet. This conversation wonderfully captures a different understanding of Islamic conversion and politics.

IBRAHIM: Here, Islam did not spread through the sword. It was the selfless Sufi's who went to the low-caste Hindus to spread Islam's message of peace and equality. The kings of Iran and Arabia conquered land, but not people's hearts. It was thanks to the Sufis that people embraced Islam. The truth is you cannot make Islam flourish with politics or arms. It is unfair to use these children for political ends.

HALIM MIAH: But in the name of secularism the Communists are endangering the very existence of Islam! Don't we need to confront them?

IBRAHIM: What is the difference between the Communists and us?

HALIM MIAH: Can you separate Islam from politics? Now Pakistan's unity is threatened, if Pakistan is torn apart, Islam will be weakened as well.

IBRAHIM (shaking his head): What makes you think that? Did Pakistan establish Islam or rather enforce military rule? (fade out)

The character of Ibrahim exhibits Sufi values of love and mercy and was modeled on Masud's real-life madrasah teacher Faiz Ahmad. His is an Islam that transcends politics and ever-evolving social crises. By situating this discussion between two teachers working in the garden with the boys reveals a kinder, more flexible version of Islam that was also influencing the boys at the madrasah.

DIVERSE CONTEXTS: THE NATION OF ISLAM IN THE USA

Muslims represent approximately 1% (3.45 million) of the U.S. population according to an Institute for Social Policy and Understanding's 2018 report. African-Americans and Blacks from other countries comprise about 25% of American Muslims and The Nation of Islam boasts about 30,000 members. Spike Lee's film based on Malcom X's autobiography therefore focuses on an racial minority who joins a small sect within a minority religion—a very different story than our film from Bangladesh, a Muslim majority context. New layers of identity and struggle are at play.

Muslims first arrived in the Americas in large number through the 17th-century slave trade; however, many slaves converted to Christianity and Muslim worship was not allowed. In the post-Civil War period various black Muslim leaders arose, including Noble

Drew Ali, originally Timothy Drew (1886–1929), who founded the Moorish Science Temple of America in Newark, New Jersey, in 1913. A member of this temple, Wallace D. Fard (or Wali Fard Muhammad), claimed he was Noble Drew Ali reincarnated and founded The Nation of Islam on July 4, 1930 in Detroit, Michigan. His disciple and protégée was Elijah Muhammad (1897–1975, born Elijah Poole) who soon left to establish the Nation's second temple in Chicago, Illinois. When Fard mysteriously disappeared one day while floating on Lake Michigan, Elijah Muhammed took over the Nation of Islam and began to further develop its separatist platform. His teachings included many of the basic tenets of Islam, including monotheism, submission to Allah, dietary, and lifestyle tenets, but he added a creation myth to appeal to disenfranchised blacks. Elijah Muhammad taught his followers they were the true Muslims destined to control the world. He told them the white race was created by Yakub, a black scientist, and that Allah had allowed this devilish race to hold power for 6,000 years. Their time was up in 1914, and the 20th century was to be the time for black people to assert themselves. This myth supported a program of economic self-sufficiency, the development of black-owned businesses, and a demand for the creation of a separate black nation to be carved out of the states of Georgia, Alabama, and Mississippi. Elijah Muhammed led the Nation of Islam until his death in 1975 and his son, Warith Deen Mohammed took over and tried to transform the Nation into orthodox Sunni Muslim group. This did not go well. The group splintered and ultimately re-grouped under the leadership of Louis Farrakhan in 1977 who revitalized the group and still serves as its leader. Today there are 20–50,000 members.

Malcolm Little, a conman, drug dealer, and hustler was introduced the teachings of Elijah Muhammed and Islam while in prison where he embraced Islam and the Nation of Islam. Malcolm X was a minister in the Temple and a direct disciple of Elijah Muhammed for 12 years. His wit and oratory skills brought many into the movement and the film captures his charisma well. Ultimately expelled from the Nation, he accepted orthodox Islam after going on the hajj, the pilgrimage to Mecca. Before he could fully articulate his new views of a racially inclusive Islam, several members of the Nation of Islam brutally killed him in 1965.

The 1992 film, *Malcolm X,* directed by Spike Lee and starring Denzel Washington depicts the power of Islam to transform a life, the dangers of mixing other social agendas with religion, and its global racial inclusivity. I will never forget viewing this film in 1992 in a packed theater in Hyde Park on the Southside of Chicago. The emotional impact of many scenes evoked tears and shouts from the predominantly African-American audience. We were sitting literally blocks away from the headquarters of the Nation of Islam and Louis Farrakan's home. It was clear that Malcolm X was a hero to those in the audience and that the battles he fought against systemic racism were still fresh.

The first hour of the film is devoted to Malcolm's sordid street hustler life after his Baptist father preacher was lynched by the KKK and his mother was committed to a mental institution. He ends up drug addicted and in jail (1946–1952), and this is where he meets brother Baynes (John Bembry) who intrigues him with the line: "I can show you how to get out of prison!" Of course, Baynes is talking about the freedom of the mind and soul that comes with embracing Islam. Slowly he disciples Malcolm and teaches him the distinct Nation of Islam Black separatist myth, that he is part of the lost tribe of Shabazz, and that all white people are evil. Malcolm ultimately converts and once released, vows his allegiance to the Nation of Islam and the honorable Elijah Muhammed. Malcolm's intelligence and charisma soon begin to attract many converts, but he is always careful to preface his sermons with "the honorable Elijah Muhammed teaches us…." In the tumult that was the 1960s in the USA, his religious message was also a political one. He advocated armed resistance against corrupt police authority and complete separation of blacks from other races. Denzel Washington's portrayal is both powerful and sympathetic.

A turning point in the film comes when Malcom X discovers his spiritual mentor Elijah Muhammed has fathered many children out of wedlock. He becomes disillusioned with the organization and their control over him. He was punished with 90 days of silence, for instance, after speaking out about the President Kennedy's 1963 assassination. In 1964 he decided to go on pilgrimage to Mecca and other holy sites in the Mid-East to perform his hajj. This Muslim experience profoundly changed Malcolm and the film depicts this

Figure 3.7 Malcolm X during Hajj in *Malcolm X* (Spike Lee, 1992).
Source: Screenshot by author.

well as only images can. He finally found himself shoulder to shoulder with Muslims of all races and cultures, those "with skin as white as snow and blue eyes" yet they were his brothers. Scenes in the film allow us to see this transformation as he eats and sleeps with fellow pilgrims of all nationalities and races (Figure 3.7).

He realizes that he is not a racist and that "the true practice of Islam can remove the cancer of racism as true Islam is about freedom, justice and equality." This trip forced Malcolm to disentangle his religion from a political, racial agenda of black empowerment. Following his Hajj, he changed his name to el-Hajj Malik el-Shabazz and began to articulate a more inclusive platform of Muslim reform. He left the Nation of Islam and formed the Muslim Mosque Inc. and converted to Sunni Islam. Unfortunately, the fruit of his maturation and re-conversion never had time to take effect as he was brutally murdered in front of his wife and children on February 21, 1965 by three Nation of Islam gunmen as he spoke in the Audubon ballroom. The film concludes with a montage of the effect of Malcolm X's life around the globe—from South Africa (inspiring Nelson Mandela) to U.S. schoolchildren (shouting "I am Malcom X"). Lee gives us a powerful story of a life transformed by Islam.

INTER-RELIGIOUS RELATIONS IN FILM

To conclude this chapter, I would like to consider two filmic models of inter-religious relations: the first film, *Earth*, portrays relations that disintegrate amidst political turmoil while *Life of Pi* offers a model of interfaith relations within oneself. *Earth* is set in Lahore during the partition of India in 1947 and focuses on relationships between Hindus, Muslims, Sikhs, Christians, and Parsees. It is an historical drama told through friendships and chronicles what happens to these friendships when religious affiliation becomes a matter of life and death. This 1998 film was written and directed by Indian-Canadian director Deepa Mehta and is the second film in her elements trilogy: *Fire* (1996) was about a forbidden love relationship between two women stuck in arranged marriages, *Earth* focuses on the politics, and *Water* (2007) centers on women and religion.

Before focusing on the interreligious lessons one can draw from this cautionary tale, mention should be made of some narrative and cinematic factors. The story is told from the perspective of a child, "Lenny Baby," and was inspired by the novel by Pakistani author Bapsi Sidhwa entitled *Ice Candy Man*. The score was composed by the legendary A.R. Rahman. Each film in the trilogy has a distinct color palette and the burnt red soil of Lahore almost becomes a character in the film. The buildup of darkening reds and browns foreshadow the threat of bloody violence to come. The blood shed was not fiction, as British officials left Lahore they had to pick their way through streets littered with dead bodies and found the railway stations flooded with blood and whole trains of Muslim refugees arriving from the south slaughtered. The 1947 Partition was a dramatic and great migration of Muslims fleeing northward and Hindus and Sikhs fleeing southward. For example, in 1941, Karachi, designated the first capital of Pakistan, was 48% Hindu and Delhi was one-third Muslim. By the end of the decade, almost all the Hindus in Karachi had fled, while 200,000 Muslims had been forced out of Delhi. Altogether more than 15 million people were displaced by the Great Partition and 1–2 million died in the process. Today the states of India and Pakistan, both nuclear powers, remain at a tense détente.

Innocent Lenny Baby, whose affluent Parsee family remains politically and religiously neutral throughout the film, narrates the story. She is cared for by a Hindu nanny, young, beautiful Shanta (played by Nandita Das). Two Muslim men, Hasan the Masseur and Dil Navaz (played by Aamir Khan, referred to as "Ice Candy Man" by Lenny) are both in love with Shanta and strive to win her hand as the story progresses. We are less concerned with romantic storylines and more concerned with religious identities, prejudices, and tensions; however, as in real life, romantic interests and politics are often influenced by religion. The Muslims in the friend group vary in their devotion: Dil Navaz is a prankster religious charlatan who calls Allah on the phone telling fortunes in the park but ultimately uses the Muslim mob to exact his revenge on Shanta, and the Romeo, Hasan, who is devout, but vows to become a Hindu in order to marry Shanta. The main Hindu figures are Shanta, the nanny/maid and her friend, Tota Ramji, who does convert to Islam to save his life (he is circumcised and learns the Shahada). People are desperate to survive and sometimes that means making unthinkable choices like marrying your 8-year-old daughter to a 60-year-old man because his Christian identity will protect you and your family. This friend group and their interactions grow increasingly tense as Partition becomes a reality, Muslim refugees begin to flood the city, neighbors betray neighbors, and sectarian violence increases.

The evolution of the tone of the conversation when these friends meet, whether it is at the park or a diner, tracks the increasing hostility between religious groups in Lahore. Let us compare a jovial, if testy, early gathering in the park with a diner scene later in the film. It is a beautiful, sunny day in the park and the Muslim, Sikh, and Hindu 20 somethings, sit in a circle. They are joking and eating sweets and ice cream and Shanta reveals that Lenny Baby is afraid of the lion in the zoo where several of them work. The Sikh bravely tells the girl not to worry, he will hold him fast which does not reassure the little girl. The nanny hugs her and tells her not to worry, a hundred ferocious lions could not break through the bars and hurt her. The guys boast they have concocted potions to grow hair or increase fertility, but soon enough the conversation turns to politics and one reports that Ghandi, Prime Minister Nehru, and British Commander Battencourt are thick as thieves to which Dil Navaz rejoins: who will represent us Muslims? who will stand with Jinnah? (leader who was campaigning for an independent Pakistan for almost a decade by this point). Shanta gets up, playfully indignant, and tells the boys if they don't stop talking politics, they will have to get along without her company. Fast forward to the diner scene where one of the Muslims chastises Lenny Baby for ordering "English pudding." Shanta quickly reprimands him and tells him not to take his anger against the British out on a little girl. They then debate whether Lahore will go to the Hindus who own most of the businesses or to the Muslims who are greater in number. Insults and threats ensue, and anger grows. Hassan tries to temper the tension by reminding his friends of their shared history: "Are you mad? We have gotten along for centuries! We share the same language, food, and enemies.... the Sikh faith came to bring us Muslims and Hindus closer together. We'll stand by each other, won't we?" Most agree to be loyal to one another; however only a few keep these promises when ethnic and religious tensions boil over into riots in the city.

I did not choose *Earth* as an exemplar of lovely coexistence between ordinary adherents of different religions; although it begins with an idyllic portrait of jocular friends, it devolves into betrayal between friends and the brutal murder of the religious other. It is a filmic and very human portrait of what can happen when religious groups demonize the other, when fear replaces friendship. Comfort was not Mehta's intention:

> I think watching *Earth* to a certain degree provides discomfort, which is excellent because we cannot be comfortable. There's a lovely quote in the film that Aamir Khan's character Ice Candy Man says about the animal within us. We all live with the animal. And the point of living is to actually make sure that the animal remains caged. If something like [*Earth*] reminds us that we cannot afford to unleash the negative aspect of ourselves as human beings, then that's a good thing.[2]

In today's world of violent religious fundamentalism, jingoism, riots in the streets, and world leaders who rise to power riding a wave of xenophobia—Narendra Modi in India and Donald Trump in the USA—*Earth*'s portrait of a society torn asunder by religious difference could not be more pertinent. We need more voices like Hassan's that remind us of our common history, ground, and interest. An alternative and more hopeful portrait of inter-religious relations in India is offered by the film *Lagaan: Once Upon a Time in India* which shows us inter-religious collaboration based on a common purpose of avoiding paying taxes to the British. Hindus, Muslims, Sikhs, Christians, and a Dalit form a winning cricket team to defeat the British, their common enemy.

INTER-RELIGIOUS HARMONY WITHIN YOURSELF: "FAITH IS A HOUSE WITH OF MANY ROOMS"

Life of Pi (Ang Lee, 2012) is a film that demonstrates how an individual from a multi-religious context (once again India) can reconcile multiple religions within himself. The protagonist, Piscine "Pi" Molitov Patel, manages to follow multiple religious traditions. Discussions as to whether this is authentic religiosity or adulterating usually follows screenings. "None of us knows God unless we are introduced" Pi explains recalling his spiritual journey as a young boy to a journalist. He was born into a culturally Hindu family and recounts his mother telling him stories of Krishna and the creation of the world. Hiding under the covers with a flashlight he would devour comic books featuring the Hindu gods who were his "superheroes." While his mother is a woman of faith and wants to preserve her link to her family and her past through her religious traditions, Pi's father is a man of science who is decidedly hostile to religious devotion, counseling his son: "religion is darkness, don't let the pretty lights fool you!"

As a boy, Pi's multi-religious quest is fueled by curiosity. He begins to explore Catholic Christianity at the age of 12 and enters a theological dialogue with a Catholic priest while on vacation in the south. He is troubled by atonement theory, sacrificing the innocent to atone for the sins of the guilty makes no sense to Pi, and he asks the priest hard questions like: why does God need us? Why did he create all this? To which the smiling priest replies "all you need to know is that God loves us." This answer and Pi's internalizing of the message of God's love is the message he takes from Christianity. Author Yann Martel does not dig deeper than this into Christianity. The gleaned message is equally simplistic when it comes to Islam. Pi is shown being drawn to the Muslim call to prayer one day while walking through the Muslim part of Pondicherry. He never learns Arabic, but the sounds bring him peace and a sense of intimacy with God. From the practice of Islam Pi finds a feeling of serenity and brotherhood.

Inter-religious solidarity is often puzzling for both religious outsiders and insiders who want to maintain their tradition's purity and boundaries. How can Christians, Hindus, and Muslims truly come together when their fundamental worldviews and beliefs are so different? In a dinner scene, Pi is being mocked by his big brother for practicing multiple religions at once and his father, who champions science and rationality, intervenes and instructs him that he cannot follow three different religions at once to which Pi innocently responds, "why not?" "Because believing in everything is the same as not believing in anything at all!" His father strives to get Pi to choose the path of science and to leave religion behind. Seeing his son is spiritually oriented, he relents and instructs him to choose one religious tradition and stick with it. Obedient Pi nods in agreement but then turns to his understanding Hindu mother and announces, "I would like to be baptized!" He is not choosing Christianity at the exclusion of other faiths however. As a grown man he explains his inter-religious inner faith thus: "Faith is a house of many rooms." He embraces truth in all religions, describing himself as Christian-Hindu-Jew-Muslim and jokes that, as a Catholic-Hindu, "I get to feel guilty before hundreds of gods instead of just one!"

In the 21st century, Pi's all-embracing inter-religious consortium is attractive, especially in cosmopolitan urban centers where one can worship at mosque on a Friday eve, wake up the next morning and go to a Zen meditation hour, enjoy a Hindu festival during the day, catch a Kabbalisitc lecture at night and finish off the weekend with a Christian church service on Sunday. Many people have created a cafeteria approach to religion that resembles Pi's. They celebrate diversity and dabble in several religions picking and choosing what works for them at different points in their spiritual journey. The problem with this, as Pi's father intuited, is that it does not go very deep. Some of these traditions, such as Christianity and Islam, are exclusivist, meaning that they demand followers accept the exclusive truth of their tradition, for example, the main proclamation of faith in Islam, the *shahada,* declares: "There is no God, but God and Mohammed is his prophet." Clearly you cannot assent to this and worship Hinduism's many deities. To authentically follow an exclusivist tradition you must decline the others. *Life of Pi* does not recognize this, choosing instead to offer and happy, easy, religious decoupage.

Inter-religious relations are complicated. Many advocates of inter-religious dialogue initially gather to dispel myths and stereotypes about the other and find common ground, or have a common social justice cause. This celebration of common beliefs and shared values is important, and this is the level of religious diversity and commonality that *Life of Pi* advocates. There is, however, a maturation in inter-religious work today that delves deeper and seeks to understand the religious other by learning about differences between religions that are not washed away in a PC celebration of diversity or a common social goal. The deeper work of inter-religious relations is far more uncomfortable, but also more mature. It is easy to say all roads lead to the same place and God wears different masks, but this is fundamentally not true from a religious studies perspective. Discovering and appreciating genuine differences without trying to force connection or utilizing what works for individual needs is the goal. Each of these films informs our understanding of inter-religious relationships. The friendships between Hindus, Muslims, and Sikhs are tested in the tumultuous tale of *Earth*. Amid societal crisis inter-religious friendships are formed and can save your life. In *Life of Pi,* religious diversity is addressed within a character who builds a house of multiple faiths within himself.

FOR FURTHER VIEWING

- Hinduism: *The World Before Her* (India, 2012) & *Darshan* (India, 2006)
- Buddhism: *Samsara* (India, 2001) & *The Cup/Phörpa* (India, 1999)
- Judaism: *The Chosen* (USA, 1981) & *Unorthodox* (Netflix, 2020)
- Christianity: *The Mission* (UK/France, 1986) & *Of Gods and Men* (France, 2010)
- Islam: *Children of Heaven* (Iran, 1997) & *Wadjda* (Saudi Arabia, 2012)

NOTES

1 David McClendon, "Sub-Saharan Africa Will Be Home to Growing Shares of the World's Christians and Muslims." https://www.pewresearch.org/fact-tank/2017/04/19/sub-saharan-africa-will-be-home-to-growing-shares-of-the-worlds-christians-and-muslims/.

2 Bilal Qureshi, "The Discomforting Legacy of Deepa Mehta's Earth," *Film Quarterly* 70:4 (Summer 2017).

FOR FURTHER READING

Hinduism: Dwyer, Rachel. *Filming the Gods: Religion and Indian Cinema.* Abingdon: Routledge, 2006.

Buddhism: Green, Ronald S. *Buddhism Goes to the Movies: An Introduction to Buddhist Thought and Practice.* London: Routledge, 2014. Suh, Sharon A. *Silver Screen Buddha: Buddhism in Asian and Western Film.* London: Bloomsbury Academic, 2015.

Judaism: Zierler, Wendy I. *Movies and Midrash: Popular Film and Jewish Religious Conversation.* Albany: State University of New York Press, 2017.

Christianity: Johnston, Robert K., Craig Detweiler, and Kutter Callaway. *Deep Focus: Film and Theology in Dialogue.* Grand Rapids, MI: Baker Academic, 2019.

Islam: Petersen, Kristian, ed. *Muslims in the Movies.* Boston, MA: Harvard University Press, 2021.

SHAKING WITH FEAR OR LAUGHTER
EXPLORING RELIGION AND FILM THROUGH FILM GENRES

FILMS ANALYZED IN THIS CHAPTER

- Sci-Fi: *Ex-Machina* (UK, 2014), *Arrival* (USA, 2016).
- Horror: *The Wicker Man* (UK, 1973), *Let the Right One In* (Sweden, 2014).
- Comedy: *The Pilgrim* (USA, 1923), *The Lizard* (Iran, 2004).
- Drama: *Andrei Rublev* (Russia, 1966), *Amazing Grace* (USA, 2020)
- Documentary Films: *5 Broken Cameras* (Israel, 2011), *Jesus Camp* (USA, 2008).
- Pilgrimage/The Quest/Road Trip: *The Way* (Spain, 2010), *Little Miss Sunshine* (USA, 2006)

Genres are a fun and popular way to approach film because we all have our favorites! We often select which movie we want to see based on how we are feeling or want to feel: do we want to gather our girlfriends at home to laugh and cry while watching a romantic comedy? Or are we in the mood for an action-packed Superhero blockbuster on an IMAX screen and Dolby sound? Perhaps we are in the mood for a good scare? Film genres have been around since the dawn of cinema, yet film historians and theorists didn't start codifying characteristics and tropes of specific genres until the 1970s. Every genre has its own conventions that influence everything from character types and narrative arc to filmic elements that include iconic scenes, stock characters, shots, cuts, music, color, and pace. Each genre selected for this chapter grapples with a different theme or concern of religion. The select genres are sci-fi, comedy, horror, pilgrimage/quest/road trip, drama, and documentary. There are many genres I will not discuss as they have been extensively explored in Religion and Film Studies, these include Action-Adventure, War, Westerns, Thrillers, Crime, Noir, Musicals, Romance, Historical Epics, Biopics, Sports, Anime, and Fantasy. The structure of the chapter will be as follows: first the general conventions of the genre will be summarized, then two films will be analyzed, and finally specific religious themes or ideas in the film will be elucidated. Sometimes, the film's reception will also be included. I hope you enjoy exploring your favorite genre and are enticed to explore other genres with new eyes.

SCIENCE-FICTION

Films: *Ex-Machina* (UK, 2014), *Arrival* (USA, 2016)
Religions: Hinduism, Buddhism, Christianity

Science Fiction (hereafter sci-fi) is an incredibly rich genre to explore in religion and film. It is a film genre that was preceded by science fiction literature. Some of the hallmarks of sci-fi include aliens, future/present/past utopias or dystopias, apocalypticism, and the threat of human or alien technology gone awry (whether through viruses, hybridization, AI, environmental disaster, etc.). There is often overlap or hybridization with other genres (Fantasy, Action, Superhero, Adventure) within the same sci-fi film, for example. One of the reasons I begin this chapter with sci-fi is due to the fundamental ontological question that undergirds many sci-fi films: what does it mean, truly, to be human? This query, of course, is one of the primary questions religions seek to address. Whether it is AI in *Bladerunner* or *Ex Machina*, the question of human nature is central. Another central conceit of science fiction has to do with the ethical or moral ends of science and the danger of scientific advancement without sufficient consideration of the ethical and physical ramifications. In sci-fi stories, from 1968's *2001: A Space Odyssey* to 2018's *Venom,* technology becomes weaponized and threatens the existence of humankind. Like Mary Shelly's *Frankenstein,* scientists become unscrupulous creator gods who lose control of their creations.

The trope that scientific experimentation can lead to disaster is common. We will focus on two films and two themes or tropes within sci-fi which specifically relate to religion. The first film, *Ex Machina* (Garland, UK, 2014) deals with the thrill and threat of artificial intelligence. The second film, *Arrival* (Villeneuve, USA, 2016), poetically explores human-alien interactions.

ANALYSIS OF *EX MACHINA*

Ex Machina, the directorial debut of British novelist-turned-screenwriter/producer/director Alex Garland, is a simple, but smart technothriller. The story revolves around three characters: Nathan Bateman (Oscar Isaac), genius founder of Bluebook (a thinly veiled equivalent of Google) and incessant inventor, his sharp, yet easily manipulated employee Caleb Smith (Domhnall Gleeson), and Ava (Alicia Vikander), Nathan's latest version of AI (Artificial intelligence). Nathan lives as a recluse thousands of miles away from any humans in a high-tech compound set in a lush forest. His gray cement bunker is cold and stark despite his art collection—even a Jackson Pollock original cannot evoke passion therein. This sterile setting is presented in stark contrast to nature outside: the vibrant greens of the forest, the thunder of waterfalls, the breathtaking blue skies. Ava is trapped in a cold room, and we viewers long to escape it with her. The film begins with Caleb having won a false lottery to be the one employee allowed to meet the founder. He nervously arrives via helicopter and soon realizes he is to part of the Turing Test of AI. He reluctantly signs a non-disclosure contract and begins his first of six interactions over the course of a week with the beautiful robot Ava.

Nathan enlists Caleb to test Ava to see if she can truly exhibit self-consciousness, empathy, emotion, creativity, etc. He congratulates Caleb for being part of a major breakthrough in human history to which Caleb responds: "if you have created a conscious machine, that is not the history of man, that's the history of gods!" Nathan, narcissist that he is, quotes him the next day, saying he "is not a man, but a god." Caleb tries to correct him, but Creator God is a mantle that Nathan enjoys and will not relinquish. The tale progresses over the course of the week as we watch Caleb and Ava become more intimate. Voyeurism is constant in the film. Nathan monitors everyone via cc tv and millions around the world via their internet searches on Bluebook. Caleb watches Ava through the monitor in his room, and we watch the watchers and watched via our screens.

The core test that Ava must pass is the test of human consciousness. Most world religions, especially Hinduism and Buddhism, understand full consciousness to be the highest goal of human life. Consciousness is much more than knowledge, Ava can be programmed to compute, to find solutions, to think, but this is not what Nathan is truly hoping to create. In fact, he explodes at Caleb in a pivotal scene in front of a Pollock painting (the artist was known for his passion), berating him to let go of his intellect, to disengage his rational mind and to feel. He asks him what if Pollock had reversed the creative order and had to understand every outcome before he painted? Caleb pauses and responds: "He never would have made a single mark." After Caleb's first encounter with Ava, Nathan brusquely dismisses Caleb's intellectual assessment of Ava's capabilities and bluntly asks him: "how do you *feel* about her?" to which Caleb admits he finds her amazing. Human consciousness involves feeling as well as cognition and Caleb comes to realize that his emotional responses to Ava are key to the experiment. In their next interaction (Session 4) Caleb changes gears and tries to explain the difference between knowledge and feeling by telling Ava the story of a scientist, Mary, who knew all about color in theory, but lived in a black and white room. The point is she never *felt* color, she never knew what it was like to see color until she was let out of the room. You can't help but imagine this anecdote is flowing through Ava's mind when she finally escapes to the vibrant greens of the forest outside the compound.

Ex Machina is a tale about the nuances of human consciousness. Consciousness not only involves emotion and thought, but also requires human interaction. Nathan is obsessed with this final element asking: "Can consciousness exist without interaction?" This is a perduring query for religionists, from the Tibetan Buddhist monk who lives for years alone in a cave to the 2nd-century Christian desert ascetic who lived atop a pillar in Cappadocia. What good is consciousness if it is not shared? Interdependency grows between Caleb and Ava. In their third session together, Ava looks directly into Caleb's eyes and asks: "Are you attracted to me?" In their fifth session she confesses she wants to be with Caleb and asks him if he feels the same.

Sci-fi films often reveal that dystopic reality is the result of unbridled scientific experimentation. Some of the most poignant scenes in sci-fi films are those moments of realization and regret that science has gone too far without considering the ramifications (recall Charleston Heston on the beach at the end of the original *Planet of the Apes* when he realized that a nuclear blast had created the dystopia, Dr. Frankenstein at the end of the tale, or the eco-activists in Garland's first sci-fi feature film, *28 Days After,* when they realize they have released the human-created virus Rage). Caleb confronts Nathan about the ethics of AI creation toward the end of the film: "Why did you make Ava?" Nathan's scientific explanation is chilling:

> Look, the arrival of advanced AI has been around for decades so the question was not *why* but *when*. So I don't see Ava as a decision, just an evolution. ...One day the AIs are going to look back on us the same way we look at fossil skeletons on the plains of Africa: an upright ape living in dust with crude language and tools, all set for extinction.

In this rare moment of human vulnerability Nathan takes off his God-like mantle and coolly explains he is just a cog in the machine of evolutionary history on planet earth.

The irony is Nathan can't seem to learn his own lessons about technology and human relations. This genius, who was coding at 13 and is a millionaire many times over, is utterly isolated. He creates, but he cannot connect to other human beings. He manufactures synthetic AI lovers who can't talk back and has closets full of them. This isolation is linked to his alcoholism. Alcohol breaks down his walls and it is when he is drunk that we see Nathan at his most human, vulnerable, and remorseful. He realizes Ava has passed the Turing Test as well as the significance of what he has created and its potential destructive power. Interestingly, with drunken bravado, he finishes Caleb's quote from Robert Oppenheimer after he had created the atomic bomb: "Now I am become Death, Destroyer of the worlds!" This declaration is a translation of a line from the Hindu text the *Bhagavad Gita*. Before he passes out on the couch, Nathan feverishly thrice recites the end of the passage: "The good deeds man has done before defends him" as if his many technological breakthroughs will compensate for his unleashing of AI which may bring the downfall of humankind.

Eva, with the help of another AI woman and Caleb, escapes her confines and brutally kills her creator Nathan. Her duped confidant Caleb is left locked inside the compound as she escapes and is whisked away to New York by the unknowing helicopter pilot. Her sheer delight in freedom and her new human skin is mesmerizing as she leaves the compound and one cannot help but recall another famous line from the *Bhagavad Gita*: "Our soul, like a bird in a cage, longs for liberty of the vast air." Can AI generate a human soul? This is but one perduring sci-fi question and one central to religion as well.

ANALYSIS OF *ARRIVAL*

The theme of technology is also explored in the film *Arrival,* a 2015 alien invasion film directed by Québecois Denis Villeneuve; however instead of technology turning against humanity as we saw with AI in *Ex Machina,* alien technology ultimately becomes a gift, not a threat-although it takes the hero-linguist professor, Dr. Louise Banks (Amy Adams), the entire movie to discover this. Twelve mysterious spaceships arrive all over the globe: from Montana to Venezuela to Russia carrying mysterious aliens (heptapods). The quest is to decipher their purpose before major military actions between superpowers usher in doomsday. Dr. Banks specializes in deciphering difficult languages and is brought to a military base in Montana to try to communicate with the aliens. She connects with the aliens and begins to decode their complex linear orthnographic language. In the end, we discover the aliens are not hostile after all, but rather have come to earth to bestow a gift (not a weapon as some the military hastily conclude). Friendly aliens (*E.T., Close Encounters of a Third Kind*) are not as common a trope as hostile ones (*War of the Worlds, Men in Black*) so you can hardly blame them. These aliens are friendlies, but their gift comes with strings attached: in 3,000 years they explain to Louise in their last encounter, the heptapods will need humanity's help (Figure 4.1).

As was the case in *Ex Machina,* the real breakthrough that technology provides is full consciousness. Dr. Banks discusses a lingual theory that suggests that learning a new language can actually affect one's brain by rerouting certain neurons. So, their technology is not vibranium (magical ore from *Black Panther*) or some nuclear breakthrough, it is their language. By learning their language their

Figure 4.1 Dr. Banks makes contact with the heptapods in *Arrival* (Denis Villeneuve, 2015).
Source: Screenshot by author

consciousness is imbibed. This consciousness moves past linear time, the future and past are accessible. At the climax of the film a desperate and alone Dr. Banks ventures to and is taken up into the spaceship by the aliens. This is when she comes to understand that the aliens know what will happen in the future. Surprisingly, they claim that she too can know the future by using the "weapon/tool." The flash forwards of her future and her life with her daughter now make sense, these visions are occurring because she is learning their language. "Weapon opens time." Dr. Banks has her aha moment and is able to return to earth and avert World War III by calling the head Chinese military commander and sharing intimate news with him from a future conversation having to do with his past. The great gift that the technology/language/weapon brought was the ability to see everything, to step outside of linear time and linear thinking. Students of religion will be quick to recognize the parallels between this full consciousness and central ideas in several world religions. The goal of any Hindu spiritual seeker is divine consciousness (Brahman) which is beyond time. The founder of Buddhism, Siddhartha Gautama, was the first to achieve moksha and full consciousness and this became a goal for bodhisattvas who followed him. The goal is also found in Jewish Kabbala and it is offered as a reward in heaven for the faithful in Christianity where they will see all reality clearly: "for now we see in a mirror, dimly, but then face to face. Now I know in part, but then I will know fully, even as I was also fully known" (1 Cor 13:12).

COMEDY

Films: *The Pilgrim* (USA, 1923), *The Lizard* (Iran, 2004)
Religions: Christianity, Islam

COMEDY GENRE CONVENTIONS

Why consider comedies in a volume dedicated to the serious topic of religion? Semiologist-philosopher Mikhail Bahktin taught that laughter can be both salvific and generative. Ingvild Gilhus, an expert on religion and humor, offers another reason explaining laughter

> …is seen as a positive contributor to human liberation, spiritual growth and wisdom. Laughter relieves tension, vanquishes rigidity and helps to cultivate a playful attitude toward life. *Homo ludens* is celebrated as one of the ideals of this century, and laughter has become a ticket to the lost paradise of play.
>
> (Gilhus, 1997, 109)

All the films considered in this section invite us to laugh, invite us to play with the serious subject of religion!

Why do we laugh? One reason is incongruity. When something does not fit, it immediately strikes us humorous. Fish-out-of-water protagonists evoke mirth, whether it is a convict disguised as a pastor (*The Pilgrim* and *The Lizard*) or Krishna riding a motorcycle through town (*OMG*). Comedy, especially satire, also has the power to subvert and challenge authority. We laugh at religious hypocrisy and superstitions. Satire, in particular, uses humor to not only expose, but to offer up a better way. There are many sub-genres of filmic comedy: slapstick, satire, adventure, romantic, screwball, musical, character, anarchic (farce or animal comedy), dramedy, even mockumentary, each with their own conventions and hallmarks. Due to the constraints of this chapter, we will only consider the first two sub-genres.

COMEDY AND RELIGION

Comedy is the least explored genre within religion and film scholarship. Theologians Terry and Chris Lindvall together with J. Dennis Bounds have taken up the challenge in their 2016 book *Divine Film*

Comedies: Biblical Narratives, Film Sub-Genres and the Comic Spirit. The Lindvalls' approach film comedies from a theological and Biblical lens asserting that humor has always been a part of the Judeo-Christian tradition. Fortified by the teachings of Erasmus and Lord Shaftesbury, they argue that wit and humor are corroborative of religion and promote true faith. G.K. Chesterton joins these two apologists and adds: "Our relations with a good joke are direct and even divine relations" (Lindvall et al., 2016, 4–5). Christian theologian Doris Donelly goes one step further arguing that humor is the heart of theology and incongruity makes us realize our limits and humbles us: "Humility and humor go hand in hand. Humor points us towards the holiness of God" by giving us perspective of our own humanness and weaknesses (Donnelly in Lindvall, 2016, 13). Comedy allows us to laugh at our own shortcomings through identification and ponder a better way, a fuller humanity.

The religions of Christianity and Islam will now be explored through the genre of comedy utilizing both a theological lens and Cultural/Reception Studies (refer to Chapter 2 for methodological details) approach. The first film, *The Pilgrim*, is a Charles "Charlie" Chaplin classic 1923 tale of an escaped convict who is mistaken for the expected small-town Christian preacher. Eighty years later, a similar mistaken identity-impersonator pastor scenario is found in the 2004 Iranian film *The Lizard (Marmulak)* but this time the escaped convict impersonates a Muslim cleric. Comparing two similar satirical stories reveals much about their different cultural contexts and eras.

FILM ANALYSIS: *THE PILGRIM*

Charlie Chaplin, one of the founding figures of Hollywood, had a complicated relationship with organized religion, especially Christianity. An avowed atheist, he nevertheless was attracted to Jesus and his films often had Christians as heroines. The ending of *Easy Street* (1917) in which Chaplin cleans up the street riffraff and herds them back into New Hope Mission could be read as championing the social gospel of the era. In *The Pilgrim* (1923) which was written, produced, and starred Chaplin, he pokes fun at the gullible straight-laced Christian congregants, but their goodness also starts to transform his sinful heart. Chaplin plays a recently-escaped convict, Lefty Lombard, aka "Slipperly Elm," who steals the clothes of a bathing minister and assumes his identity (Rev. Phillip Pim). He soon finds himself in Devil's Gulch where the small town is anxiously awaiting their new minister. He is rushed into the church where the congregation is waiting to hear his first sermon. Lefty is a fish-out-of-water in the church and the scene is series of unexpected events: he is startled to come upon the 12-person choir which he mistakes for a jury and assumes he is in another courtroom; he is delighted to find the parishioners part so easily with their money in the collection and he is completely out of his element when asked to give a scripture-based sermon. He quickly decides to retell the story of David and Goliath which he dramatically pantomimes to the delight of a distracted young boy in the front pew. The convict has intuited that his new role involves performance, and after his show (sermon) he takes multiple bows before the "audience." He assuredly is capturing the bravado of successful mega-preachers of his day such as his friend Aimee Semple McPherson who opened Angelus temple January 1 of that year (Figure 4.2).

Some could see the parody as anti-religious and clearly Chaplin highlights some believer's hypocrisy such as the deacon who has a whiskey bottle in his back pocket or the judgmental congregants. However, if you consider how his heart changes after lodging

Figure 4.2 David and Goliath sermon in *The Pilgrim* (Charles Chaplin, 1923).
Source: Screenshot by author

with church members Mrs. Brown and her fetching daughter, Miss Brown (played by Chaplin's long-time leading lady Edna Purviance) one could argue their Christian virtues challenge and change the long-time thief. Their naiveté, hospitality, and trust in him instigate his moral shift. When an ex-con robs the Browns, Chaplin chases after him and returns their money. At the end of the film, the sheriff apprehends Lefty and carts him off but heeds Miss Brown's plea for mercy and her forgiveness of the theft. The final scene finds the Sheriff choosing mercy over justice as he leaves the tramp at the border of Mexico instead of sending him back to jail.

RECEPTION OF *THE PILGRIM*

The Pilgrim was a box office success for Chaplin. Certain conservative Christians protested its release and depiction of believers as simpletons. The Evangelical Minister's Association of Atlanta demanded a boycott of the film calling it an "insult to the Gospel." Reviewers called it "vulgar, distasteful, offensive." The Ku Klux Klan claimed the film ridiculed all Protestant ministers. The film marked an end of an era for Chaplin as it was his third and final contract film for First National and freed him to go on to make longer features with his new company, United Artists, which he founded with Mary Pickford, Douglas Fairbanks, and D.W. Griffith.

FILM ANALYSIS: *THE LIZARD*

Over 80 years later and a world away, *The Pilgrim* inspired a wildly popular Iranian film entitled *Marmulak* (*The Lizard*, 2004). Approaching this film using history, Religious Studies, and Reception Studies allows us to better understand Islam as it has developed in Iran. With the rise of the Safavid dynasty in 1501, Shiism became the official religion of Iran and the power and political influence of Iranian Shiite clergy grew with each century until it culminated with the Islamic Revolution in 1979 when the Grand Ayatollah Ruhollah Khomeni came to power. In addition to this rise to supreme authority at the state level, it is also important to note that Iran has a centuries-long tradition of revering imams at the local level. Believers are dependent upon imams for spiritual and social guidance. Their opinion on all matters, both domestic and spiritual, are held in high esteem. Understanding this, we can better appreciate the immediate deference and honor the townsfolk in the film show their new imam who they turn to for all sorts of advice. Shia choose a certain teacher (Mujtahid) to be their own spiritual guide and his opinions on life and morals are binding. Realizing this religious tradition, viewers can better appreciate how Reza's actions are immediately emulated by the whole community.

The Lizard is a tale that mirrors the basic plot line of *The Pilgrim*. It was the first comedy about religion in post-revolutionary Iran and surprisingly it was the biggest box office hit in Iranian cinematic history. It is a parable that follows the foibles of an escaped thief, Reza Marmulak (Reza the Lizard), who steals an imam's clothes while he is showering in a hospital and walks out to freedom. The authorities quickly realize he has escaped and launch a relentless search for him. Reza's goal is to make it to the border, pick up his forged passport, and escape to freedom. Of course, his plans are comically and repeatedly thwarted by the fact that he is mistaken for the long-anticipated cleric in the small town near the border. The comic mainstay of incongruity is constantly invoked as he fumbles with his cloak (several slapstick moments) and is daily thrust into situations for which he is not prepared, like offering domestic counseling or answering cosmic theological questions. In attempt to get his forged papers, he knocks on many doors late at night in the poorer part of town. His disciples discover his covert actions and assume he is clandestinely serving the poor so the entire mosque is inspired to do the same and launch a campaign to feed and aid the poor. Although he is a criminal, Reza has a heart of gold and proves this to the audience time and time again (much like the good-hearted thief in *The Pilgrim*).

There are two primary ways in which *The Lizard* differs from *The Pilgrim:* (1) there is a much more thorough critique of the abuse of power clerics hold in Iranian culture, as well the vacuity of going through the religious motions, advocating instead for spiritual reform based on love; (2) the endings of the films are dramatically different. When first thrust into the role of religious leader during a call to prayer at a train stop you see Reza frantically trying to get the bodily mechanics correct and he mumbles a quick prayer no one can make out; however, as the film progresses, he begins to relish his role of teacher and moral guide. His first official sermon

Figure 4.3 Reza the Lizard is besieged by eager townsfolk in *The Lizard* (Kamal Tabrizi, 2004).
Source: Screenshot by author

begins as a reflection on the filmic theological gem *Pulp Fiction*, a work made by "brother Tarantino a great Christian filmmaker." His humorous ad-libbed sermon resembles Chaplin's David and Goliath pantomime. By his last sermon, when he finds himself preaching to prisoners, he exhibits how he has grown spiritually by playing the role of a preacher. His tone is one of compassion and sincerity as he tells the convicts "The gates of the prison may be closed to you, but the gates of God's blessings are always open to you" for "God does not only belong to good people." He refers to God as "the heaviest dude" in forgiveness, kindness, and friendship. He ends by declaring that the way to God is not through the rule of law and punishment but rather by taming their selfish nature through love. Finally, *The Lizard* ends with the lawmen arresting Reza and taking him off to jail as opposed to the merciful sheriff in *The Pilgrim* releasing the thief due to his good deeds in town (Figure 4.3).

RECEPTION OF *THE LIZARD*

The criticisms we saw levied against *The Pilgrim* by conservative, and fundamentalist Christians were echoed and deepened by conservative Iranian Muslim clerics. For example, one critic, Javed Hoseyni, said the film should be called "the Scorpion" for its poisonous sting, a film he found socially, morally, and theologically deviant. He cites three ways the film is dangerous and deviant: (1) it promotes pluralism, permissiveness, tolerance, and compromise (he found the fact that audiences applauded such statements while watching the film only proves their theological ignorance); (2) the film mocks religious believers' basic intelligence and portrays the devout as simpletons; (3) the portrayal of the clergy is an affront, "what takes place in the film goes beyond error, challenging religious values and social norms instead."[1] The film was allowed to play in most provinces, however only for a few short weeks. At least three provinces banned the film altogether. Of course, banning *The Lizard* from public screens only made the film more popular and pirated DVDs flooded the marketplace. This, in addition to screenings at international film festivals around the world, meant that *The Lizard* had wide unofficial distribution.

HORROR

Films: *The Wicker Man* (UK, 1973), *Let the Right One In* (Sweden, 2008)
Religions: Paganism, Christianity

Horror is an ideal genre to consider in religion and film. Why? The genre deals with the dark side of the human psyche, the reality of evil, and the forces that fight against it. One of the reasons we are drawn to horror is our innate fear of the unknown. The Latin root of the word, horrere, means "to bristle with fear." As H.P. Lovecraft explained: "the oldest and strongest emotion of mankind is fear, and the oldest and strongest kind of fear is fear of the unknown" (Lovecraft, 1973, 6). Filmic tales of horror, whether it is a malevolent spirit or monster or a serial killer, let us explore these mysteries in the relative safety of our seats. They can, therefore, serve a valuable cathartic psychological purpose that allows us to grapple with our fears or violent sides. Good horror shows us elements in our own psyche that we may not comfortable acknowledging, but may need to consider anyway. Horror films can affect us deeply, they can stir up deep fears or desires within us. They also often deal with the struggle between good and evil or death-dealing supernatural forces versus defenders of life. The dark side of human nature, the battle between good and evil, supernatural realities…these are the mainstays of religion!

Horror films have been around since the dawn of cinema. Some consider George Méliès' 1896 short film *The Devil's Manor* as the first true horror film which he followed two years later with *The Cave of Demons*. The genre has always appealed to filmmakers around the globe, for example, Japan produced *Bake Jizo* (*Jizo the Spook*) and *Shinin no sosei* (*Resurrection of a Corpse*) in 1898. Over time the genre has grown and evolved to include many sub-genres (each with its own icons, rules, and cadences): monsters, pagan-folk horror, hauntings/ghosts, paranormal, demons/Satan/possessions, slasher, teen-fright, witchcraft, occult, etc. This section will focus on two of these sub-genres: folk-horror/paganism is central in *The Wicker Man* (Hardy, UK, 1973) and vampire-monster films are explored in *Let the Right One In* (Alfredson, Sweden, 2014).

ANALYSIS OF *THE WICKER MAN*

The first example of horror we will consider is a simple little "B-film" called *The Wicker Man* which was the brainchild of screenwriter Anthony Schaffer, Christopher Lee (an actor in many vampire movies) and small-time director Robin Hardy. Like the campy *Rocky Horror Picture Show*, the film has developed a cult following of loyal fans and is considered a classic story of pagan horror (a more recent example would be *Midsommar* (2019). The plot involves a virginal, devout, and strait-laced Scottish policeman from the mainland, Sergeant Neil Howie (Edward Woodward) who ventures to a remote Hebridean island to investigate the reported disappearance of a young girl: Roan Morrison. As he investigates, he discovers that Christianity has been discarded by the islanders in favor of the more ancient practices of paganism. Pagan symbols abound and he comes to learn that paganism is taught in the schools and practiced by all. The crops have failed that year for the first time in over a century and the locals have lured him there in order to offer him as a human sacrifice to the gods of the sea and fields in order to ensure next autumn's harvest is bountiful. The conclusion of the film, as he is burned alive inside the towering Wicker Man structure, is truly horrific.

Religion and film scholars can find much to discuss in *The Wicker Man*, in particular, the questions raised about inter-religious tensions, ritual, and the role of religion and culture. The influence of one of the pioneers of the academic study of religion, James Frazier, and his opus magnus *The Golden Bough* (1890) is explicit in the film. Screenwriters Hardy and Schaffer read all 12 volumes of it and Sergeant Howie loosely quotes from it in his research into paganism in the Summerisle Library. Lord Summerisle intones a Frazierian-English sense of intellectual superiority as he explains to Sergeant Howie how his scientific botanist grandfather came to the island in 1868 and resurrected the Old Religion to inspire his workers, his father continued this practice and taught him to revere the dramas and the rituals. He then wryly surmises he may be "a heathen, conceivably, but not an unenlightened one."

There is clearly a Marxist interpretation at play with religion being used by those in power to control and manipulate the workers (Figure 4.4). The pagan rites make the villagers feel a certain sense of control, for example, preschoolers march in line carrying a pagan baby figure chanting: "we carry death out of the village." The pagan villagers, explains Lord Summerisle, are "a deeply religious people," who have chosen a religion other than the dominant English one

Figure 4.4 Lord Summerisle leads a ritual before burning Sergeant Howie alive in *The Wicker Man* (Robin Hardy, 1973).
Source: Screenshot by author

(Christianity) which "had its chance" on the island and has been abandoned, its churches left to ruin, and its priests exiled. Sergeant Howie defends orthodox Christianity to the end (his faith is an odd mix of Scottish Presbyterianism and Anglicanism). As he is being led to his fiery sacrificial death he screams: "I am a Christian and hope for resurrection. *I* will live again…not your damn apples!" Throughout the film the music stops whenever Howie enters the room as song is a key part of the islanders' spiritual practice; however, as he peers out from the Wicker Man totem he fights back with song and passionately sings Psalm 23. He dies calling out for mercy from God and Jesus. Many read the film as anti-Christian and clearly *The Wicker Man* can be read as a triumph of paganism over a dying religion; however, Lord Summerisle himself (Christopher Lee) did not view the film as an attack on Christianity, but rather as commentary on the potential for all religions to be exploited by despots. This tale is horrific in the sense it displays the power of religious belief to override basic moral norms such as the taking a human life. Finally, *The Wicker Man* is a vivid communal example of one of the mainstays of horror: the dark side of the human psyche. This theme, the dark impulses innate in all humans, are also deftly exemplified in the second film highlighted in this genre: *Let the Right One In*.

ANALYSIS OF *LET THE RIGHT ONE IN*

Let the Right One In (Alfredson, Sweden, 2014) has many of the tropes you expect in a vampire film: the mysterious figure who sleeps during the day, avoids sunlight, can fly, climb with suprahuman powers and whose evil presence is sensed by animals, and victims who survive turn into vampires; however, the film is original and unconventional in having the vampire be a 12-year-old girl and providing us with a relatively happy ending. The story begins with two new neighbors moving in next door to lonely, bullied Oskar. Oskar (Kare Hedebrant) slowly befriends the mysterious Eli (Lina Leandersson), and they bond over Rubik's cubes and use Morse code to communicate through the walls. Oskar, who fancies himself a detective, slowly comes to realize Eli is a vampire. For our purposes, I will focus on two horror genre themes present in the film: the violent, vengeful impulses within us and the monster longing for human relationship.

Most religions ultimately formulate ethical codes and guidelines to tame violent desires in human nature, for example, The Ten Commandments' prohibition against murder or the Buddhist and Hindu mainstay *ahimsa* (do no harm). Horror films expose and demonstrate these destructive desires in a variety of ways, from the sadistic cannibalism of *Texas Chain Saw Massacre* (1974) and a host of slasher-splatter films to the more restrained threat in *Cat People* (1942) or *Silence of the Lambs* (1991). The very first line of *Let the Right One In* is Oskar muttering: "Squeal, squeal like a pig" as he sits alone in the dark rehearsing his revenge on the bullies at school who torment him and call him a pig. Of course, Eli hears this through the wall. His fascination with murder is reflected in the scrapbook he has compiled of newspaper clipping of various murders. Oskar studies them, the weapons used, he is fascinated with death. Eli encourages him to fight back, to "hit them hard" when the schoolboy bullies next confront him. He follows her advice and ends up sending the bully to the ER with an injured ear. In the reveal scene when Oskar confronts Eli about killing people he disagrees with Eli's suggestion that they are alike. "I don't kill people!" Oskar protests to which Eli sincerely responds: "No, but you would like to." Vampires act on the violence that lays deep within us all. One way in which horror films can be cathartic is witnessing the monster act out our own violent impulses. Eli, however, unlike stalkers and murders in many horror films, feels a bit of remorse in some cases as we see her weep after killing her first victim in the story.

The second trope in classic monster films is the sympathetic monster longing for relationship and love. The early Frankenstein films capture this longing poignantly as does *Let the Right One In* and the recent award-wining *The Shape of Water* (Guillermo del Toro, USA, 2017). Murderous monsters, from Mr. Hyde to Dracula know they must live in the shadows and are not allowed human intimacy. The very first thing Eli says to Oskar is "I want to be left alone" the classic vampire line. Since Oskar is desperate for companionship, he ignores her rebuffs and loans her his Rubik's cube as a gesture of friendship. One night, after sucking the blood of another victim, she appears at his fourth story window and asks to come in (as everyone knows one of the cardinal rules of vampire etiquette is that they must be invited in). Another's blood has quelled Eli's physical appetite but not her emotional one. She admonishes Oskar not to look at her and she slips into his bed naked. He remarks that she is cold, but accepts it and sleepily asks her if she will be his girlfriend. She remarks she cannot for she is not a girl. He again, ignores her confession and says going steady will not change their relationship and so Eli acquiesces and slowly entwines his warm hand in hers. It is a beautifully shot scene full of tension…will she bite his neck and suck his warm blood? We see her tempted, but she is ultimately won over by his love and innocence. Lonely monsters (from the creature in *The Shape of Water* to King Kong) force us to reflect upon the value of human intimacy and our need to be in relationship. Religions have long held this to be critical, from the Hebrew scripture's creation story of Eve who is formed after God has reasoned "it is not good for man to be alone" to Gautama Buddha's teaching that community (the Sangha) is one of three jewels of Buddhism. *Let the Right One In* ends affirming this religious tenet of relationship as Oskar and Eli ride off in a train with Eli safely ensconced in a trunk tapping Morse code messages to her new companion Oskar.

DRAMA

Drama: *Andrei Rublev* (Russia, 1966), *Amazing Grace,* (USA, 2006)
Religion: Russian Orthodox and Protestant Christianity

Drama, perhaps the most familiar cinematic genre, has also been around since the early days of cinema. Dramas usually contain well-developed characters with clear developmental arcs, a serious dilemma or quest, conflict, resolution, or realization after a lesson learned, and clear conclusions. Subgenres of drama include historical, biographic, war, romance, political, and courtroom. We will examine two dramatic narrative films set in different cultures and eras, both stories of internal, spiritual conflict in a context of political tumult and social tensions. The first film, *Andrei Rublev,* is the second film of the great Russian filmmaker Andrei Tarkovsky (1932–1986). The 1966 historical epic follows the journey of Russian icon painter Andrei Rublev in 12th-century Russia, a land ravaged by Mongol invasions and a land where Orthodox Christianity is under threat. The second drama, *Burden* (2018) takes place in Laurens, South Carolina, USA in 1996 and tells the story of African American Rev. Kennedy who confronts racism head-on by befriending a Ku Klux Klan leader and changing his life.

ANALYSIS OF *ANDREI RUBLEV*

Andrei Tarkovsky's epic *Andrei Rublev* was the first film I watched and discussed as a graduate student to better understand religion, in this case Orthodox Christian spirituality, and the artist's role in history. It would be fair to date my love of religion and film to that experience in the den of my professor's home in Hyde Park in 1989 and being surprised and overwhelmed after being enveloped in this moving black and white film. This Russian film was made by Tarkovsky in 1966 and is a good example of "slow cinema." I often host screenings for students in my home. It is well worth your three hours and is considered a cinematic masterpiece. It also illustrates the mainstays of the dramatic genre. Many of Tarkovsky's convictions about the role and purpose of true art (detailed in Chapter 2) are grappled with by the protagonist of the film, famous Russian icon painter Andrei Rublev (c.1360s–1430) played by Anatoliy Solonitsyn. His iconography shifted the tone of Russian icons from ones that portrayed Christ's suffering and a judgmental God to a more compassionate divinity and human figures.

Rublev's quest is to be a true Christian artist, but life, war, paganism, people, politics, and princes get in his way. Early in the film his fellow monastic Kirill criticizes his paintings saying they lack "faith that comes from the depth of his soul." Feofan Grek (Theophanes the famous Greek icon painter) summons the talented Rublev to Moscow to paint with him. Many temptations befall Rublev enroute: from a pagan orgy where he is captured and tempted to conflicts over his commission. When they finally arrive, Danil, his fellow monk and icon painter, wants to paint the assigned Last Judgment on the cathedral walls and relishes painting sinners burning in pitch and the devil with smoke coming out of his eyes, but Rublev is tired of these damning depictions rooted in fear saying it "disgusts" him. He wants to change the portrayal of divinity, sensing its power over people. His assistants wait and wait for his artistic and theological block to lift and when it finally does, he declares: "it should be a feast!" They finally begin to paint but their beautiful frescos are barely dry when Prince Vladimir launches a violent raid on the town destroying people, animals, and the church. At the end of the raid the compassionate Rublev kills a soldier about to rape the "Holy Fool" peasant woman. After this act and the destruction of his art in the cathedral, Andrei takes a vow of silence and abandons his art. Before he leaves the ghost of Theophanes appears and they discuss human beings' propensity to sin and their violent nature. "How long will this go on?" asks a defeated Rublev to which the ghost replies: "Forever," but then gazes at what is left of the paintings and sighs "yet, how beautiful all this is!" Theophanes is channeling Tarkovsky here with a message to another century filled with war and death. Rublev upholds his vow of silence for the next decade until the closing scene of the final chapter of the film ("The Bell"). Only then, when the unexpected success of a fraudulent teen bell forger leaves the youth overcome and sobbing with relief in the mud, does Rublev speak. Moved with compassion, Rublev comforts him and breaks his silence: "Come on, let's go together you and I, you'll cast bells and I will paint icons." Tarkovsky leaves us with a very earthbound human pieta with Rublev cradling the tired, muddied boy in his lap. The camera pans to the thick mud and then to the fire which dissolves into a red color and expands to the glory of Andrei Rublev's famous icons. Three hours of black and white dour images are crowned with the colorful triumph of Rublev's vision of God. The last image in the film is his famous Trinity icon where three figures, who look almost identical, sit equally around a table with their heads tilted in compassion toward one another. Art can shape theology and Rublev's journey concludes with a vision of Christianity rooted in love, a God who wants to feast with us, not condemn us. The film is a perfect example of a dramatic journey of a nuanced central character who faces obstacles and ultimately overcomes them.

RECEPTION OF *ANDREI RUBLEV*

Andrei Rublev was quickly taken out of theaters and banned for five years in Russia. It was considered too politically provocative and likely to inspire anti-totalitarian critique. It was also considered by some to be too experimental in form and graphically violent. It was lauded outside of Russia and won the International Critics Prize at the Cannes film festival in 1969. Today, *Andrei Rublev* is considered one of the best films ever produced in Russia and is often included in lists of Best Films ever made not only for its lyrical poetic style but as an enduring portrait of an artist grappling with the purpose and power of art itself.

DRAMATIC SPIRITUAL JOURNEY CAPTURED IN FILM:
AMAZING GRACE

Amazing Grace is a perfect drama: it offers us a well-developed character, William Wilberforce, who has a clear developmental arc (from carefree student to Christian statesman), who goes on a serious quest (the abolition of the slave trade), endures numerous conflicts and setbacks, has a legal epiphany, and conclusively achieves his goal by the end of the film. It is based on the life of William Wilberforce (1759–1833) was raised in the Church of England and was exposed to Nonconformist and Methodist faith-inspired moral ideas by his aunt and uncle as a boy. After rather licentious college years at Cambridge University, he had an evangelical awaking at the age of 26. Wilberforce stands out in Christian history as someone who dedicated his life to social reform based on his faith. He took the injunction to care for those who had no social power, "the least of these" referenced in Jesus' Sermon on the Mount seriously and his position as a Member of Parliament from the age of 21 until a few years before his death at 73 afforded him the societal influence to affect change. Foremost among his social reform efforts was the abolition of the slave trade. His campaign, supported by the Society for Effecting the Abolition of the Slave Trade (organized by Quaker and Anglican Christians), is considered the first grassroots human rights campaign. Wilberforce's battle to end the British slave trade and commerce was a very long and arduous one: 46 years in all!

Amazing Grace was directed by Michael Apted, produced by Patricia Heaton and Terrence Malick, et al. and it centers on Wilberforce's struggle to translate his Christian convictions into political and societal change. It stars Ioan Grufford as William Wilberforce, Benedict Cumberbatch as Prime Minister William Pitt, and Albert Finney as Wilberforce's spiritual mentor John Newton, a man haunted by his former life working in the West Indies as a slave trader who is working through his penance as an Anglican monk. As with most dramas, there are internal and external conflicts. Not only does he struggle with opium addiction, but he cannot reconcile his secular political career with his Christian commitments. Early on in the film the tension between private faith and public work is made clear. It is a lesson that different characters repeatedly teach the protagonist. At a dinner scene with members of the socially progressive Clapham sect, Wilberforce admits his confusion as to whether he should be a secular statesman or a Christian. One guest, Hannah Moore, gently replies: "we humbly suggest, sir, that you can do both." After several defeats in Parliament regarding abolition, Wilberforce seeks Newton's counsel and seeks his blessing to quit political life. Newton instructs him that his place is *in* the world, as a politician. Pitt, his best friend and ultimately Prime Minister, challenges Wilberforce: "will you praise the Lord or change the world?" reminding him that "the principles of Christianity can lead to action as well as meditation."

What are these Christian principles? Christianity has inspired followers to pursue social justice for "the least of these" since the times of Jesus. A central passage in the Christian scriptures is called The Sermon on the Mount (found in the Gospel of Matthew 5–7). Here Jesus lays out a moral and ethical lifestyle and orientation for his followers and expects them to be counter-cultural. Several of The Beatitudes (Matthew 5: 1–11) pertain to social justice activists including[6] "Blessed are those who hunger and thirst for righteousness, for they shall be satisfied[7]; "Blessed are the merciful, for they shall obtain mercy[10]; "Blessed are those who are persecuted for righteousness' sake, for theirs is the kingdom of heaven; and finally,[11] "Blessed are you when men revile you and persecute you and utter all kinds of evil against you falsely on my account.[12] Rejoice and be glad, for your reward is great in heaven, for so men persecuted the prophets who were before you." Wilberforce, often mocked by his fellow parliamentarians, was one such prophet.

Film is powerful because it *shows* you rather than *tells* you. Case in point, we can tell you about Wilberforce's 46-year-long campaign to end slavery, but a dramatic dinner party scene shows you how his faith-based convictions were sparked into action. The dinner at his home is attended by a group of abolitionists including Hannah Moore, Thomas Clarkson, and a former-slave-turned-author and activist, Olaudah Aquiano. Wilberforce asks Aquiano if he has something to discuss with him to which he abruptly replies: "No! Because we hear you are a man who does not believe what he hears until he sees it with his own eyes!" Without missing a beat, Clarkson pushes away his china plate and slams heavy iron shackles down on

Figure 4.5 Aquiano explains to Wilberforce how shackles are used on slaves in *Amazing Grace* (Michael Apted, 2007).
Source: Screenshot by author

Wilberforce's fine cherrywood dining table and proceeds to explain how slaves are shackled and confined during their passage from the Africa to the West Indies closing the dense iron band around his own neck while a disturbed Wilberforce looks on (Figure 4.5).

Next Aquiano unbuttons his shirt and displays his slave master's brand burned into his chest, explaining "this is how they let you know you no longer belong to God, but to a man." This is a perfect scene to exemplify the power of the visual not only to motivate a character, but to move audiences as well. Wilberforce repeats this lesson when he brings fellow politicians and their wives on a tour of the port and then stops at a slave ship where we see them recoil in disgust at the stench of human death that still lingers on the ship. *Amazing Grace* is a well-done historical drama of one Christian who was motivated by his faith to change the world. He faces many obstacles in his battle, but his faith, his strong wife, and his spiritual mentor John Newton help him persevere and achieve his goal in the end. We in the audience are much like Wilberforce, we are not moved by merely hearing his story, "we must see it with our own eyes" and this film helps us do just that.

PILGRIMAGE/QUEST/ROAD TRIP

Films: *The Way* (Spain, 2010), *Little Miss Sunshine* (USA, 2006).
Religions: Catholicism, Judaism, Buddhism.

Pilgrimage/Quest/Road Trip films are an ideal genre for those exploring religion and film as the religious life is often equated with a journey. While there might be a concrete goal or mission, it is often the inner discovery and transformation of those on the road that is the true story. The formula for these films usually includes a dramatic inciting incident, an urgent need to complete a task that involves a journey, a mismatched crew that must journey together despite tensions, many obstacles and hardships along the way, increased camaraderie built on co-suffering, self-discovery, and new sense of community at the end.

ANALYSIS OF *THE WAY*

The first film considered in this category is a pilgrimage film *The Way* (Estevez, Spain/USA, 2010). This road trip takes place on *El Camino*, a 1,000-year-old, 800-km/500-mile pilgrimage route from the French Pyrenees to Santiago di Compostela in northern Spain. Although many undertake the trek for religious reasons, none of the four central travelers in the film initially do so. The inciting incident is the freak accidental death of the central protagonist's (Tom Avery) estranged son, Daniel, on his first day of his pilgrimage. Tom (Martin Sheen) travels to France to retrieve his son's ashes and decides to cremate his remains and finish the journey his son began. Of course, the 60-year-old ophthalmologist is ill-prepared for such a journey and emotionally raw. He is soon befriended by a jocular Dutchman named Jost who is on the pilgrimage to lose weight. They ultimately are joined by an emotionally damaged chain-smoking Canadian woman named Sarah, and a hyperbolic verbose, annoying Irishman, Jack, who is suffering from writer's block and hiding from his editors. Tom clearly does not want their company on the long trek, but circumstances ultimately see the motley crew coalesce over the weeks. This film offers two lessons related to religion: human beings need each other and rituals are a powerful part of life.

As we saw in our discussion of *Ex Machina,* humans need each other in order to thrive. This is a lesson Tom learns over the course of the film. Any pilgrim must undertake the journey for themselves, you must carry your own 40-pound pack and your own demons, but the lesson of film is: you can't do it alone. Martin Sheen's son, Emilio, who wrote and directed the film, explains that the film is fundamentally about reconnecting with yourself and others. The four main characters: Tom, Jost, Sarah, and Jack are about as different as four figures can be and certainly get on each other's nerves. Have you ever been on a road trip stuck with traveling companions who drive you crazy? Watching the characters argue and ultimately bond is part of the gentle grace of the film. Toward the end of their journey Tom splurges one night and buys them all rooms in a fancy hotel. One by one, however, they all end up together in Tom's suite drinking herbal brandy, comically acknowledging they have grown to need each other.

Road trip films are often as much about healing as they are about the quest. *The Way* proposes two ways to promote this healing: confession and ritual. The confessions in the film are not formal Catholic confessions, they occur along the dusty road. In one scene Sarah lashes out at Tom and struggles to explain her reaction. She later relates that her husband beat her and, in her desperation to avoid more abuse, she had an abortion that she now regrets. Both she and Tom have lost a child and this shared loss connects them. Later, Tom confesses his struggles with his son to Jack, the writer he strongly dislikes, knowing it will end up in his book, but sharing it anyway with the admonition that he "write the truth."

The second tool for healing is ritual. None of the four pilgrims is a practicing Catholic. In fact, Jack the writer, is openly hostile to the Catholic Church and refuses to enter any church along the way. At one point along the *camino* pilgrims are supposed to toss their stone at a shrine and say a prayer. Sarah tries to complete the ritual but stops halfway, it is too painful, Tom completes the prayer for them both and tosses his stone into the pile. This action brings unspoken peace. They have all evolved by the end of the journey when they arrive at the Cathedral of Saint James. Each places their hand in the worn hand-shaped space on marble pillar holding up a statue of Saint James. Much like the marble steps in Rome worn down by the knees of thousands upon thousands of pilgrims over the ages, this ritual act connects them to a journey that is much larger than their own. Each of the four reacts differently after having reached the end of their journey: Jost enters on his knees, Tom goes to a side chapel with his son's ashes, and Jack begrudgingly decides to enter the church. All are moved and let the immense incense holder being swung by six monks waft over their tired, but healed bodies and souls. *The Way* is a pilgrimage film, at times poignant, at times comical, that highlights our need for community, connection, and the role ritual can play in healing.

ANALYSIS OF LITTLE MISS SUNSHINE

The second road trip film we will consider is *Little Miss Sunshine* (2006). It is also a story of healing; however, their quest is very different. The inciting incident of this hilarious dark comedy is a phone call which interrupts a very awkward family dinner to inform seven-year-old Olive Hoover (Abigail Breslin) that she is now eligible (due to a contestant being disqualified after taking diet pills) to compete in the youth Little Miss Sunshine beauty pageant in California. This news compels the family to band together and pile into an old VW bus with ignition issues and hurriedly drive from New Mexico to California to enter the pageant. As was the case with *The Way,* each member of the Hoover family has their own issues: Richard, the father (Greg Kinnear) is so wrapped up in writing and promoting his self-help book on the "9 Steps to Success" that he can't communicate past his own rules for being a "winner"; the teenage son, Dwayne, played to sulking and angry perfection by Paul Dano, refuses to speak to anyone until he becomes an Air Force pilot (and because he hates everyone); Olive is the bubbly, innocent, positive youngest member of the family, and she is especially close to her foul-mouthed and drug-addicted Grandpa (Alan Arkin); the frazzled mother, Sheryl (Toni Collette) is doing her best to keep the family together and her suicidal brother Frank alive (Steve Carell).

This independent film is a blend of farce, satire, drama, and comedy that takes place on the road. As with most films in this genre, the road is filled with obstacles and challenges, some of which are quite absurd. The challenges include the time pressure of travelling from Albuquerque, New Mexico to Redondo Beach, California in a mere three days. Their vehicle is ramshackle and the starter breaks which forces them to physically push the vehicle and jump into it while it is rolling each time they need to start it. The van's horn also jams at the most inopportune moments. When Grandpa dies of a drug overdose in Arizona, they steal his corpse and stick it in the van's trunk in order to make it to the beauty pageant in time. The more difficult obstacles have to do with interpersonal tensions and self-doubt. Critiquing America's celebration of winners and distaste for losers is ever-present as is truth telling versus spin and self-help platitudes.

Little Miss Sunshine is not an overtly religious pilgrimage; however religious topics and themes are central to the plot. Christian theologian and film scholar Craig Detweiler has analyzed the theme of community in the film (Detweiler, 2008). I would like to focus on another religious theme central to the story: compassion. Amidst the many roadblocks they encounter, this is a lesson everyone learns. Most world religions hold compassion as a fundamental human ideal. For example, in the Hebrew scriptures there is a form of compassion exhibited by Hashem which is referred to as *nichum* which means to "be sorry for," "regret," "comfort," "console" yet the term connotes more than emotion, it includes a will to change the situation. This Jewish idea that compassion is more than co-suffering, that it involves action, is picked up in the Christian tradition. Jesus was often "moved with compassion" and then acts on this feeling, for example, healing a leper (Mark 1:41) or feeding the 5,000 (Mark 6:34–44). *Splagchnizomai* is one of eight terms in Greek that translates as "compassion" and connotes being moved from one's bowels (thought to be the seat of emotions). Followers of Jesus are told to "cloth themselves in compassion" (Col. 3:12). Finally, compassion is the cardinal virtue or aspiration in Buddhism. The word usually translated as "compassion" is *karuna*, which is understood to mean active sympathy or a willingness to bear the pain of others. As in Christianity, it is an active term beyond feeling emotion but there are different motives and nuances involved. One is the realization that we are all connected therefore compassion for another is really compassion connected to your own self (or non-self). In Tibetan Buddhism this practice of compassion toward oneself is called *toglen* and involves self-compassion that recognizes a far larger view of reality: the unlimited spaciousness and lack of divisions that Buddhists call *shunyata*.

One wonderful aspect of learning more about religion through film is the opportunity to take religious concepts, such a compassion, and see them actualized in story form. In addition, knowing the generic formula for a road trip/pilgrimage film readies the viewer to go with the flow. So what can *Little Miss Sunshine* teach us about compassion? There are three particular scenes where you see compassion in action. The first occurs when the family is in the waiting room of a hospital expecting news that grandpa has died. Holding back tears, the mother tries to prep the kids for grandpa's impending death, stressing that they need to stick together as a family as she confesses how much she loves them. Uncle Frank says nothing but rests a hand of comfort on his sister's knee and her non-verbal son scribbles a note to his sister that reads: "Go hug mom!" It is a great visual tableau of compassion in action. Compassion is a lesson they are still learning as this tableau portrays their separation in the waiting room (Figure 4.6).

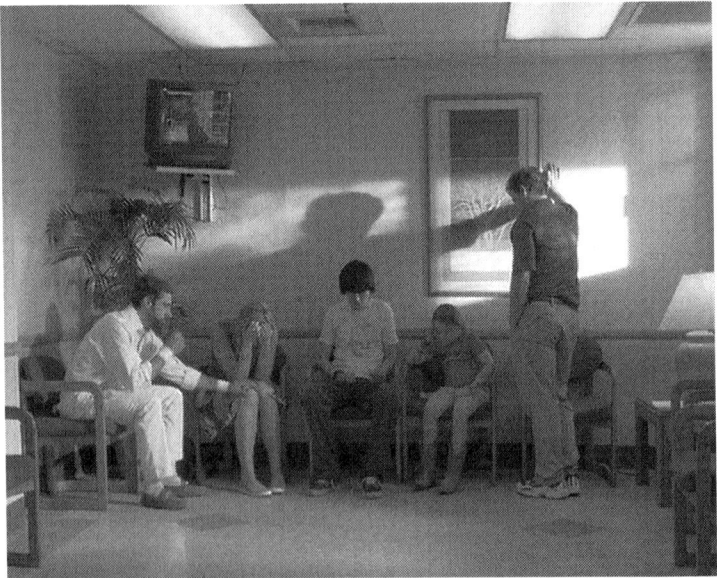

Figure 4.6 Learning compassion as a family in *Little Miss Sunshine* (Jonathan Dayton, Valerie Faris, 2006).
Source: Screenshot by author

Another poignant example of compassion occurs when Dwayne has discovered that he is colorblind and will never achieve his dream of becoming a pilot which results in a severe panic attack and his meltdown by the side of the road. The grownups fail to console him, but Olive instinctively knows what to do. In her little red boots, she marches down the hill to her sobbing big brother and gently lays her head on his shoulder. No words are spoken, but her compassionate action and physical connection are enough to break through his despair, he shrugs and says "O.K." and he lifts his little sister up the hill as they return to the car together. Uncle Frank, a Proust scholar, in a scene toward the end of the film with the depressed Dwayne on the end of the pier shares the wisdom he learned from Proust that applies to both himself and Dwayne: that we learn the most from the periods of our life when we are suffering. This is a moment of compassion and Dwayne decides to embrace the suffering of high school, those "prime years of suffering" and uncle and nephew find a moment of self-compassion and connection. In the final scene of

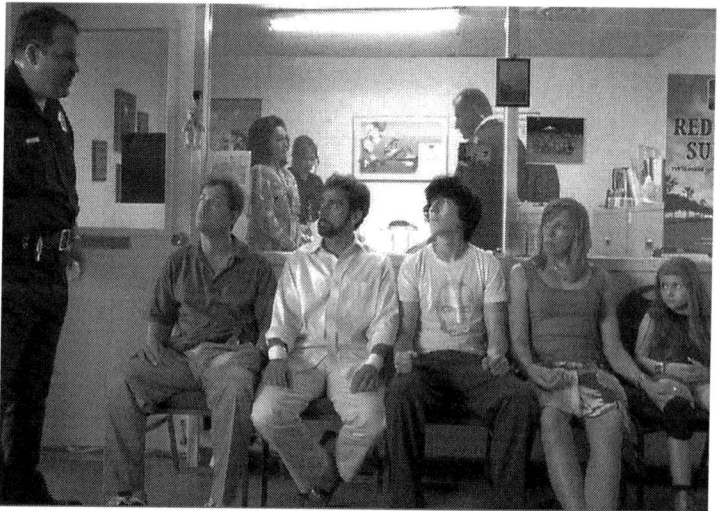

Figure 4.7 The Hoovers sit together, touching, and look with one accord as they are sentenced by security guard in *Little Miss Sunshine* (Jonathan Dayton, Valerie Faris, 2006).
Source: Screenshot by author

the film Olive is humiliating herself by doing a wildly inappropriate striptease for her talent portion of the pageant. Rather than let her suffer alone, her dad jumps onstage with Olive and is then followed by the rest of her family and they hilariously complete her dance together. The family ends their journey much closer to whole, despite losing grandpa. They have learned how to be vulnerable and compassionate with their broken selves and with each other (Figure 4.7).

DOCUMENTARY FILM

Films: *5 Broken Cameras* (Israel, 2011), *Jesus Camp* (USA, 2008)
Religions: Islam and Pentecostal Christianity

Perhaps more than any other type of film, documentaries have the potential to dramatically impact our understanding of religion. Religion and documentary film profess to share a common goal: the revelation of what is really real. When the two converge in documentaries about religion or religious figures, the terrain is fraught with latent hazards and pregnant possibilities. So, how do we approach this final genre of film? One common way to approach religion in religious studies is the Insider-Outsider perspective. I will apply this lens to two different films. The first film, *5 Broken Cameras*, was made by a Muslim insider and offers an insider's view of the Palestinian-Israeli conflict. *Jesus Camp* (2007) is an example of two religious outsiders making a documentary film about a Pentecostal youth camp. What assumptions do you make when you choose to watch a documentary? Most likely you expect a filmic slice of real life. You expect the subjects of the film to be real characters, not paid and coached actors. You may acknowledge that the bias of the director will influence the final product, however most expect a certain critical ambivalence or at least the presentation of two points of view as well as minimal narrative coercion and manipulation. Documentary films are a wonderful way to explore religion and the genre itself is being examined by religion and film scholars such as Justin Wells in his recent book *How to Film Truth: The Story of Documentary Film as a Spiritual Journey*.

"Documentary" film was officially christened as such in 1926 by John Grierson in reference to Robert Flaherty's film, *Moana*. The explorer-turned-filmmaker, Flaherty, in many ways, was the father of what we now call documentary film. Flaherty did not approach a subject with a preconceived notion of a filmic narrative, but rather immersed himself in the lives of his subjects, observed them, shot numerous reels of footage and only later, in the editing room, did he tease out what was "significant, beautiful, or interesting." Flaherty's editing process raises important questions for us: To what degree should a director of a documentary film manipulate the subject matter? Where do you draw the line between creative representation of lived reality and capturing reality? The term "documentary" has its root in Latin term *docere*, literally "to teach." Today most understand the term "document" however, to refer to a factual record. Film has a unique ability to capture, document, and record reality. These dual understandings of documentary "to document" with an added desire to teach or reveal reality are fundamental to what most viewers expect of documentaries today. Most documentarians retain a sense of didactic intent while maintaining they are presenting audiences with a window into reality. Early documentarian John Grierson defined documentary film as "the creative treatment of actuality," a short definition which still enjoys widespread use. It is a definition which allows for directorial influence and creativity while still maintaining the notion that reality is being presented.

Documentary film has evolved dramatically since the 1920s. British documentarians, such as Scotsman John Grierson, brought a new politicized lens to the genre. The 1960s and 1970s brought two new schools/theories to documentary film: Direct Cinema and Cinéma Vérité. Direct Cinema refers to a style of filming in which the director and camera person are largely flies on the wall. Adherents to this approach believed in non-directed, "objective" capture. Robert Drew and Richard Leacock, leaders of U.S.-based Direct Cinema taught that once the subjects were chosen, the filmmakers should not participate in or influence the scene in any way. Cinéma Vérité (film truth) refers to the French school led by Jean Rouch that found inspiration in Russian filmmaker Dziga Vertov's Kino Pravda. Rouch rejected the idea that the filmmaker could be an unobtrusive presence who quietly captured reality. He believed the camera was a stimulant to action. At an infamous 1963 conference of filmmakers sponsored by Radio Television Francaise, Rouch argued that direct and honest interviewing could tease out reality while Leacock claimed the only way to really discover the truth about people was to not intrude and wait for moments of self-revelation. Leacock accused Rouch of coercing his subjects and Rouch accused Leacock of being an uncritical, too-accepting passive American.

INSIDERS AND OUTSIDERS IN THE STUDY OF RELIGION

Scholars of religion have struggled with the issue of outsiders trying to present the insiders' religious experience since the beginning of *Religionswissenschaft*. German theologian Rudolph Otto declared that outsiders could never truly understand religious experience and they should not try. On the other hand, Joachim Wach, one of the founders of the academic study of religion, taught that while religious insiders may have more access to the inner intention of a particular religious experience, they may be hindered by their lack of distance. Our exemplar of a religious insider documentarian is Emad Burnat creator of the Palestinian film *5 Broken Cameras* (2011).

ANALYSIS OF *5 BROKEN CAMERAS*

This film was shot in the village of Bil'in located in the West Bank (Palestinian territory). Burnat, who began filming when his fourth son, Gibreel, was born in 2005. Over the course of five years, Emad filmed the border struggle, which is led by two of his best friends, alongside filming how Gibreel grows and is affected by the border violence and encroaching Jewish housing settlements. The fence that dissects their land becomes the focus of weekly demonstrations by local residents and foreign and Israeli human rights activists protesting against what they call the "apartheid wall," a 600 km complex of walls and fences built mostly on and between occupied Palestinian areas. At Bil'in the barrier dipped deep into the West Bank to carve off 60% of the village's farmland, land designated by Israeli authorities for the future expansion of the nearby illegal Jewish settlement of Modiin Illit. The quotidian border conflict is punctuated by Emad's 5 broken video cameras—which usually last about a year before being destroyed in Israeli-Palestinian scuffles. One camera after another is shot at or smashed exemplifying the constant violence their community faces.

There have been many documentaries on Palestinian-Israeli tensions over the past 20 years (*To Live and Die in Jerusalem* (Israel, 2007) et al.). This personal film gives the conflict a human face by chronicling the birth and development of one little boy, Burnat's son Gibreel, from innocent baby to hardened "little man" celebrating his fifth birthday. At three he is seen gingerly giving an armed Israeli soldier an olive branch, but by the end of the film his innocence is crumbling and being replaced with frustration and anger. In one heart-wrenching scene near the end he asks his papa: "why don't you kill the soldiers with a knife?" to which his father responds, "why do you want to hurt them?" Gibreel explains: "because they shot my Phil" (his favorite jocular uncle who he saw gunned down and die). Another poignant moment happens when the wire fence is bulldozed only to be replaced with a bigger cement wall. Little Gibreel scribbles his name in chalk on the new cement border wall—if only to faintly assert his existence (Figure 4.8).

Burnat explains that his filmmaking, which got him in trouble on several occasions, is also part of his healing:

> Healing is a challenge in life. It's a victim's sole obligation. By healing, you resist oppression. But when I'm hurt over and over again, I forget the wounds that rule my life. Forgotten wounds can't be healed. So I film to heal. I know they may knock at my door at any moment. But I'll just keep filming. It helps me confront life. And survive.[2]

Figure 4.8 Gibreel surveys the disputed border between Israel and Palestine in *5 Broken Cameras* (Emad Burnat, 2005).
Source: Photo courtesy of Emad Burnat.

Not only is his filmmaking part of his testimony and process of healing, but it serves to educate others around the world about the daily reality Palestinians face, a reality where 12-year-old boys are arrested, and your unarmed favorite uncle can be killed before your eyes while marching in a protest.

The film has been screened at film festivals around the world. It won the Audience award for best documentary and was nominated for an Academy Award in 2012 for Best Documentary. Islamophobia is not reserved for the war-torn borderlands of Israel and Palestine, as the Burnat family's reception at LAX testifies. When they arrived in Los Angeles to attend the awards ceremony, they were detained for hours at the airport until hard copies of the Academy Award invite letter could be procured.

ANALYSIS OF *JESUS CAMP*

Outsiders can bring a critical eye to religion. They may see connections or complexities that would never occur to the insider. However, outsiders are always at a distinct disadvantage when it comes to truly understanding a religious insider's actual experience. Ecstatic behavior, for example, glossolalia or speaking in tongues, may sound like incoherent gibberish to an atheist cinematographer standing on one side of the subject, while a member of the same community might interpret the sounds to be the sweetest praise refrain or a prophetic warning. If representing truth is the goal, documentarians must be hyper aware of their outsider biases.

The documentary *Jesus Camp* (2007) follows three Pentecostal children: Rachael, Levi, and Tory from their Missouri homes to the family "Kids on Fire" camp in Devils Lake, North Dakota run by Becky Fischer. The focus on the spirituality of the children takes place in the charged context of the national debate in the USA over religion and politics. At camp, the battle lines of the culture wars are clearly drawn and the children are taught to become dedicated soldiers in God's army in effort to "take back America for Christ."

Heidi Ewing and Rachel Grady established themselves as talented documentarians with the award-winning *The Boys of Baraka* (2005). After meeting the charismatic Fischer (a fourth generation Pentecostal) and watching one of her recruiting sessions at a church, they decided to focus on her ministry. Neither of the filmmakers are religious insiders. Their general lack of familiarity with Protestant Evangelical Christian faith expression and worldview impedes their final product. Outsider filmmakers don't need to become religious practitioners, but they should do their homework and be honest about how their presence influences their film. Ewing is crystal clear about their method:

> Our job is to capture the essence of situations and to try to show the audience what it is like to be there. We don't make personal movies! We are not activist filmmakers, we are extraordinarily curious people, we want to learn along the way.[3]

They were clear about their motives and mission behind *Jesus Camp*: (1) to spark a conversation about the growing cultural divide in this nation; (2) to shatter stereotypes and provoke new ways of thinking; (3) to teach their audience about Evangelical subculture. While this film sparked a conversation, they reified negative Pentecostal caricatures and augmented the ignorance, contempt, and disdain many non-Evangelicals feel toward this powerful and large subculture of 80–100 million Americans.

The filmmakers should have done some research into the nuances and differences that exist both historically and today within Evangelical Christianity. While Fischer is identified as a "Pentecostal Evangelical," the directors never mention her denominational background which is a huge omission as she hails from the Word of Faith Movement which does not represent the majority of Pentecostal Christians, let alone Evangelicals! Word of Faith preachers are known for their dramatic style (for example healer Benny Hinn) and penchant for hyperbole. In her faith tradition, such methods are the norm, while to many Americans who viewed the film, she appears to be extreme.

These filmmakers crossed the line with the editorial decisions they made which not only stilted the viewers' understanding of the sequence of events, but, in some cases, fabricated reality. I will offer a few examples of how Ewing and Grady violated the ethics of documentary film editing. In one scene at camp a very emotional boy, Andrew, shares his doubts and struggles with God. As he publicly confesses his doubts about God and the Bible, the camera pans to faces of the children who look horrified and confused. They appear to leave Andrew standing there alone. This scene struck me as inaccurate. I suspected that he was not left to stand there alone and vulnerable, but would have been comforted by those around him during this moment. Of course, I had no way to prove it until I stumbled upon the blog of Levi's father, Tim O'Brian, who explained what really happened:

> The scene in the movie shows Andrew freely sharing his doubts and struggles about God. I was in the room during that moment. I really don't like the way the editor cut the scene. She purposely used shots of kids that looked confused or troubled when I am sure those shots were not taken during that moment. That moment was, in reality, a beautiful moment. The kids really embraced Andrew as he shared and there was an atmosphere of, "Hey, it's safe to share here.... Any shot of the audience is suspect in the film.[4]

Another example of editorial adulteration of reality involved the portrayal of Pentecostal mom, Tracy O'Brian, who home schools Levi. One of Tracy's more provocative quotes was: "There are two kinds of people in the world: those who love Jesus and those who don't...." Of course, taken alone, this statement might offend many viewers and portray Tracy as a judgmental xenophobe; however this quote was cut mid-sentence in editing. The rest of the sentence was "...and they are both worthy of dignity and respect." When the editors excised the second half of her sentence, they erased her instruction for her children to recognize each person's human dignity and to respect them. Ewing and Grady decided they wanted to portray conservative, homeschooling moms in a negative light to the detriment of a fascinating film. Viewers should always consider the background, biases, and agenda of the documentarians, especially when the subject matter is religion.

RECEPTION OF *JESUS CAMP*

Popular reactions to *Jesus Camp* ran the gamut from glowing praise to passionate denunciation. The film garnered an Academy Award nomination for best documentary. It never cleared 1 million dollars in the theaters and nationwide release was limited. The subjects of the film have been supportive of the documentary with some important reservations. Becky Fischer (the most polemical, controversial adult in the film) has attended many public screenings and has endorsed the film with some misgivings while welcoming the increased publicity.

> I was in shock because I have never viewed what we do with children as political in any way. It was a blow and I have been on a roller-coaster emotionally over it, but not having any editorial rights to the film there was not much I could do about it.[5]

Some of the subjects' parents lamented that Ewing and Grady never came to truly understand them, something that they did not realize while being filmed, but discovered after viewing the edited film. "Disturbing" was an oft-cited descriptor followed closely by "fascinating." Kenneth Turan, the Los Angeles Times lead film critic, called *Jesus Camp* "one of the most unnerving films of the year." Many viewers left the theater repulsed at what they viewed as nothing less than child abuse along with political and religious indoctrination.

Ewing and Grady claimed to provide audiences with a fair and truthful portrait of Evangelical children and their world. Unfortunately, their editorial choices belied this goal leaving us with what one reviewer called a film with

> more than a faint whiff of hypocrisy and condescension… [as]… the filmmakers are out to demonize, not humanize, which means their movie ends up preaching to the liberal choir instead of shedding any real light into the Evangelical Christian movement.[6]

In the end, *Jesus Camp* is a cautionary example of the possible shortcomings of outsiders creating a documentary on religion. Thankfully, there are many examples of outsider filmmakers making enlightening documentaries on religion, for example, *Waiting for John* (2014) about a cargo cult on Vanuatu, et al. This analysis of *Jesus Camp* is meant to raise your awareness of activist editing and the nuances of religious experience that may be eclipsed by outsider documentarians who desire to sensationalize religion in order to sell their film, a more recent example is *Wild, Wild, Country* (Netflix) about the Rajneeshpuram movement.

FOR FUTURE VIEWING

Sci-Fi: *Avatar*, (2009), *Inception* (USA, 2010), *Annihilation* (USA, 2018), *Star Wars* (USA, 1977–2019).

Horror: *Midsommer* (Sweden, 2019), *Us* (USA, 2019).

Comedy: *Life of Brian* (UK, 1979), *Dogma* (USA, 1999), *PK* (India, 2007) *Halal Love Story* (India, 2020).

Drama: *Clemency* (USA, 2019), *Higher Ground* (USA, 2011).

Pilgrimage/The Quest/Road Trip: *The Lord of the Rings trilogy* (2001, 2002, 2003), *Paths of the Soul* (China, 2016), *The Motorcycle Diaries* (Argentina, et al., 2004).

Documentary Films: *Wild, Wild Country* (USA, 2018), *The Vow* (2020), *Holy Hell* (2016).

NOTES

1 Jomhuri-ye Eslami web site, Tehran, 4 May 2004. "Iran Commentary Says Film has "Fundamental Deviations." BBC Monitoring Middle East, May 10, 2004.
2 Emad Burnat, "Quotes" on imdb.com page for *5 Broken Cameras*. imdb.com/title/tt2125423.
3 Heidi Ewing, interview with David Poland, 4 April, 2007. http://www.menblogs.com.
4 Tim O'Brian interview on www.jesuscampers.com accessed October10, 200.
5 Becky Fischer, http: www.kidsinministry.org accessed August, 2007.
6 Glen Whipp, "Does Jesus Love You? Ask these happy campers," http://www.daily news.com, 28 September, 2006.

FOR FUTURE READING

Cowan, Douglas E. *Sacred Terror: Religion and Horror on the Silver Screen*. Waco, TX: Baylor University Press, 2008.

Lindvall, Terry, J., Dennis Bounds, and Chris Lindvall. *Divine Film Comedies: Biblical Narratives, Film Sub-Genres and the Comic Spirit*. New York: Routledge, 2016.

Lyden, John C. "Part II: Genre and Film Analysis." in *Film as Religion: Myths, Morals, and Rituals*, second ed., 119–250. New York: New York University Press, 2019.

Neale, Steve. *Genre and Hollywood*. New York: Routledge, 2000.

Wells, Justin. *How to Film Truth: The Story of Documentary Film as a Spiritual Journey*. Eugene, OR: Cascade Books, 2018.

DEMONS, REDEEMERS, GHOSTS AND MORE
RECURRENT TROPES IN RELIGION AND FILM

Beyond genres, another way to approach religion and film is to consider religious tropes (repeated motifs and ideas) in film. I have selected six prevalent or socially significant tropes for exploration: evil and suffering, sex/gender roles, race, redemption and healing, reincarnation and karma, and finally, death and the afterlife. I will utilize a variety of the approaches outlined in Chapter 2 to comment on the different ways these themes are presented. Some of the films, such as *Water*, feature religion; however, most of them are popular films (for example, *Get Out* or *Magnolia*) that nonetheless have profound things to say on the topic. As we have seen throughout this book, religion is concerned with more than the transcendent realm, it is intimately concerned with human life, therefore cinematic portrayals of human life in all its messiness are the perfect place to find religious themes and concerns. Each trope will be elucidated by two films.

FILMS AND TROPES ANALYZED IN THIS CHAPTER

EVIL AND SUFFERING

Films: *The Exorcism of Emily Rose* (USA, 2005) & *Get Out* (USA, 2017)
Foci: External evil, demonic possession, the systemic moral evil of racism.

SEX, GENDER ROLES, AND RELIGION

Films: *Water* (India/Canada, 2005) & *God Loves Uganda* (USA, 2013)
Foci: Hinduism, patriarchy and women's roles in India and sexuality/homosexuality and Christianity in the USA and Uganda.

RELIGION AND RACE

Films: *The Other Conquest* (Mexico, 1998) & *Burden* (USA, 2020)
Foci: European Hispanic Colonial racism and indigenous religion in Mexico and black-white racial tensions and Christianity in the Southern USA.

REDEMPTION, RECONCILIATION, AND HEALING

Films: *Central Station* (Brazil, 1998) & *Magnolia* (USA, 1999)
Foci: Interpersonal human redemption and generational healing.

KARMA AND REINCARNATION

Films: *It's a Wonderful Life* (USA, 1947) & *Uncle Boonmee Who Can Recall His Past Lives* (Thailand, 2010)
Foci: Karma restoration, edification, and reincarnation.

DEATH AND AFTERLIFE

Films: *Biutiful* (Spain, 2010) & *From a Whisper* (Kenya, 2009)
Foci: Fear, negotiation, and coming to terms with death and the afterlife, mourning.

EVIL AND SUFFERING

Evil is slippery. Definitions of evil have evolved over time. Saint Augustine gave us an ontological definition: evil is the absence of the good. Jung proffered it was the shadow side of human nature. I define evil as that which destroys life. There are many types of evil: natural evil (like natural disasters, cancer, or Covid-19), personified external evil (demons, evil spirits, monsters), moral evil (when humans choose to act in a life-destroying way), and systemic evil (institutionalized racism, for example) that has been created over time by immoral choices that constrain, corrupt, and destroy life. Cinema has explored all of these manifestations of evil over the past 130 years from George Mélies's gothic *Le manoir du diable* (1896) to Universal's iconic monsters movies of the early 1930s (*Dracula, Frankenstein, The Mummy*) to demon-possession tales of the 1960s and 1970s (*Rosemary's Baby, The Exorcist, The Omen*). We will focus on two types of evil: demonic, external evil and the systemic evil of racism.

"SO THAT THEY MAY KNOW THAT EVIL IS REAL" (ANNALIESE MICHEL)

The horror movie *The Exorcism of Emily Rose* (2005) was selected as a representative story of external evil in the form of demonic possession amidst dozens of choices for two reasons: it is based on a true story of the exorcism of Anneliese Michel (1952–1976) in Germany and the director and writer, Scott Derrickson, is a Christian and articulate about how the horror genre relates to religion. Whether Annaliese was suffering from epilepsy that led to psychosis or actually possessed by external evil entities is something that was debated at the trial of her parents and two priests following her death. Anneliese experienced her first episode in 1968 at the age of 16 and suffered increasing physical and psychological afflictions over the next five years, despite being under medical and psychiatric care. In 1973, her parents turned to the church for help and the Bishop of Wurzburg finally authorized an exorcism. From September 1975 to June 1976, she underwent over 67 exorcisms at the hands of two priests following the official Catholic *Rituale Romanum*. She died on July 1, 1976 of malnutrition and both her parents and the two priests were tried and found guilty of negligent homicide. Despite the German Bishop conference officially denying her demonic possession, Anneliese is now considered a martyr, a heroine who valiantly fought the Enemy, and her gravesite has become a shrine. Derrickson, who co-wrote the film that is part courtroom-drama, part-horror, followed the fundamentals of what happened but collapsed the timeline into less than one year and set the story in the USA. Emily Rose (Jennifer Carpenter) is a devout Catholic who is delighted to earn a full scholarship to her local university however, her joy is cut short as a demonic attack occurs shortly after arriving on campus. Her story is told in flashbacks interwoven into the courtroom drama in which Father Moore (Tom

Wilkinson), her exorcist and parish priest, is on trial for her murder. Laura Linney plays Father Moore's agnostic defense attorney Erin Bruner and exemplifies the struggle between scientific rationalism and supernatural evidence. Despite medical intervention for supposed epilepsy (Gamutrol), Emily's condition worsens, and she ultimately returns home where she harms herself and refuses to eat. Family, Father Moore, and her boyfriend all try to help her and one stormy Halloween night the demons reveal themselves to be many: Legion, Beliel, Lucifer, and various evil humans who had passed: Hitler, Nero, Judas. After a vision of the Virgin Mary, Emily chooses to continue to suffer, so others will know that evil is real, and dies shortly thereafter.

Using the auteur approach is fruitful in analyzing this film. Derrickson has carved out a niche for himself as a director and writer of horror films: *Dracula 2000* and *Hellraiser: Inferno, Sinister, Deliver Us from Evil*, et al. He feels horror is "the perfect Christian genre" explaining:

> this genre deals more overtly with the supernatural than any other genre, …it distinguishes and articulates the essence of good and evil better than any other genre, and my feeling is that a lot of Christians are wary of this genre simply because it's unpleasant. The genre is not about making you feel good, it is about making you face your fears. And in my experience, that's something that a lot of Christians don't want to do. To me, the horror genre is the genre of non-denial. It's about admitting that there is evil in the world, and recognizing that there is evil within *us*, and that we're not in control, and that the things that we are afraid of must be confronted in order for us to relinquish that fear.
>
> (Derrickson, 2005)

He adapted the story of Anneliese Michel to provoke people to ask themselves what they really thought about evil, as well as God, memory, morality, and truth.

This story is an excellent cinematic example of a religious worldview that believes this world is a battleground between forces of evil and forces of good. Helping the agnostic, skeptical lawyer Erin Bruner to accept this reality is part of Father Moore's mission in the film. When odd supernatural things start happening to Erin alone at night in her apartment such as smelling something burning or the alarm clock going off at 3 a.m. (the hour of demons mocking Christ's death), Father Moore explains to Erin that she is "under attack." He explains that by helping him she is now in a spiritual battle and the forces of darkness are trying their best to keep her out of the light. Erin, like most late moderns in the audience, believes in science but her character does evolve throughout the film. She does not become a believer, but she has opened up her mind to the possibility of external evil forces. Her closing argument captures this transformation well, while she does not admit to believing in the "the work of the devil," she urges the jurors to consider if it could be possible.

Christian viewers may be troubled that a sincere believer could be attacked and inhabited by demons. How could God allow this? Doesn't her faith in Jesus protect her? It is the age-old question of why bad things happen to good people, albeit in an extreme form. How could a good, all-knowing, loving God allow this to happen? Many horror films simply present the battle between good and evil, but Derrickson offers a theodicy by allowing Emily Rose a moment of free will amidst this cosmic battle. There is a short, but crucial dream scene near the end that is narrated in Emily Rose's voice through a letter she gave to Father Moore in a rare lucid moment after a failed exorcism. In it she describes a realistic out-of-body experience where she is walking in the mist and sees the Virgin Mary who tells her: "Heaven is not blind to your pain" and gives her the choice to come with her to heaven then and there or she can make the choice to stay knowing there would be more horrific bodily and spiritual suffering. Why would anyone choose the latter? Emily chooses to stay to prove to a secular world that hears her story that the realm of spiritual evil is real. "People will say God is dead," Emily writes, "but how can they when they see the Devil is real?" She makes her choice and dies a gruesome death believing that good will triumph over evil in the end. Free will and human choice is part of the answer to the problem of evil. *The Exorcism of Emily Rose* presents evil personified in demonic forces locked in battle with God and believers. Another external evil is examined in the next film; however, this time its origin is all too human....

"RACISM IN ITSELF IS A DEMON, AN AMERICAN MONSTER" (JORDAN PEELE)

Get Out (2017) is a horrifying genre-melding work, a satire/horror/thriller with laugh-out-loud moments of comedy sprinkled in (mostly thanks to scene stealer Lil Rel Howery who plays Chris' best friend Rod). The film was a first for comedian Jordan Peele who wrote and directed it after several years of fundraising. *Get Out* won Best Original Screenplay at the Academy Awards and became a cultural phenomenon earning more than 272 million dollars worldwide. The racialized meet-the-parents story is one we have seen before in films like *Guess Who Is Coming to Dinner*. Chris (David Kaluuya), who is black, has been dating his Caucasian girlfriend, Rose (Allison Williams) for almost five months when she decides it's time for him to meet her parents in their country manse upstate. He asks: "Do they know I'm black?" She smiles and assures him not to worry, they adore President Obama and "They are *not* racist." When a racist cop stops them enroute Rose defends Chris after he is racially profiled and harassed. They arrive and Chris meets Rose's parents, her neuroscientist father Dean Armitage (Bradley Whitford) and her mother Missy (Catherine Keener), a psychiatrist. Both are white and woke and eager to prove how un-racist they are to their new houseguest. Chris is not the only black character, there are the servants: Georgina (Betty Gabriel) the creepy housekeeper and Walter (Marcus Henderson) both of whom are dutiful, but almost catatonic. As the weekend unfolds, we discover the true horror of the situation which includes robbing Chris of his life force, his agency, his humanity. At the end of the garden party, we discover that the Armitage's hunt and auction black bodies for rich white people to be able to inhabit by inserting their brains into strong black bodies through the "Coagula procedure" perfected by the secret Crimson Society. This film is so complex that to unpack all the ideas, allusions to other films, genre innovations, mis-en-scéne elements, etc., would merit its own chapter. Here we will focus solely on the following: the director's intention, how cultural context shaped the story, the evil of racism/white supremacy, The Sunken Place, and reception.

AUTEURIAL INTENTION AND THE ROLE OF CULTURAL CONTEXT

Peele began to write the screenplay during Barack Obama's first term as President of the USA (2008–2012). Having elected a black man to the highest office in the land, there was much talk of the USA being "post-racial," something Peele knew was far from the terrifying truth. People were smiling and celebrating the cultural moment as if the country was finally moving past the evil of slavery and the disenfranchisement of blacks. Peele believed that the way we talk about race in the USA was "broken" and therefore he wanted to create something new: "Woke Horror" a subgenre within horror that incorporated all the expected tropes of horror and pulled back the veil on the evil of white supremacy and racism. "This movie is about a lot of things," confessed Peele, "definitely about the way America deals with race…I hope [post-screening] they have a discussion about race or horror films they have not had before." *Get Out* is also an interesting example of how much cultural context can shape a movie. For example, Peele changed the original ending of the film after they shot it. In the original ending Chris strangles Rose to death, white cops arrive, and he is sentenced to a long prison sentence. The final shot was Chris dressed in an orange prison jumpsuit walking back into prison after telling Rod to stop fighting the system to free him. This is the reality for far too many young black people in the USA, where blacks comprise approximately 13% of the population but 33% of prison population. Peele was more hopeful about black lives in 2017 when they finally shot the movie for several reasons, the Black Lives Matter movement (founded 2013) was spreading, many whites were becoming racially "woke," i.e., more aware of systemic and interpersonal racism, and the incarceration of black men was decreasing. In addition to these hopeful cultural trends, Peele changed the ending of the film to allow for a triumphant black hero who does not succumb with reactive brutality by killing his evil girlfriend and is reunited with his true brother, Rod, who leaves us with a laugh.

EVIL WITH A SMILE: WHITE SUPREMACY

Although the director calls racism a "demon," there is no satanic external force at play here, there is white supremacism and racism with a smile. The film is replete with verbal racist micro-aggressions and they abound at the garden party. Besides the help and an oddly dressed young black man, Logan, Chris is the only black person in a sea of older, rich white folk. Guests take turns trying to interact with Chris, making offensive comments with a smile, like how being black is "fashionable now" or mentioning that they "know Tiger Woods." One woman takes it further asking Rose about if it is true about black men's sexual stamina as she squeezes Chris's bicep. As

Chris tries to escape, the niceties cease and Dean explains that "we [Whites] are divine, we are the gods trapped in a mortal cocoon." These whites are part of secret Crimson Society who have discovered a way for their "superior" brains to be implanted into stronger black bodies. Part of the pre-op has the white person who has purchased the black host at auction explain to them what will transpire next. Through a screen, Jim Hudson (who has purchased Chris's body) explains to the strapped-down Chris that a "slice" of him will remain, but this existence "will be as passenger." Chris' voice will be muted, he will be trapped while the white man is in control (Figure 5.1).

Horror films allow us to visualize evil. Peele's "Sunken Place" is a memorable example of this. In a scene eerily reminiscent of the manipulative Hannibal Lector and Clarise in *Silence of the Lambs,* Missy manages to get Chris to speak about his most painful memory: the night he lost his mom who died in a car crash and bled out on the side of the road. He was a young boy who sat paralyzed watching TV and "did nothing." Missy ends up hypnotizing Chris, and this is how she controls him. She sends him into "The Sunken Place" which is depicted as a black, starry sky (reminiscent of the Twilight Zone) into which one falls endlessly. There is a window, a screen by

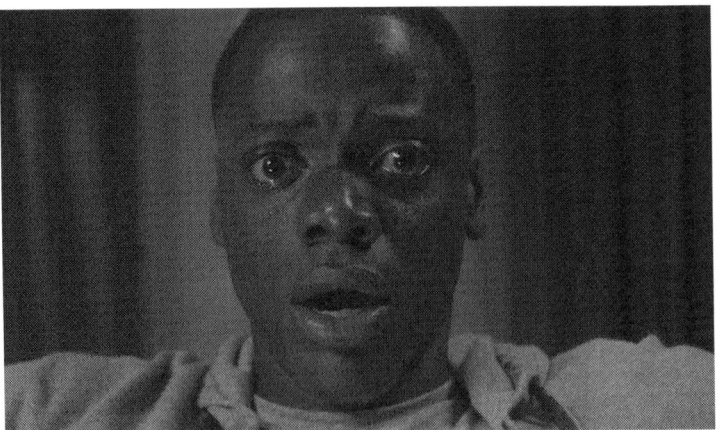

Figure 5.1 Chris is trapped in the Sunken Place in *Get Out* (Jordan Peele, 2017).
Source: screenshot by author

which you can see the outside world, but you cannot communicate, you are trapped. Peele explains that "black souls are in the Sunken Place and they can't escape." In some ways, Peele sees our modern prison system as a Sunken Place, "where black men are abducted, tossed in a hole, relegated to the back of our minds. No matter how hard we scream, the system silences us."[1] Reception of the film was varied: some white viewers became "woke" to racial injustice while others just could not believe it, nor accept that Rose was part of the deception. Many whites asked Allison Williams (Rose) after screenings if her character was really a victim of her family or perhaps, she too was hypnotized by her mother to which Williams incredulously responded: "No, she is just evil! How hard is that to accept?" *Get Out* is a clever, layered look at the evil of racism.

SEX, GENDER ROLES, AND RELIGION

AUTEUR AND CULTURAL STUDIES ANALYSIS OF *WATER*

Water (2005) is the third and final film in Deepa Mehta's Elements Trilogy that began with *Fire* (1996) and *Earth* (1998, detailed analysis in Chapter 4). *Water* is set in 1938 and explores the lives of Hindu widows at an ashram in Varanasi, India. The film is visually stunning, the spiritual score by Sufi A.R. Rahman moves you, and the mis-en-scéne is striking. The film begins with eight-year-old Chuyia (Sarala Kariyawasam) being brought to live the rest of her life in a widows' ashram. Her adjustment to the austere life of a widow brings moments of humor and heartbreak which is softened a bit by her friendship with Kalyani (Lisa Ray), a beautiful young widow who has been forced into prostitution by the head of the destitute ashram, Madhumati (Manorma). At this time, Hindu widows had three choices: death on her husband's funeral pyre, marriage to his brother, or she could live out the rest of her days as an aesthetic in an ashram. Widows are considered half a human based on the ancient Hindu text, *The Manusmriti* (laws of Manu). They are considered polluted and are shunned by society. Shakuntala (Seema Biswas), a devout and literate Hindu from the Brahmin caste, takes Chuyia under her wings. Shakuntala is middle-aged, second in command at the ashram, resigned but questioning. Through Chuyia's misadventure running through town, Kalyani meets Narayan (John Abraham), a law student from a wealthy family who is a true believer in the civil disobedience campaign of Mahatma Gandhi, and they fall in love. Unfortunately, Madhumati forbids their marriage (as the ashram would lose their income). Kalyani's only way out is suicide and her role as prostitute is forced on Chuyia. Alongside this romantic story, Shakuntala continues to question the religious basis for their gender-conscribed lives. She has a breakthrough, rescues Chuyia, and sends her off to Gandhi with Narayan in the end.

Using a Cultural Studies lens, the tumult surrounding the film's production is almost as interesting as the film itself. It inspired an entire book entitled *Shooting Water* by Mehta's daughter Devyani Saltzman. After many years raising funds, Mehta arrived in the holy city of Varanasi, India to film. Protests led by the Hindu fundamentalist political parties soon filled the streets and surrounded their hotel chanting "Death to Water Picture! Death to Deepa Mehta!" The protestors burned the film's sets and tossed them into the river as well as burning Mehta in effigy. They accused her of defiling Hinduism and the holy river. It is no coincidence that members of the Hindutva party were keen to shut down production of a film that questioned women's gender roles as one of their founders, Sri Aurobindo, felt Hindus suffered from effeminacy and inspired Hindus to return to hypermasculinity, even violence, if necessary, becoming worthy of their Kshatriya warrior caste. Despite approval from the ministry in charge of film production, Mehta made the difficult decision of shutting down production because of death threats against herself and her crew. It took three years before Mehta could resume production in Sri Lanka.

The auteur reveals the film's symbolism and deeper message:

> Water can flow or water can be stagnant. I set the film in the 1930s but the people in the film live their lives as it was prescribed by a religious text more than 2,000 years old. Even today, people follow these texts, which is one reason why there continue to be millions of widows. To me, that is a kind of stagnant water. I think traditions shouldn't be that rigid. They should flow like the replenishing kind of water.[2]

Mehta does not consider *Water* to be an anti-Hindu film, in fact she self-identifies as Hindu, but she is calling for a reevaluation of what she calls a "misinterpretation of religion." She was asked, after the five-year struggle of making *Water*, financial loss, threats to her life, being burned in effigy, if it had been worth it and if she felt vindicated by the international success of the film. She replied "I feel a quiet sense of justice-not vindication." She hopes that *Water* will break what she terms the "conspiracy of silence" that surrounds the treatment of India's 34 million widows today (11 million of whom live in ashrams).

HINDUISM AND WOMEN'S ROLES

There are three main storylines in *Water:* Kalyani's romantic-tragic story, Chuyia's coming-of-age story, and Shakuntla's religious awakening story. Shakuntala's story directly pertains to our focus on gender roles and religion. By looking at her three riverside encounters with her guru Sadananda (played by veteran actor Kulbhushan Kharbanda) we can trace her spiritual evolution. As part of their ascetic pursuits the widows often gather around the local guru to listen to Vedic chants and receive Hindu wisdom. During her first encounter/conversation with Sadananda inquisitive Chuyia dares to ask Shakuntala where the men's ashram is. The other widows abruptly chide her and say they "hope her tongue burns" for daring to suggest that widowers would suffer a similar bleak fate as widows. Chuyia finds refuge from their castigation in the folds of Shakuntla's robes. The second encounter finds Shakuntala alone with her guru. She busies herself in this scene with cleansing the ghat area where the he will sit and teach for the day. She bends her body and performs her cleansing duties by sprinkling holy water around, but has a troubled look on her face. Sadananda inquires if, after all her labors, she feels any closer to "self-liberation" the goal of Hindu life. Shakuntala, as she continues to clean, responds, "If self-liberation means freedom from worldly desires, then no." It is a powerful line. Despite her bleak life, she admits she still has hopes, desires, and dreams for *this* life. Sadananda responds with sincere advice: "whatever happens, do not lose your faith." Her third encounter/conversation occurs after the narrative has taken a tragic turn as Kalyani has been shorn and locked in her room by Madhumati after telling her she planned to break free of her religiously prescribed role and marry Narayan. Shakuntala seeks

Figure 5.2 Shakuntala learns the truth about the treatment of widows from her guru Sadananda in *Water* (Deepa Mehta, 2007).
Source: screenshot by author

out her spiritual mentor and demands to know if it is written that widows should be treated so badly (Figure 5.2).

In response Sadananda recounts the three options for widows written in the *Manusmriti* a 2,000-year-old religious code. The dating is significant because the work was written during the period when Brahmanical tradition was seriously threatened by non-Vedic movements. In other words, these social codes were written when the culture was in a defensive fundamentalist posture and they felt orthodoxy was under assault by alien cultures. These gendered prescriptions are not taken from one of the fundamental religious texts of Hinduism: the *Vedas, Upanishads, the Bhagavad-Gita*. Sadananda, who truly is a compassionate mentor, tells Shakuntala of a new civil law that overturns this religious dictate and allows widows to remarry. This is a revelation to Shakuntla and she incredulously responds: "why didn't I know about this law?" He admits: "We ignore the laws that do not benefit us." In a patriarchal society, it simply does not benefit males to allow widows agency. This is the turning point for Shakuntala. This knowledge of the law, this realization that traditions can change, inspires her to confront the matriarch of the ashram, to demand the keys, and to liberate the imprisoned Kalyani. She manages to save Chuyia in the end. Mehta does not tell us

Shakuntla's fate, but leaves us with a powerful tale that ends with theological discovery and hope that the next generation will break free of life-denying religiously sanctioned gender roles.

CHRISTIANITY, THE LAW, SEX, AND NEOCOLONIALISM: *GOD LOVES UGANDA*

A complicated portrait of northern faith-based neocolonial influence is drawn in Roger Ross Williams' 2013 documentary *God Loves Uganda*. The director follows an American team of eager young missionaries from The International House of Prayer (IHOP) on their short-term mission trip to Uganda. Additional North American figures profiled include: Rev. Scott Lively of Abiding Truth ministries in the USA, red-headed missionary matron Joanna Watson, and IHOP founder Ron Engle. Ugandan anti-homosexuality leaders include politicians such as David Bahati and President Yoweri Museveni as well as Christian pastors like Rev. Robert Kayanja, leader of Uganda's largest mega-church The Miracle Center, and Rev. Martin Ssempa founder of Makerere Community Church. As a counter voice we hear from Ugandan retired Bishop Christopher Senyonjo who supports LGBT people unconditionally, exiled Rev. Kapya Kaoma, who provides shocking undercover footage and academic conclusions, and LGBT rights activist David Kato who is murdered for his work and whose funeral concludes the film.

This documentary film is a striking example of the power certain branches of the Christian church have in influencing not only private sexuality, but politics and law in Uganda. The film argues that anti-homosexuality legislation is a North American neoconservative Evangelical import. However Ugandan political opposition to homosexuality had been brewing for over a decade when David Bahati introduced an anti-homosexuality bill in 2009 which passed parliament in 2013 and was signed into law in February, 2014. Clergy who presided over gay marriages could also be legally penalized. International pressure including economic sanctions by the USA, Europe, and the World Bank immediately ensued and the bill was overturned in August 2014 on "procedural grounds."

The documentary footage is a montage of William's trip following the multicultural teen missionaries from IHOP, "undercover" clips from Kaoma's earlier work in Uganda, street scenes of both evangelism and violence against gays, anti-gay protests, and interviews with the figures listed above. Scenes of Rev. Scott Lively show him fanning fears of "gays trying to recruit your children...Uganda don't let that happen to you!" He preaches "when the righteous rule, the people rejoice." Rev. Lively is featured on television and speaks for five hours to the Ugandan parliament teaching them how homosexuality harms society. Parliamentarian David Bahati does not mince words: "It [homosexuality] is not the change the world is looking for, it is the evil it should fight."

Being against homosexuality became a major way for Ugandan political and religious leaders to assert their ideological independence of liberal Northern influences. There is a dramatic clip featuring Rev. Ssempa illustrating this independent stance: he reads from a letter he sent to President Obama calling him a hypocrite for approving abortion while telling Ugandans how to care for their children. The screen behind him shows graphic pictures where he shows his congregants "the truth" gleaned from his "research" about homosexual sexual activities which include images of a man licking the anus and "poo-poo" of his sexual partners. "Say no to homosexuality! Say no to sodomy! This is a spiritual battle!" Ssempa adjures his horrified audience who are seen taking notes.

Speaking up in defense of the civil rights of the LGBT community comes at great cost. Bishop Senyonjo was relieved of his priestly duties for not condemning homosexuals and has been ostracized by his church. Rev. Kaoma had to leave the country due to death threats and David Kato was brutally bludgeoned to death for his LGBT activism. When protests broke out at Kato's burial, Bishop Senyonjo delivered the following politicized eulogy:

> His death is a result of the hatred planted in Uganda by U.S. Evangelicals. But I have known these people who are LGBT. I respect them for who they are. I believe they are going to heaven. God created you. God is on your side!

Bishop Senyonjo explained that his Christian convictions caused him to stand with the Ugandan LGBT community, "it simply comes down to this" he confessed, "what is the most loving thing to do?"

SEXUALITY AND THE CHURCH: A COMPLICATED AFRICAN CONTEXT

The context is more complicated than the film portrays it to be. Same-sex relations have been criminalized in Uganda since British colonial times, they are not simply a result of recent U.S. incursions. Articles on "unnatural offenses" and "indecent practices" have been retained in the penal code since independence in 1962. Williams' sympathies clearly lie in support of homosexual civic rights and the missionaries and evangelists are portrayed to be simpletons at best, coercive imperialists at worst. He highlights the most outrageous footage of speaking in tongues and passionate clips without contextualizing them. The clear heroes of the film are Kato, Kaoma, and Senyonjo. Many Christians in Uganda felt that U.S. LGBT rights groups were forcing them to change their culture too rapidly. For example, the African bishops at the 1998 Lambeth global conference of Anglican bishops voted overwhelmingly against affirming same-sex relationships. One third of Ugandans are members of the Anglican church and another third are Roman Catholic, another Christian denomination that does not condone homosexual activity or same-sex marriage. So, the thesis that anti-homosexual sentiment is primarily the work of Evangelicals from the USA is simply not true. As we saw with Ewing and Grady's *Jesus Camp*, be sure to clarify the agenda of the filmmakers and always be conscious they are crafting a story, not solely capturing reality. That being said, *God Loves Uganda* is a powerful chronicle of the power of religion to shape public sentiment surrounding human sexual behavior and politics.

RELIGION AND RACE

This section will delve into filmic presentations of religion using the interpretive lens of race. Race is critical part of human experience and, as such, central to religion as well. The following two films were chosen explicitly because they highlight how religion can reinforce racism and prejudice. Below we will focus on how medieval Iberian Catholicism confronted indigenous people and their spirituality in the Mexican film *The Other Conquest* (1998) as well as consider how

Protestant Christianity supported the ideology behind the Ku Klux Klan and provided the antidote for dismantling racism and bringing about racial reconciliation in a small southern town in the film *Burden* (2020).

RACISM IN MEXICO: COLONIAL ROOTS, *MESTIZAJE*, LEGACY

The Other Conquest was a seven-year-long passion project for Mexican filmmaker Salvador Carrasco who wanted to make a historical film that dealt with the complicated racial and spiritual legacy of the Spanish conquest of the Aztecs. It is a beautifully shot fictional story featuring Topilztin, a codex painter and son of Moctezuma, who has survived the initial destruction of the main temple of Tenochtitlán (present-day Mexico City) in 1521 and is captured by Spanish soldiers. Topiltzin (Damien Delgado) soon encounters Hernan Cortes who spares his life due to the intercession of his half-sister, princess Techuicho (Elpidia Carillo), the captured lover of Cortes (Iñaki Aierra). She pleads for his life and Cortes agrees but only after his public "conversion" and torture by the sadistic Capitán Christóbal Quijano. The second half of the film is focused on the complicated process of trying to convert Topilztin and his relationship with Fray Diego, his spiritual director. Topiltzin comes to identify the blond Spanish statue of Mary with his own mother goddess Tonantzin. The film's merger of Maria with the Aztec goddess foreshadows the brown-skinned mestizo Madonna of Tepeyac, The Virgin of Guadalupe. It is a wonderful story to explore Mestizo, borderland Christianity; however, here we will focus on scenes directly related to race and religion. The 500-year anniversary of the Conquest in 2021 will bring a re-release of the film.

REGARDING THE OTHER: INDIGENOUS-SPANISH RELATIONSHIPS

The action begins with a small unit of soldiers accompanied by a priest (Fray Diego) on a "maneuver of purification"—a scouting mission to find any remnants of indigenous holdouts, then capture and convert them. They arrive moments after an Aztec human sacrifice of a virgin with the priest holding her bloody heart in his hand. A horrified Fray Diego exclaims "you really do come from another world"

Figure 5.3 The public torture of Topiltzin by Capitán Cristobal with Maria and Fray Diego looking on in *The Other Conquest* (Salvador Carrasco, 2000).
Source: Photo by Andrea Sanderson, used with permission.

and crosses himself for protection against the evil alien. Topiltzin's brother whispers that the Spaniard "barbarians" will not let them be with their gods, demonstrating that the demonization and distrust went both ways. The Spaniards destroy the goddess stone statue and Fray Diego tries to explain that the goddess Tonantzin is "nothing but a handful of stones" to a distraught Topiltzin who finds some solace in the maternal gaze of the very white Maria (Figure 5.3).

Spanish xenophobia is represented by Capitán Cristobal who warns early on that mixing with other cultures is detrimental to pure Spanish culture using the infiltration of Muslims in Spain as an example. He disapproves of Hernan Cortes' indigenous lovers: first *La Malinche* and now the daughter of Moctezuma, Techuipo. He hisses at her "your mixture is disgusting to God." He sadistically relishes publicly whipping Topiltzin and burning his feet proclaiming all of it is for the natives' benefit to insure their eternal salvation as Christians. The Capitan's racist actions are commissioned by the Catholic Church whose Papal bull condoned the forced conversion

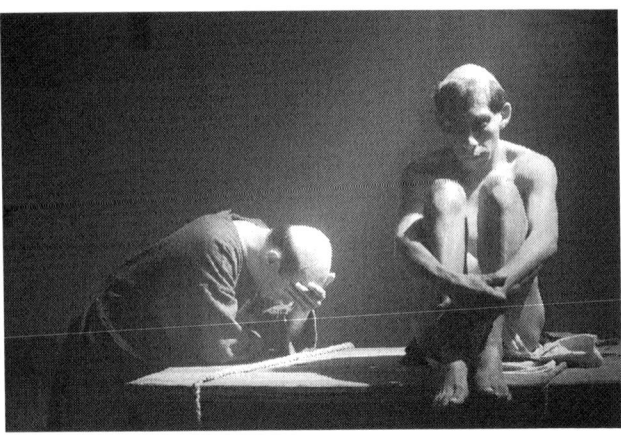

Figure 5.4 Fray Diego realizes Topiltzin's conversion to Christianity is mixed with indigenous beliefs in *The Other Conquest* (Salvador Carrasco, 2000). Photo by Andrea Sanderson, used with permission.

of native peoples. Cortes represents the European mentality that saw native people as sub-human and believed their customs, religious history and cultural identity must be obliterated. *On the Just Causes for War Against the Indians* by Juan Ginés de Sepúlveda (1489–1573) articulates the European mentality that justified the rape and enslavement of indigenous peoples. Sepulveda argues in the 1544 text that "Indians" were morally inferior, did not have human souls, had no governmental order or laws, therefore civilized Christians could legitimately evangelize and enslave them. Conquest was sanctioned by the Roman Catholic church and enforced by the military (Figure 5.4).

Fray Diego views the new world through a racist lens, but he sincerely cares for Topiltzin, recognizing his intelligence and spiritual sincerity. Their theological discussions slowly teach him the beauty of Aztec spirituality, at least devotion to the goddess. As Topiltzin descends into a fever and a mental breakdown, he becomes fixated on the blond Madonna. Fray Diego begins to accept the symbolic merger of the two figures and even encourages the syncretism: "Yes, she is just as lovely as yours [Tonanztin] what matters now is that this is a new world." As kind and gentle as he is with Topiltzin, he is always clear that his white Maria and his European translation of

Christianity is the only allowable religiosity in this "new world." It is only after the dramatic death of Topiltzin who is crushed under the weight of the Marian statue that Fray Diego has his racial breakthrough. As he lays out Topiltzin's broken body alongside the Virgin (whose broken arm drips with blood—whose we do not know) he calls for Cortes to come to the monastery to witness "the miracle of how two races can be as one through tolerance." A bit heavy handed, but Carrasco ends his historic portrayal of race and religion with a hopeful note. Perhaps religion, which often girds racism, can help abolish it as we will see in the next film.

The racial tensions at the heart of *The Other Conquest* are alive and well in the 21st century. Many Latinx people today have the blood of Aztec warriors *and* Spanish conquistadores running through their veins. Many Mexicans are reticent to speak about the racism that permeates their society. There are no discrimination laws in Mexico and discrimination against indigenous peoples is deeply entrenched. For instance, Carrasco was told in no uncertain terms by the Director of the Mexican Institute of Cinema that the lead actor Damien Delgado was "too ugly and no one would ever go to see a film with an indigenous actor." He refused to support the film financially unless Delgado was replaced with a whiter, green-eyed established Mexican actor. Carrasco refused and the ministry made filming on location extremely difficult. Film is often the spark that get people talking about racism. Most recently this racism was exposed when a famous Mexican actor, Sergio Goyri, called the Oaxacan indigenous actress, Yalitza Aparicio, the lead of Alfonso Cuarón's 2018 hit *Roma*, a "f—ckin Indian" and passive dolt in the hands of the director. In the 20 years since the Mexican film board urged Carrasco not to use an indigenous actor, little has changed in Mexico.

THE KKK AND THE BLACK CHURCH: RELIGION AND RACE IN *BURDEN*

A newspaper story about a Ku Klux Klan museum in a small Southern town caught the eye of actor/director Andrew Heckler in 1996. It took him over 20 years to realize his dream of telling this true story cinematically. *Burden* (2020) takes place in Laurens, South Carolina, USA in 1996 and tells the story of African American Rev. Kennedy who confronts racism head-on by befriending a Ku Klux Klan (KKK) leader and changing his life. The KKK is an American white supremacist organization that was founded in 1865 after the American Civil War. It has a long history of violence and intimidation against blacks as well as other immigrants, Jews, and Catholics. It is known for lynching, burning crosses and their pledge to preserve the "purity" of the white race. As we saw with *The Other Conquest,* the Christian religion was used to sanction racial purity and enslavement of "inferior" people. The group's popularity has waned and risen in waves over the past 170 years with crests occurring in the 1920s, 1960s, 1980s, and 2010s (aided by internet anonymity and communication). Real-life Mike Burden was an orphan and raised by a KKK family. He became a "grand dragon" leader of the group in South Carolina and the story opens with the renovation of an old movie theater (The Echo) into a KKK museum and Redneck store. Burden is an Army vet, under-employed and his life is one full of violence and hatred. He is given the deed of the newly-opened store/museum as a reward for his loyalty to the group. While Klan members quote Christian scriptures and try to preserve what they consider to be their divinely granted racial superiority, Christianity can also inspire social justice and change. This faith-inspired courage is represented by the African-American Rev. Kennedy (Forrest Whitaker) who leads a small Southern Baptist church in town. He organizes peaceful daily protests outside the KKK museum and store. He consistently preaches the biblically based belief that "perfect love casts out all fear" (1 John 4:18) and the only way to defeat racism and hatred is with love. His family and congregation are with him, but wary.

Tensions come to a head as these two groups build to a violent confrontation at a protest. Mike is on the rooftop as a sniper and comes very close to killing the Reverend and his son, but he holds back, not because he is questioning his racism, but because he has fallen in love with a woman named Judy and her young son is in the riotous mix. Judy presents him with an ultimatum after the Klan patriarch gives her young son a hunting knife and instructs him to use it to carve "dark meat"—a thinly veiled symbol for black bodies. Mike chooses Judy and leaves the Klan. The consequences of this choice are dire. Due to the KKK connections all over town, Mike loses his job as does Judy, his car is repossessed, and they are evicted from their rental home in the middle of the night. They are left sleeping in her car, destitute, and hungry. Enter Rev. Kennedy who is now faced with his own dilemma: demonstrate Christian mercy, help the young couple, and practice what he preaches, or leave them to suffer the consequences of their fate. He quickly chooses the former and brings the white couple and her son home to his shocked black family.

Burden's well-developed characters who examine themselves, who resolve both internal and external conflicts, offer up a hopeful story when it comes to race relations in the USA and the positive power of religion to change both hearts and communities. The difficulty of forgiveness is shown for both blacks and whites. The Rev. Kennedy admits to his son, he does not want a vicious KKK leader under the same roof as his family. He begins to forgive Mike only after learning of his painful backstory and realizing his humanity. Recognizing the humanity of the Other was one of the main goals director and screenwriter Heckler wanted to accomplish. The KKK members are not racist one-dimensional caricatures, nor are the Reverend's family saints (although they come close). Burden begins to unpack his abusive childhood where he learned there was no room for compassion and violence was the only way to resolve things. It takes time for Burden to learn to confess and ask forgiveness of the people he has hurt. This culminates in his river baptism where he confesses to his racist wrongdoings and later, confesses to police that he brutally beat a black teen (for which he goes to prison). He has learned to face himself, take responsibility for his actions, and rebuild friendships with people like Clarence, his black childhood friend (played by singer/actor Usher).

FOR SUCH A TIME AS THIS: CULTURAL CONTEXT AND PRODUCTION OF *BURDEN*

The Cultural Studies lens is fascinating applied to this film's production. Like many independent films, *Burden* has had a long and circuitous road to final distribution. The screenplay was completed in 2000, however the funding and casting of the film took over a decade. One significant problem was that this film features the deep-seated painful reality of racism in the USA. Heckler received industry "condolence calls" in 2008 when Barack Obama was elected to office as many believed the USA was now "post-racial" (KKK hatred was surely past). Unfortunately, racism has become increasingly visceral and public since the election of President Donald Trump in 2016. Political urgency made *Burden* socially relevant once again and Heckler secured investors. The film was shot in 2017, finished in 2018, but did not secure a distributor to invest in marketing it until 2020, a year in which Black Lives Matter protests raged throughout the USA and the world. The reality is films like *Burden* or *Clemency* (2019) or films by Ava DuVernay or Spike Lee make white viewers uncomfortable and force them to begin to understand the complexities and pain of black Americans. As students of religion and film the fact that both the KKK and Baptist Church members appeal to the same religion makes this film a springboard for uncomfortable, but necessary post-screening discussions about racism and Christianity in the USA.

REDEMPTION AND HEALING

What is redemption? Redemption literally means re-purchasing and is related to the idea of atonement and reconciliation with God. For Hebrews this involved temple blood sacrifice (Lev. 17:11). Christians understand Jesus' sacrifice of himself as being the ultimate act of redemption (Romans 3:22–24; 5:18). Christ followers are also called to lay down their lives for others (1 John 3:16). Theologian Bradley Hanson has outlined four distinct ideas associated with Christian redemption: sacrifice, victory over evil, doing justice, and revealing love (Hanson, 1997, 155–182). Jesus's confounding of demons, healing of the sick, and his death on the cross are read as triumphs over evil and followers are promised this victory as well (Galatians 1:4). Explaining how Jesus' person and death satisfy God's sense of justice is more complicated. Theological explanations from Pauline substitutionary atonement theory to Anselm's compensatory satisfaction theory to Calvin's classic substitutionary punishment explanation fail to fully satisfy both our notion of a loving God and a just system. Many postmodern theologians have moved away from traditional atonement theories toward an understanding of the heart of Jesus' work being about setting people free, restoration, and reconciling them with God.

A BRAZILIAN TALE OF DUAL REDEMPTION

Central Station is a memorable road film set amidst the scorched earth of northeastern Brazil and provides us with an interesting filmic tale of redemption.[3] The plot of *Central Station* is fairly straightforward: a jaded retired schoolteacher, Dora, poignantly played by Brazil's premiere stage actress, Fernanda Montenegro, supplements her retirement by writing letters for the illiterate hoards who pass through Rio de Janeiro's Central Train station. A woman, Ana, and her son Josué (Vinícius de Oliviera), approach Dora to write a letter to his father, Jesus. Ana is killed by a bus moments later and Josué turns to Dora. Dora sells him to clandestine adoption agency for $1,000R. Irene, her best friend, is horrified at the news and explains that it is an organ-harvesting scheme. Dora rescues Josué and the rest of the story chronicles their tumultuous relationship and journey in search of his father. They face many adventures together including being befriended by an Evangelical truck driver. They make money on the road working as a team with Dora writing letters (and actually mailing them this time) and Josué hustling sales. Dora helps Josué reunite with his two brothers before setting off for a new chapter of her own life. The film was a global success: it won the Berlin Film festival's coveted Golden Bear award for Best Film and Best Actress and was nominated in both these categories for the Academy Awards.

Central Station is a tale of dual-redemption as we watch each character heal and be transformed through their relationship with the other. *Central Station's* message of redemption does not fit neatly within traditional definitions of Christian redemption. The film offers a more Hebraic notion of redemption as being concerned with the transformation of self and society into good, life-giving, justice-seeking relations. It reinforces redemption theories which interpret the heart of Jesus's mission as reconciliation. It also is closer to an Eastern Orthodox understanding of redemption involving full restoration of human and divine relationship. At the end of the film Josué is reconciled with his brothers and we hope this will extend

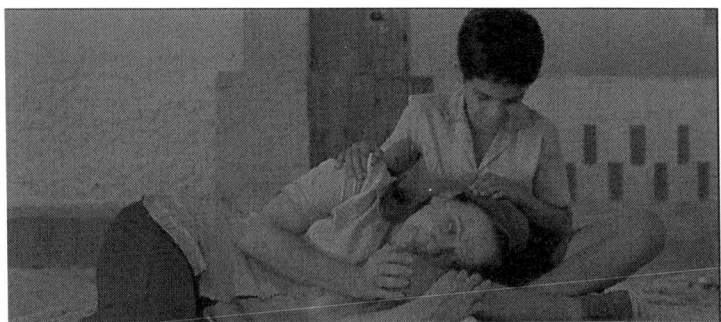

Figure 5.5 Josué comforts Dora after her collapse in the House of Miracles, an inverted pietà in *Central Station* (Walter Salles, 1998).
Source: screenshot by author.

to his father as well. Dora is reconciled with her past, remembers the good in her formerly despised father, and is emboldened to begin a new life at 67. She is saved from loneliness, ennui, and cynicism (Figure 5.5).

Unlike many redemption narratives, *Central Station* has no singular heroic, sacrificing savior figure; alternatively, both Josué and Dora function as savior figures for one another. As they travel together, Dora becomes increasingly warm and motherly toward Josué. She literally saves him from death twice and Josué (Joshua) returns the favor after her collapse in the House of Miracles shrine. His name is not accidental: Joshua was the leader of the road-weary Israelites who led them to the Promised Land after wandering 40 years in desert. Joshua's original name was Hoshea which meant "salvation;" however, Moses changed his name to "Joshua," which means "The Lord saves or the Lord gives victory." Joshua's 1250 BCE. conquest of the land of Canaan concretized God's redemption of the Israelites. The wary, yet idealistic orphan and the cynical retired teacher function as unlikely, but remarkably effective co-redeemers in the tale, challenging viewers to reconsider the possibility that savior figures can be less-than-perfect. This film forces the viewer to critique traditional notions of redemption and redeemers. Plucky Josué and jaded Dora are not your typical redeemer figures; however, as their love grows, they are both restored and redeemed. Although there is nothing supernatural occurring in *Central Station's* human redemption tale, it raises many questions about the process and ends of redemption.

WISING UP AND RECONCILING IN *MAGNOLIA*

As with *Central Station,* familial reconciliation, restoration, and redemptive action are found in Paul Thomas Anderson's 1999 operatic, complex drama *Magnolia.* The action takes place one rainy 24-hour period in the San Fernando Valley (Southern California) and reveals the intersecting lives of nine main characters. Jason Robards plays Earl Partridge, a television producer who is literally on his death bed dying of cancer and attended to by his guilt-stricken trophy wife Linda (Julianne Moore) and the compassionate hospice worker, Phil Parma (Philip Seymour Hoffman). Earl is filled with regret for having cheated on and abandoned his wife, Lily, and leaving his 14-year-old son to tend her. That estranged son Jack is now an over-the-top self-help guru Frank T.J. Mackey (Tom Cruise) who specializes in training sheepish men to tame and control women—especially sexually. He loathes his father and publicly claimed he died long ago. Earl produces a TV kid game show whose 30 year-long host, adulterer Jimmy Gator (Philip Baker Hall) is also dying of cancer. He is also guilty of molesting his own daughter Claudia Wilson Gator (Melora Walters). Stanley (Jeremy Blackman) is the recent incarnation of the famous 1962 "Quiz Kid Donnie Smith" (William H. Macy) who is now a pathetic failing electronics salesman. Finally, there is the divorced, lonely, and friendless moral pillar of kindness: police officer Jim Kurring (John C. Reilly). As with all P.T. Anderson films, music plays a key role. *Magnolia* is divided by three powerful Aimee Mann Songs: *One, Wise Up,* and *Save Me.* The first song plays over the opening montage introducing the nine lonely characters, *Wise Up* surprised audiences as Anderson has each of the main characters sing it aloud to themselves in the middle of the film, and *Save Me* aurally bathes the audience as they watch scenes of reconciliation, resolution, and healing at the end of the film. Anderson, director of many lauded films including *There Will Be Blood* (2008), *The Master* (2013), and *Phantom Thread* (2017), confessed: "For better or for worse, *Magnolia* is the best movie I will ever make." This author agrees.

REGRET, LAW, FORGIVENESS, LOVE, AND RECONCILIATION

We will focus on two main sets of relations as they pertain to the trope of reconciliation and redemption: the Earl Partridge melodrama and the Officer Kurring-Claudia relationship. The film shows us plenty of relationships that are irredeemable due to the sins of the father (Deuteronomy 5:9): Jimmy Gaynor and the daughter he sexually molested, Earl and the wife he cheated on repeatedly, Donnie Smith and his parents who robbed him; however, there are two tales that leave the audience with hope of reconciliation, healing, and redemption.

Earl Partridge's death scene is one of the most memorable in cinematic history. Perhaps it is so heart-wrenching because it is imperfect and awkward. Perhaps his scattered speech rings true because only one year before he shot *Magnolia* the director watched his own father die from cancer. Perhaps it was the breathless pathos of Robards himself sensing it was his very last scene in his very last film (he died of lung cancer a year after filming). The following are some key lines from his ten-minute-long confessional monologue:

EARL: "I cheated on her over and over and over again because I wanted to be a man and I didn't want her to be a woman, you know smart, who was something…I f-cked other women and then I crawled in her bed and said "I Love You" That was Jack's mother…these two that I had…and I lost. This is the regret that you make. Mistakes like this…you don't make. […] She has cancer and I am not there and he is forced to take care of her. …the biggest regret of my life: *I let my love go*. Don't ever let anyone tell you you shouldn't regret anything…use it, use it. Love. Love. Love."

FRANK: "You prick, cocksucker that's what you used to say…It hurts doesn't it. You in a lot of pain? She was in a lot of pain, I know because I was there….She waited for your call, for you to come. I want you to know I hate your f-ckin guts…."

Nurse Phil then gives Earl a fatal dose of liquid morphine. Frank/Jack enters soon thereafter. He is angry, yet he goes to his bedside (Figure 5.6).

Anderson cuts to other stories and then returns to a sobbing Jack begging his father not to leave. Earl stirs and sees son Jack at his side. Recognition, forgiveness, and reconciliation are *shown*, not said.

Figure 5.6 (a and b) Frank Mackey confronts his father Earl on his death bed in *Magnolia* (P.T. Anderson, 1999).
Source: screenshot by author.

His father takes his last breath, his son's presence is enough. Later we see Frank/Jack curled up on his father's couch like in a fetal position (so far from the bravado of Frank Mackey), he is allowed to hurt, to self-comfort, to begin to heal from the loss of his dad. Grace, the TV interviewer was right, he needed to face his past to move on. Part of his healing means establishing a relationship with the only family he has left and we last see Frank going to hospital to see his stepmother, Linda.

The last two elements of Bradley Hanson's theological definition of redemption referenced above: doing justice and revealing love, are central in officer Jim Kurring and Claudia's relationship. Kurring's job is to bring justice to the streets of L.A. He is a Christian who lives to serve, a flawed savior figure in a uniform. We are introduced to Kurring walking to his squad car alone when everyone else has a partner and we hear his recorded dating service introduction. Claudia is also alone as well as addicted to cocaine and meaningless sex with strangers. An unlikely romance begins to blossom between them. They meet when he is called to her apartment on a disturbance call. He tells her to "keep her chin up and her music down" and they decide to go on a date. Over dinner later that night they both desperately want to connect but don't know how, so coked-up Claudia suggests they tell each other everything and try to get past the "piss and the shit and lies" that kill relationships. Her forthrightness stuns him, they kiss, she runs away.

Driving home from this botched date, Kurring gets caught in apocalyptic rain of frogs (Exodus 8:2) and ends up heroically helping Donnie return money he has stolen from the electronics store safe. As he helps him, we hear his thoughts about the dilemma he constantly faces between upholding the law and acting with mercy and grace:

> Sometimes people need a little help and sometimes people need to be forgiven and sometimes they need to go to jail. That's the tricky thing on my part, making that call. The law is the law and heck if I'm gonna break it. But if you can forgive someone...that's the tough part. What can we forgive? Tough part of the job, tough part of walking down the street.
>
> (Officer Kurring, *Magnolia*)

In the very last scene of the film Jim comes to Claudia's apartment where she is sitting in bed tearful, the rain has passed, and we see sunshine through the red sheet on the window. Jim enters, but keeps his back to the camera, all we see is her reaction to his healing words. Aimee Mann's lyrical "Save Me" plays as Jim tells her there were things he still wanted to say at dinner, mostly that "she is a good and beautiful person." Claudia listens, raises her chin, and smiles for the first time—this is last flickering image.

Magnolia is a tapestry of the woes of late modern society: absent parents who neglect, ignore, or exploit their children, drug addiction, broken marital relationships, misogyny, a crisis of male identity, alienation, etc.; however, I see the saga as a testament to love, reconciliation, healing, possibility for change, compassion, forgiveness, and redemption. Truthtellers (Jim, Claudia, Earl) are given hopeful, partially happy endings. The difference between Jimmy Gaynor dying alone and Earl dying with his son by his side is that the latter confessed his wrongdoing and learned from it. His son is re-deemed—bought with his regret. Claudia and Jim vow to tell the truth and be there for each other. Their future gives us hope that humanity can learn to forgive, listen, and support each other. *Magnolia* shows us that is all that matters in the end.

KARMA AND REINCARNATION

What is Karma? Karma means action, work, or deed. In many religious systems (Hinduism, Buddhism, Jainism, Sikhism, Zoroastrianism) it refers to a system were beneficial action results in beneficial effects and negative action results in negative effects in both this life and the next. A similar idea exists in Abrahamic-based faiths which teach one will be judged on their good or bad actions by God on Judgement Day and the sins of the father will negatively affect his offspring (Deuteronomy 24:16). In the Asian-based traditions listed above, the judgmental God is replaced with karma and the cycle of rebirth (reincarnation). Both are strong ethical tools to encourage morally upright action. The Hindu system refers to merits (punya) and demerits (papa). The Hindu scripture of the Upanishads 5:7 describes it thus: "we wander in a cycle of transmigration according to our deeds." Karma is, therefore, directly related to the idea of reincarnation. Your karma determines your reincarnation in your next life—whether you will be born as an animal or a human being (the highest incarnation). The ultimate goal in both Hinduism and Buddhism is the get off the wheel of life and death/samsara, become one with Brahman or achieve enlightenment.

KARMIC REWARD FOR A LIFE OF SERVICE

It's a Wonderful Life (1946) was directed by Frank Capra and adapted from Philip Van Doren's self-published short story *The Greatest Gift*.

When first released it was a box office flop (due in part to coming out the same month as *The Best Years of Our Lives*) but after wide exposure during the holidays Capra's favorite film is now in the top ten of many esteemed Best Films of All Time lists. The film stars James Stewart as George Bailey, a man who always postpones his dreams and ambitions in order to help others. Other main characters include his wife Mary (Donna Reed), Clarence Oddbody (Henry Travers) as George's guardian angel, and the villain, Mr. Potter (Lionel Barrymore). The inciting incident happens on Christmas Eve 1945 when the absent-minded Uncle Billy loses the Baily Building and Loan's $8,000.00 deposit at the bank. This loss (which was really a theft by Mr. Potter) threatens George with jail time and forces him to humbly go to Mr. Potter, the richest man in town, for a loan. Mr. Potter laughs at his collateral: a $5,000 life insurance policy, and comments that George is "worth more dead than alive." Pushed to the brink, George prays for God's help, crashes his car, and goes to a bridge to throw himself off. Enter his guardian angel who must earn his wings by helping George realize that he really does have a wonderful life by showing him what a difference his life has made for people of Bedford Falls. The first two thirds of the film replay George's life from a 12-year-old-boy to a 38-year-old married father of four in order to aid Clarence in this task.

Through angelic intervention Clarence shows how George's generous good actions have touched and transformed many. Bedford Falls would have been a much different town if George had never been born. Without George and his father Bedford Falls has no businessman champion to thwart the heartless capitalism of Mr. Potter who has transformed the town, now called "Potterville," into a hamlet of bars, crime, and dance halls. They visit the cemetery and discover that Harry, George's little brother, died at age eight because George was not there to save him when went under the ice at the lake. This also means that Harry was not able to become a World War II hero and many lives were lost as a result. Mr. Gower becomes a murderer and a drunk after poisoning a customer because George, who worked in his drugstore as a boy, was not there to stop him. George touched many lives in town by keeping the Building and Loan open amidst the Great Depression and then helping many poor renters in town own their own new home. Mary, his wife, never marries in this alternative vision and becomes an anxious "old maid" librarian. In Buddhism, and many other religions, being a person who puts others before themselves is highly valued. As his father did before him, George constantly does this with his money and his dreams. For example, after his father dies, 22-year-old George foregoes a trip to Europe and his plans for college in order to save the Baily Brother's Building and Loan, giving the funds he saved toward his own tuition to his brother Harry so he can prosper. This generosity is his *modus operandi*. A needlepoint sign hangs in his father's office that reads: "ALL YOU CAN TAKE WITH YOU IS THAT WHICH YOU GIVE AWAY" which perfectly captures George Bailey's character. For example, he and Mary are about to depart on their honeymoon when the Great Depression run on the banks happens and they sacrifice all their honeymoon money to keep the Building & Loan solvent. Karma operates in this life and the next. The good karma he has engendered results in his friends and bride springing into action and creating a memorable, terribly romantic "bridal suite" in a broke-down mansion complete with Bert the cop and Ernie the cab driver serenading them.

After Clarence has shown him the worth of his individual life, George recognizes his riches and begs to be able to "live again," jail time be damned. God grants his wish and he races home through the streets of a charming Bedford Falls screaming "Merry Christmas" to his many friends. He arrives home, embraces his four darling kids, but Mary is not there. The authorities are there to arrest him. Mary bursts through the door followed by the townsfolk who begin to dump all their spare change and cash on the table. The dozens of people whose lives he has transformed through his good actions return the blessing. A telegram arrives from a rich friend authorizing $25,000 to be wired to George and it is addressed to "the richest man in town." Surrounded by joyous family and friends they all toast George and sing *Auld Lang Syne*. This memorable closing scene is a wonderful portrait of karma in action. His beneficent actions, done selflessly, result in a dramatic beneficent reward. *It's a Wonderful Life* is a fictional narrative that portrays karmic retribution in this life while our next film illustrates how your karmic choices and actions determine your life after death.

REINCARNATION PERSONIFIED IN UNCLE BOONMEE WHO CAN RECALL HIS PAST LIVES

Many films depict reincarnation: from the 1991 noir thriller, *Dead Again,* to the transnational drama *Little Buddha* (1993) to the 2007 fantasy Bollywood melodrama *Om Shanti Om.* To exemplify reincarnation, I have selected the award-winning Thai film *Uncle Boonmee Who Can Recall His Past Lives* (2010) which was inspired by the 1983 book *A Man Who Can Recall His Past Lives* written by Buddhist abbot Phra Sripariyattiweti. It premiered at the 2010 Cannes Film Festival, where it won the Palme d'Or. The film's experimental director Apichatpong Weerasethakul explains: "The film is not about Boonmee, but about my take on the idea of reincarnation. It naturally developed into an homage to the cinema I grew up with. A cinema that's also dying or dead."[4] The film opens with an epigraph which reads: "Facing the jungle, the hills and vales, my past lives as an animal and other beings rise up before me." The film recounts the last days of Uncle Boonmee (Thanapat Saisaymar), a Northeastern Thai farmer, who is dying of kidney failure. In these final days his sister-in-law, Aunti Jen (Jenjira Pongpas), and her son, Tong, are at his side. His dead wife Huay and his long, lost son Boonsong (who has transformed into a Monkey Ghost that looks like a black Chewbacca with glowing red eyes) appear one night at dinner and are accepted nonchalantly and welcomed. The mood of this dinner scene powerfully communicates a Thai Buddhist worldview (Figure 5.7).

Uncle Boonmee knows his time is short and tries to give Jen his farm. Huay escorts the trio of the dying Boonmee, Aunti Jen, and Tong to a cave filled with stalactites and pools that may be a metaphor for a womb. Uncle Boonmee is certain he was born there. It is also the site of his death as his dead wife disconnects his dialysis tube. We attend his funeral and follow Auntie Jen to a sparse hotel room where Tong arrives, weary from monastery life. He showers and as they are leaving to go out to eat, they see themselves transfixed watching various images loop on the TV from the hotel bed, a duplication created by double exposure. The dual realms of reality that have been hinted at throughout the film are presented on the screen side-by-side. The film was shot on 16 mm film, with the stated purpose of emulating the look of the classic Thai films that

Figure 5.7 The ghost of Huay manifests as Tong and Auntie Jen look on in *Uncle Boonmee Who Can Recall His Past Lives* (Apichatpong Weerasethakul, 2010).
Source: screenshot by author.

Apichatpong watched as a child. This is pure Asian slow cinema: it is hypnotic and languorous, with images, especially from nature, that give rise to thought.

KARMA'S POWER

In *It's a Wonderful Life* we found a cinematic narrative demonstrating how karma might work in this life. Weerasethakul's characters sincerely believe in karma and how it influences this life and the next. Auntie Jen jokes at dinner that her nomadic life is "my karma for being stubborn." When she allows her son the monk to take a hot shower in her hotel room she notes "I am earning future merit." In one scene outside in the field, a remorseful Uncle Boonmee confesses

BOONMEE: "You know, this is a result of my karma."
JEN: "What is?"
BOONMEE: "This illness. I killed too many communists."

JEN: "But you killed with good intentions."
BOONMEE: "I killed too many bugs on the farm."
JEN: "It depends on your intentions."

As far as the comment about killing communists, the farm is set in the Northeast of Thailand, near the Laos border. Many leftist guerillas fled there in the 1960s and were exterminated by the Thai army. Her insistence on intention being key is based on the Buddhist belief that one's intentions are critically important.

REINCARNATION AND MEMORY

Memories, dreams, "flashbacks" are purposely opaque in the film as the director explains this is how our minds actually work, especially in regard to memory. Often our memories are episodic, partial, and do not make sense. Images help us ground memory which is why they are central to this story. For example, in order to help his transformed Monkey ghost son remember his past, Boonmee hands him a photo album and to jog his ghostly wife's memory, he hands her an album of her funeral. Unfortunately, no one remembers to take pictures at his funeral. Through mnemonic content Apichatpong's film explores the way that spirituality is strongly linked to queries about the constancy and reliability of human memory and the complexities of the relationship between Thai Buddhist-shamanist spirituality. Your memory is your connection to history and other temporalities/realities. Andrei Tarkovsky wrote in *Sculpting in Time*,

> Memory is a spiritual concept! [...] Bereft of memory, a person becomes the prisoner of an illusory existence; falling out of time he is unable to seize his own link with the outside world – in other words he is doomed to madness.[5]

Cinema is memory. Memory of one's past lives is a result of awakening, a goal of all Buddhists. It was during meditation that the real-life Uncle Boonmee saw his past lives as if "a film was playing beneath his closed eyelids." Cinema is a uniquely appropriate way to tell a story about reincarnation, as the director explains:

> I believe in the transmigration of souls between humans, plants, animals, and ghosts. Uncle Boonmee's story shows the relationship

between man and animal and at the same time destroys the line dividing them. When the events are represented through cinema, they become shared memories of the crew, the cast, and the public. A new layer of (simulated) memory is augmented in the audience's experience. In this regard, filmmaking is not unlike creating synthetic past lives.

(Weerasethakul, 2010)

The film can become confusing for those expecting a clear explication of which of the scenes depict Uncle Boonmee's past lives: was he the water buffalo or the Monkey Ghost? The catfish or the princess? Weerasethakul wanted to allow space for the audience to wander through the memories and use their imagination: "...for me, he could be every living thing in the film, the bugs, the bees, the soldier, the catfish and so on. He could even be his Monkey Ghost son and his ghost wife."[6]

Memory, images, seeing are intertwined themes in this film about the transmigration of souls. His son Boonsong took up still photography to connect with his dead mother. Using her old Pentax camera, he becomes an avid photographer and ends up capturing images of the mysterious spirit animals in the forest, the Monkey Ghosts. After mating with one, he begins to transform, not only by growing hair, but his eyes dilate like all night creatures. The aged princess distrusts her eyes as she gazes in a much-younger figure reflected in the water and challenges the catfish saying his "eyes must be distorted" to which he responds he sees her true beauty. When Boonmee is dying in the cave he asks: "what's wrong with my eyes, they are open, but I cannot see anything." Jen assures him to be patient, his eyes will adjust to the darkness and he will see. We spectators in a theater are asked to do the same with experimental slow cinema about metaphysical themes, be patient, watch the film several times, your eyes will adjust and you will begin to see....

DEATH AND THE AFTERLIFE

For many *cinephiles,* the relentless pursuit of the Swedish knight in Ingmar Berman's 1957 film *The Seventh Seal* by the hooded grim reaper is their first association with a filmic portrayal of death. Or perhaps films like *Meet Joe Black* (1998) or various wartime dramas spring to mind. I have chosen two very different films about death, one Kenyan drama and one from Spain by a Mexican director to explore how humans mourn, try to evade, and finally accept death and the afterlife.

From a Whisper (Kenya, 2009), Wanuri Kahiu's first feature film, was inspired by the 1998 U.S. Embassy bombings in Nairobi (and Tanzania) that killed 213 and injured 4,000. Al-Queda was linked to the bombing as well as Egyptian Islamic Jihad. The film has screened around the world: from Cannes to Los Angeles at the Pan African Film Festival where it won Best Narrative Feature as well as five awards at the African Movie Academy Awards, including Best Director and Best Screenplay. The story is anchored by Abu (Ken Ambani) a police intelligence officer and Tamani (Corinne Onyango) a young, rebellious artist both of whom lost somebody in the U.S. Embassy bombing ten years prior. Through flashbacks their losses emerge and together they learn how to confront their loss, mourn, and forgive. This story explores how one might approach their own death through the character of Fareed (Abubakar Mwenda) the suicide bomber and Abu's best friend, as well as how families and friends deal with death. Abu is haunted by the knowledge that he did not do more to stop his friend from driving the truck into the embassy. Tamani's mother was killed in the bombing when she is only eight years old. Although he knows the truth, her father cannot bear to tell Tamani, so he tells her she is just "missing" and shuttles her off to America to live with her auntie until she is 18. Upon returning to Kenya, Tamani gets in trouble with her graffiti art that always includes a Bansky-like signature "J.K." for her mother Joyce Kenzio who was also an artist. Abu makes the connection and ultimately gives Tamani her mother's police death file which she angrily confronts her father with, accusing him of killing her again. Abu convinces her to try and reconcile with her father and in the final scene she does just that at the memorial park surrounded by her artwork in a moving mourning installation.

WELCOMING DEATH

In the months following the release of *From a Whisper* Kahiu had to have an armed security escort due to death threats from Islamist groups. In the film she humanizes Fareed, the character who ends up driving the truck loaded with explosives into the embassy. We first we meet Fareed as he is joking around with his best friend Abu, borrowing his car, eating too fast at a restaurant, flirting with a waitress. We see Fareed come under the influence of Fazul Abdullah Mohammed the coordinator of both the U.S. Embassy bombings in Nairobi and Dar es Salaam in1998 and the Paradise Hotel bombing in Mombasa in 2002. Mohammed explains that the West and the USA, in particular, have invaded Muslim Holy Lands and must be punished for their "evil deeds." Fareed reads Mohammed's words on a pre-suicide video explaining his "blessed raid" against "the American Crusader government." This motivation is familiar to many. Kahiu presents Fareed as devout and thoughtful, very aware of the path he had chosen and where it led. On the morning of the bombing he shows up to pray one last time with Abu. He has paid his debts and wants to put his spiritual life in order. When Abu tries to talk him out of it, Fareed explains "I can't, my death was determined before I was born. You can't run from death." In fact, he consoles Abu, "my death saves the soul of seventy of my family." Abu uses scripture from the Qur'an to convince him not to kill, but it falls on deaf ears. Fareed responds: "Some must die so others may live" and warns him to stay home that day. After unsuccessfully trying to stop the bombing, Abu tries to wash his guilt off as he washes off the blood from the crime scene before going into the mosque to pray.

THE IMPORTANCE OF MOURNING

This film demonstrates the role mourning plays in healing. Neither Tamani, nor her father Sam have been able to mourn the loss of Joyce. He throws himself into his real estate business and allows the building he bought his wife to use as an art studio to fall into decay. Tamani is shipped off to Michigan, far from the pain of Nairobi. Fast forward ten years, Tamani returns to Nairobi, yet they are estranged and angry at one another. As he drives her to the airport to send her away once again, she asks to stop at the memorial park at the site of the bombing. Abu has filled the park with red hearts each with the name of a victim. At the center of the memorial he lays out a circle of Tamani's graffiti art. The ritual moment and the images are powerful. Tamani sits down, leaning against the engraved names of the victims, and takes it all in. Her father joins her, she apologizes and he simply replies "it's my fault, I forgot how to trust life." What a wonderful response in the face of death, trusting the life that follows. They embrace, paralleling a poignant image ten years earlier where a grief-stricken father in shock held his daughter the night of her mother's murder. This time the daughter squeezes him, a wonderful tableau of forgiveness and mourning together. Humans need each other to mourn and move on. They also need each other to face death, as our final film, *Biutiful*, demonstrates.

MEXICAN VIEWS ON LIFE AND DEATH: A DIALECTICAL CELEBRATION IN *BIUTIFUL*

Reflecting on the reality of death and grappling with its reality is a perduring theme in Alejandro González Iñárritu's films. His first three films, *Amores Perros*, *21Grams*, and *Babel* are called the "death trilogy" yet all his films include death. Even when Iñárritu turned to satirical comedy in *Birdman*, death was still whispering in Riggen's ear and surely *The Revenant* is about cheating death and seeking revenge. I argue that, despite moving to LA in 2001 and achieving Hollywood commercial success as an Academy Award winning director, Iñárritu's films have a Mexican and Catholic after-image, especially when it comes to death. Mexicans engage with the dead in a more purposeful way that most. Starting with the passing of a body, the corpses are not immediately shuttled away to a sterile storage unit in a mortuary. For the first day the body is kept in the home and a vigil is kept. For nine days following this, the novena is observed. Although the body has been buried, the mourning continues to cover the soul in their journey in the afterlife. Most importantly, the dead are not forgotten after this. Traditionally, *Los Dias de los Muertos,* Nov. 1 and 2 are days when families visit and tidy up their dead loved ones' gravesites, bring the deceased's favorite treats, eat together, and reminisce graveside. The living family members and the dead celebrate together on these days when the veil between the living and the dead is thinnest. Three central Mexican beliefs about death include: (1) Death is not something to be feared-grapple, dance, have fun with it! (2) Death is generative; (3) Death is a natural part of life and our lives are enhanced by acknowledging this dialectical relationship.

Biutiful is a powerful, unforgettable, difficult story of Uxbal (Javier Bardem), father to five-year-old Mateo and ten-year-old Ana and his estranged bi-polar wife Maramba (Maricel Álvarez) set in a bleak barrio in Barcelona, Spain. Uxbal is a hustler and genuine psychic medium who is in the terminal stages of prostate cancer. Iñarittu calls his first three films "melodramas" and refers to *Biutiful* as his first "true tragedy." It took him took four years to make: two years to write and produce, five months to film and direct and a year and a half to edit. It won multiple awards including Best Actor for Javier Bardem at BAFTA-the British Academy Awards in 2010. It is a grueling, yet glorious film, my favorite of his films because I think it is closest to his lyrical soul. There are many rich veins to mine: from themes of redemption and forgiveness to ghosts, death, and the afterlife. It has many parallels to Kurosawa's classic film *Ikiru* which chronicles a Japanese man dying of cancer. Iñarritu acknowledged *Biutiful* exposes the ugliness of bodily decay and societal inequities: "My films are not decoration pieces. Art should provoke. It should be about love, emotion, catharsis and I hope the Academy can *get* this film, get behind the scheme of pain and see the light behind it." Indeed, there is light behind this grim, but achingly honest human story about death. Iñárritu actually equates this Mexican dialectical grounding with his spirituality: "I have always considered myself to be spiritual in a way that has less to do with religion and more to do with an awareness that you have…of being alive and the consciousness that you will be dead." Despite the centrality of death in his films, Iñarritu protests they are all ultimately life-affirming: "*Biutiful* is not about death," he protests, "it is about Life. It is a hymn to life" (Iñárritu, 2010).

What does *Biutiful* teach us about death? Uxbal is very close to the dead, he makes a little money on the side connecting with the recently deceased and helping them pass on. He later hears and sees the ghosts of the Chinese indentured sweatshop workers he accidently murders by buying cheap heaters that spew carbon monoxide. The film is bookended with a scene of a young man walking in a snowy forest of skeletal birch trees. Later we come to realize that this is Uxbal's father who died in his twenties of pneumonia while in political exile. While Uxbal fears his own death, he is not afraid of the dead. Uxbal sees his father for the first time in the flesh after his father's body has been exhumed in order to be cremated (the cemetery is being moved to make room for a shopping mall). He loving touches his father's decomposing face, neither repulsed, nor fearful. There is only love and a sense of loss in this scene. The irony is, despite knowing death is not the end, Uxbal runs from his own death, like the knight runs from the hooded specter in *The Seventh Seal*. He refuses to accept that he will soon die and the film traces his slow, painful acceptance of his impending death. He flees to Beatrice, his spiritual mentor, to see if she can stave off his fast-approaching death. Unfortunately she cannot, the prostrate cancer has spread too far. She tells him to get his affairs in order, he is dying.

UXBAL: "I don't want to go, Bea. I am afraid to leave the children on their own. I can't."
BEA: "You think you take care of the children? Don't be naïve, Uxbal. The universe takes care of them."
UXBAL: "Yes, but the universe does not pay the rent. When I was Ana's age my mother died, I hardly remember her. My father died before I was born, I never met him. I don't want that for my children."
BEA: "Tell them. Tell them everything. You and I know the dead suffer if they leave debts behind."
UXBAL: "Why is this happening to me? Is it a punishment?"
BEA: "You can give up and let yourself go or grit your teeth and hang on like stupid people do. It is a long, exhausting road, Uxbal. Death is not the end. You know that."
UXBAL: "No, I am not going to die. No, no, no…"

Uxbal slowly comes to terms with his own death. He is given a bit of time to find a caretaker for his kids and give them a few more happy memories together. In the penultimate scene he lies his cancer-ravaged body down in bed for the last time with his daughter Ana by his side. They whisper in hushed tones and he tenderly gives her his mother's wedding ring, their fingers intertwining. We then see his spirit sitting in a chair watching the two figures in bed. He is now ready to pass and with masterful sound and light editing, the opening dialogue in the snowy wood replays and a close-up dissolves his grizzled ghostly face into an illuminated healthy visage in the snowy wood. This time Iñarritu shows us the same encounter from a different angle-focusing on Bardem's reaction to his father's ghost. They share a cigarette. Uxbal inquires "what's over there?" smiles and follows his father in the great beyond, footsteps crunching the freshly-fallen snow. Uxbal was now ready for death, ready to explore

Figure 5.8 Uxbal looks towards his deceased father in the snowy wood and crosses over at the end of *Biutiful* (Alejandro González Iñárritu, 2010).
Source: screenshot by author.

"over there." *Biutiful* is a poignant portrait of life's fragile beauty. This hymn of life and death as part of Iñarritu's commitment to telling stories about the human condition. Iñarritu explains: "You can't understand or speak in any depth about life except from the perspective of death." Tarkovsky taught us that art should prepare a person for death (Tarkovsky, 1986, 43). Iñarritu's films do just this through broken characters and haunting images that help us discover the beauty of life and encourage us to gently walk into that snowy forest without fear (Figure 5.8).

FOR FURTHER VIEWING

Evil and Suffering: *Mother!* (USA, 2017) & *A Hidden Life* (Germany/USA/UK, 2019).

Sex, Gender Roles, and Religion: *Osama* (Afghanistan, 2003), *Eyes Wide Open* (Israel, 2009) & *The Vow* (USA, 2020).

Religion and Race: *Eve and the Fire Horse* (2004) & *Selma* (USA, 2014).

Redemption, Reconciliation, and Healing: *Silence* (USA/Japan, et al., 2016), *California Solo* (USA, 2012) & *Beautiful Boy* (USA, 2019).

Karma and Reincarnation: *Little Buddha* (France, 1993) & *Brother Bear* (2003).

Death and Afterlife: *The Seventh Seal* (Sweden, 1957) & *Heaven is For Real* (USA, 2014).

NOTES

1 Jordan Peele, tweeted on March 16, 2017 and quoted in "Jordan Peele Explains the Sunken Place," *The Wrap*, https://www.thewrap.com/get-out-director-jordan-peele-explains-the-sunken-place.
2 Deepa Mehta quoted in article by Nabeela Jamil "Institutional Oppression to Spiritual Awakening: *Water* and the Journey of Its Women," November 13, 2018 in https://feminisminindia.com/2018/11/13/water-movie-review-widows/.
3 For a fuller reading of redemption in this film please read my article "Blessed Broken Bodies: Exploring Redemption in *Central Station* and *Breaking the Waves*," *Journal of Religion & Film* 8:2, Article 16.
4 Apichatpong Weerasethaku "Q&A with Apichatpong Weerasethaku," in *Spirituality & Practice*, http://spiritualityandpractice.com/films/features/view/20854/qa-with-apichatpong-weerasethakul.
5 Andei Tarkovsky, *Sculpting in Time*, translated by Kitty Hunter-Blair. Austin, TX: University of Texas Press, 1986, 57.
6 Apichatpong Weerasethaku, "Q&A with Apichatpong Weerasethaku," in *Spirituality & Practice*, http://spiritualityandpractice.com/films/features/view/20854/qa-with-apichatpong-weerasethakul.

FOR FURTHER READING

Bell, Jamel S.C. and Ronald L. Jackson, eds. *Interpreting Tyler Perry: Perspectives on Race, Class, Gender, and Sexuality*. London: Taylor & Francis Group, 2013.

Brode, Douglas and Leah Deyneka, eds. *Sex, Politics, and Religion in Star Wars: An Anthology*. Lanham, MD: Scarecrow Press, 2012.

Cho, Francisca. *Seeing Like the Buddha: Enlightenment through Film*. Albany, NY: SUNY Press, 2017.

Cutrara, Daniel S. *Wicked Cinema: Sex and Religion on Screen*. Austin, TX: University of Texas Press, 2014.

Rankin, Phillip. *Film and the Afterlife*. London: Routledge, 2020.

Ver Straten-McSparran, Rebecca. *Lars von Trier's Cinema: Excess, Evil, and the Prophetic Voice*. London: Routledge, 2021.

BEFORE THE CREDITS ROLL
A CONCLUSION

Most audience members tend to get up and leave as the credits roll at the end of the film while cineastes and filmmakers tend to remain in their seats and read the credits. Those who linger ponder what they have just experienced and those who have made films appreciate recognition of the entire cast and crew, post-production elements, locations, musical details, etc., that are revealed. Sometimes viewers are rewarded with a final clip of a future film (especially Marvel films). We have reached that point. Before you get up and close the covers of this introductory text, I want to remind you of the many elements that make up this work, comment on and critique the field today, offer suggestions for the future of Religion and Film Studies, and finally leave you with a personal commission.

THAT'S A WRAP!

When the principal photography is complete, the director traditionally exclaims: "That's a wrap!" and the cast and crew cheer and breathe a sigh of relief tinged with nostalgia. Before the credits roll, I would like to review what we have covered in *Religion and Film: The Basics*. Our first chapter began with exploring the chemistry between film and religion, grounded you in the history of the relationship between religion and film and the development of the field of Religion and Film Studies. An analysis of Lois Weber's 1915 film, *Hypocrites*, was the first of 39 films examined and highlighted the early connection between religion and the film industry.

Chapter 2 was perhaps the most practical and useful of all the chapters as it introduced you to a variety of approaches to film and encouraged you to try them all using "methodological bricolage." In this chapter I described the basic ideas of each approach, offered examples from select scholars who employ these methods, and highlighted what each contributed to the study of religion and film. Methodological bricolage encourages interdisciplinarity and questions whether any one approach should be normative when approaching a film. As each film engenders different approaches, the layering, the artistry of analysis should be idiosyncratic.

Despite prognostications at the turn of the 20th century that religion would wither away, 120 years later, religion remains a fundamental and pervasive part of human existence around the globe. Chapter 3 took a different approach than most religion and film readers that use film to teach you the basics about the major world religions or trace its depiction through film history. Instead, it honed in on one of three aspects: (1) diversity within the religious tradition; (2) lived religion: examples of how a practitioner of that religion would face the world and live out their faith; or (3) explored key ideas unique to that religion put into practice, grappled with, or exemplified.

Genres were our entrée into religion and film in Chapter 4. Every genre has its own conventions that influence everything from character types and narrative arcs to filmic elements that include iconic scenes, stock characters, shots, cuts, music, color, and pace. Each genre selected for this chapter grappled with a different theme or concern of religion, for example, Buddhist and Christian ideas of pure consciousness were explored in the sci-fi films *Ex-Machina* and *Arrival*. The select genres of sci-fi, comedy, horror, pilgrimage/quest/road trip, drama, and documentary were explored.

Exemplifying how one might go about exploring religious themes or tropes in film was the concern of Chapter 5. Six perduring and socially significant tropes were explored: evil and suffering, sex/gender roles, race, redemption and healing, reincarnation and karma, and finally, death and the afterlife. Each trope was elucidated by two films chosen to examine a different aspect, for example, the problem of supernatural evil and human suffering in *The Exorcism of Emily Rose* was juxtaposed against the evil of racism in *Get Out*.

THE PRESENT AND FUTURE OF RELIGION AND FILM

SPECIALIZED STUDIES OF RELIGIONS, AUTEURS, TOPICS, FILM ELEMENTS

The first two decades of the 21st century have allowed increasingly focused studies in religion and film. Moving beyond Christian theological analysis and broad collections of essays addressing various themes and religion, the field has matured and diversified. Today you can find books on religion and film from a variety of religious perspectives which no longer simply trace the depiction of that religion in film. An example of this theoretical hermeneutical maturation is found in Wendy I. Zieler's *Movies and Midrash: Popular Film and Jewish Religious Conversation* (2017) which begins with key ideas within popular films like *Memento, Forrest Gump, and The Hunger Games* and then turns to Jewish tradition, texts, and theological concepts, using an "inverted midrash" method. Buddhism has inspired several texts, such as Francesca Cho's thought-provoking work connecting Buddhist concepts and epistemology to film. In *Seeing Like the Buddha: Enlightenment through Film* (2017), Cho considers film as a site of religious practice as film re-presents reality and can be a site of enlightenment. While Cho examines concepts like discernment, emptiness, and "seeing like the Buddha" in relation to film, others, such as Sharon A. Suh in her nuanced *Silver Screen Buddha: Buddhism in Asian and Western Film* (2015) begins with Cultural Studies categories of race and gender in her analysis of Buddhism in film. Suh moves past the peaceful, if mysterious, monks in Frank Capra's Shangri-La (*Lost Horizon*) to the lived Buddhism of women and non-monastics in contemporary films. Examples of more popular film-based studies that are widening readership and influence of the field, include Jeff Bridges and Bernie Glassman's *The Dude and The Zen Master* (2012) and Cathleen Falsani's *The Dude Abides: The Gospel According to the Coen Brothers* (2009). Focused philosophical works such as *Taking the Red Pill: Science, Philosophy, and the Religion in the Matrix* (2003) by Glen Yeffeth are further evidence of a broadening field. *Faith, Film, and Philosophy: Big Ideas on the Big Screen* (2007) edited by Douglas Geivett and James Spiegal is a collection of essays that combines religion with philosophy in the analysis of film. Philosophical themes such as the moral life, the nature of knowing, and the human condition are explored in films such as *Citizen Kane*, *Pretty Woman*, *Contact*, and *Mystic River* in the text.

Maturation in religion and film has also produced some wonderful in-depth studies of certain film auteurs whose films consistently deal with religious or spiritual themes. One example of an in-depth auteur study is found in Lauren Hubner's 2007 work *The Films of Ingmar Berman Illusions of Light and Darkness*, which delves into everything from religion, truth, and symbolism in the *Seventh Seal* to dreams, ghosts, and death in *Cries and Whispers*. More contemporary auteur studies include Elijah Siegler's *Coen: Framing Religion in Amoral Order* (2016), which unpacks religious elements such as community in *The Hudsucker Proxy*, Christian moralism and postmodern irony in *Fargo* and absence in *Inside Llewyn Davis*. Another example is Rebecca Ver Straten-Mcsparran's *Lars von Trier's Cinema: Excess, Evil, and the Prophetic* (2021) in which she considers his prophetic, difficult films with the help of the book of Ezekiel and Paul Ricoeur.

Thankfully more genre studies within religion and film are being produced. Today you can find helpful and insightful guides to exploring your favorite film genre as it relates to religion. Like to laugh? Read Terry and Chris Lindvall and Dennis Bounds' 2016 text, *Divine Film Comedies: Biblical Narratives, Film Sub-Genres, and the Comic Spirit* which brings together human/comedy studies, film studies, and theology. This superb, eclectic collection examines everything from screwball and slapstick comedies to parody and satire and finds filmic narratives can inspire new readings of biblical stories as well as discovering embedded theological truths in film comedies. Comedies not your cup of tea? There are several provocative horror and religion texts to delve into, for example, Douglas E. Cowen's *Sacred Terror: Religion and Horror on the Silver Screen* (2008) or a more recent title, *Scared Sacred: Idolatry, Religion and Worship in the Horror Film* (2020) edited by Rebecca Booth et al., which explores demonic possession films like *The Omen* and *The Conjuring* as well as lesser-known international horror films like Korea's *The Wailing* (2016).

As religion and film dialogue enters its fifth decade, in-depth topical phenomenological and ideological tomes have emerged. For example, religion and race are central to Judith Weisenfeld's

Hollywood Be Thy Name: African American Religion in American Film, 1929–49 (2007) and sexual transgression and traditional belief systems are the focus of Daniel S. Cutrara's *Wicked Cinema: Sex and Religion on Screen* (2014). Routledge Press has published more than a dozen monographs in their *Religion and Film* series that focus on topics or auteurs; for example, Antonio D. Sison's *World Cinema, Theology and the Human* (2012) or *Transcendence and Spirituality in Chinese Cinema: A Theological Exploration* by Chris H.K. Chong (2020) as well as volumes devoted to the work of singular filmmakers such as Darren Aronofsky or Terrence Malick. Finally, another sign that the field has matured is the publication studies of singular elements of film explored in-depth such as the role of music in Kutter Callaway's *Scoring Transcendence: Contemporary Film Music as Religious Experience* (2013). In sum, in addition to excellent readers and primers, highly specialized studies of auteurs and film elements are enriching the field.

INCREASED INTERNATIONAL SCHOLARLY DIALOGUE, COLLABORATION, CONFERENCES

Another manifestation of the growing significance of Religion and Film Studies around the world are the increasing number of international conferences devoted to increasing the dialogue. The International Religion and Film Conferences sponsored by *The Journal of Religion and Film* and other civic and academic institutions is one example. These international gatherings began in 2014 when the first conference was held at the University of Nebraska. This inaugural conference brought together scholars predominantly from the USA, Canada, and Europe. The following year the conference was held in Istanbul, Turkey and the global diversity of the presenters attests to worldwide developing expertise: speakers hailed from throughout Europe (Finland to Azerbaijan), Malaysia, Pakistan, as well as Turkey and the USA. The topics addressed at this conference are a clear example of the generative nature of the field. Papers analyzed films from Tunisia to Nigeria to Japan and, although Islamic topics predominated, there were also papers on Neopaganism, Shintoism, Self-Realization, and Tibetan Buddhism. This conference is a striking example of the growing global interest in Religion and Film Studies. International Religion and Film conferences were also held in 2017 in Syracuse, in 2018 at the University of Toronto, Canada, and 2019 at St. Mary's University in Nova Scotia, Canada. Future International Religion and Film conferences include a summer 2022 conference (rescheduled from 2020 due to the Covid-19 crisis) sponsored by the Vrije Universiteit Amsterdam and *The Journal of Religion & Film* whose theme is: "Visions of a Better World: Film and the Politics of Lived Religion." An unforgettable International Religion and Film conference is being planned for the summer of 2024 in Hollywood, California and will feature historical Hollywood sites, film museums, and dialogue with directors, producers, and other industry professionals as well as academics in attempt to increase critical appreciation for each other's craft and expertise.

Across the world other academic groups are forming and holding international conferences related to film and religion, such as the CINESPI Research Group of the Catholic University of Louvain (Louvain-la-Neuve) which most recently organized an international conference on "Visions and Prophecies in Cinema" in December 2019. This group is connected to the European Network of Cinema and Media Studies. The Center for Media, Religion, and Culture (University of Colorado, Boulder) hosts an international Religion and Media conference every two years with film being among the variety of media forms discussed. Eleven of these conferences have taken place since 1994 around the world: from Uppsala, Sweden and São Paulo, Brazil to Toronto, Boulder and Louisville in North America, to Seoul, South Korea.

THE WINDRIDER FORUM AND THE SUNDANCE FILM FESTIVAL

In 2005, entrepreneurs John and Ed Priddy joined professors Will Stoller-Lee and Dr Craig Detweiler to create an immersive educational experience at the annual Sundance Film Festival in Park City, Utah to connect students with independent filmmakers. The event grew each year and by 2019 over 250 students and faculty from over 20 undergraduate and graduate programs were gathering to attend Sundance screenings and special Windrider in-depth discussions with filmmakers. The year 2019 was also a significant turning point for Windrider as they had grown to become the biggest parafestival group and were officially sanctioned as an Associate by the Sundance Film Festival. The fact that a secular, premiere festival like Sundance recognizes the value of the conversations conducted by Windrider speaks volumes about the importance of religion and film. Beyond Sundance, the Windrider Forum has grown to serve as a leadership forum, international short film showcase around the USA, producer, and resource provider to inspire people to create, view, and discuss visual media that address life's ultimate questions.

CROSSING CREATIVE BOUNDARIES: RELIGIONISTS AND SCHOLARS AS FILMMAKERS

In addition to increased dialogue with secular filmmakers at forums like Windrider and panels at various film festivals around the world, people of faith are increasingly articulating and divulging the role that faith plays in their own creative work. I am not speaking of the growth of explicitly religious films, for instance, the many films produced by the Kendrick brothers (*Overcomer, War Room, Fireproof,* etc.) and, of course, people of faith have long been filmmakers; I am noting how there increasingly seems to be more space for revealing the connection between one's faith and religious commitments and the filmmaking process. I will mention a few Christian and Muslim filmmakers, writers, and producers to illustrate this growing trend that extends to all faiths.

Camille Tucker is representative of many who earn both theological degrees and film degrees and strive to incorporate their faith into their creative work. Tucker has earned two Masters degrees, one from Fuller Seminary and another from Loyola Marymount in Screenwriting and Film. She is a member of the Writers Guild of America and has sold screenplays to Sony, Universal, New Line, Fox TV, and Disney. Tucker's made-for-TV film, *The Clark Sisters: First Ladies of Gospel,* premiered on the Lifetime Channel in April of 2020 she has recently optioned her screenplay of "Blessed in the City" an inspirational romantic comedy. I interviewed Tucker regarding how her faith has influenced her creative career. Tucker's journey with film reflects that of many Protestant Christians, she explains:

> I am a non-denominational Christian, a Neo-charismatic in the Protestant camp. Some African-American traditions taught that movies are dark, movies were a sin...my parents were Southern Baptist and

> Church of God in Christ…there was a disconnect between church and movies. Either you were a good Christian or you were working in the belly of the beast, the Entertainment industry, that is not Godly! I remember going to my grandmother's house and being told movies were "worldly" …pretty archaic ideas, but that is where I came from.

When I asked her, "Do you feel your religious commitments are a help or a hindrance in Hollywood?" she replied:

> It is important for people in Hollywood to see Christians as individuals, I am a filmmaker who happens to Christian, I don't think it is "us" against "them," what I have experienced is in order for us to make an impact as Christians in ANY setting…first people have to know us, then they have to trust us, then, hopefully they will want to hear our message. I don't think storming the gates is necessarily the strategy Christians ought to have. The entertainment industry is cutthroat, we are talking millions of dollars at stake …there is a competition for resources….. your talent should be up to a certain standard.[1]

Tucker is one of many Christian creatives working in film today. While most of their films and scripts are not explicitly religious, there is an acknowledgement that their creativity and commitment to write powerful, transformative stories is in some way related to their religious grounding. Producer-writer-directors Destin Daniel Cretton (*Short Term 12* (2013), *Just Mercy* (2019) and Marvel's *Shang-Chi and the Legend of the Ten Rings* (2021) and Scott Derrickson (*Sinister* (2012), *Deliver Us from Evil* (2104) and *Doctor Strange* (2016) are two examples of people of faith who have made it big in Hollywood. Seminary graduates have gone on to successful careers in television and film include Craig Detweiler, Chris Retts, Joshua Lim (Singaporean), Justin Bell, Eugene Suen (Taiwanese), TC Johnstone, Jeremy Seifert, and Native American actor/playwright Jason Grasl among others.

Another recent example of a Christian screenwriter and director naturally integrating his faith into his work is Lee Isaac Chung whose 2020 film, *Minari,* won multiple top-tier film awards in 2020 (from Sundance to the Golden Globes to the Oscars). The semi-autobiographical film portrays a Korean immigrant family struggling to create their own version of the American Dream on a farm in Arkansas and religion is part of their story. Chung, who was raised Baptist, Methodist, and is now Episcopalian, explains:

> I didn't want to set out to make a Christian movie, if that makes sense, like in the sense that I'm preaching to the choir, or just trying to preach the Gospel. I didn't want this film to be that. I just wanted this film to capture a certain perspective and experience that I have of wrestling with God. The name of the main character is Jacob, and he's wrestling with God in this film.[2]

Minari is, above all, a family drama with very human and fallible characters, religion is part of their lives, but Chung wanted to move beyond the all-too-common filmic and political caricatures of Christians in the South. Chung created authentic characters in this quietly moving immigrant story of perseverance and familial struggle. Benjamin Lee of *The Guardian* described *Minari* as a "richly-textured, yet restrained…portrait of a family figuring out their place in the world [which] is both small and somehow rather grand" (Lee, 2020). Universal (grand) tales are the films that will be discussed for years to come. Chung is another example of how people of faith are simply producing quality stories and providing us with richer fodder for discussion. Spirituality is part of the story not simply in "religious" scenes, but in the family's relationships with one another, especially between the five-year-old David (Alan S. Kim) and his feisty grandmother Soonja (Yuh-Jung Youn) who won the Academy Award for Best Supporting Actress for her portrayal. "I feel a lot of our spirituality" explained Chung, "is worked out in our relationships with other people and the way we choose to look at other people" (Seun, Interview, 2021). Religious ideals of compassion, reconciliation, restoration, and intergenerational healing are central to the film.

In addition to writing and directing films, many people of faith have forged successful careers as producers. For example, Fr. Ellwood Keiser (1929–2000) produced several films based on the lives of Catholics who spent their lives fighting for justice for the least of these such as El Salvador's Oscar Romero (*Romero*, 1982) or *Entertaining Angels* (1989) based on the life of Dorothy Day, founder of the Catholic Worker Movement. Ralph Winter is another film producer (*X-Men, Star Trek, Planet of the Apes, The Promise, Reagan*, et. al) who is outspoken about being grounded in his Christian faith.

Of course, Christians do not have the corner on the film market. Creatives of all faiths are filmmakers. Muslims too are increasingly finding success in film and television and bringing their lived religious experience to the screen. Nia Malika Dixon is a Muslim poet, screenwriter, and director who exemplifies this increasing presence. She has written and produced several short films that portray the tensions of being a Muslim in contemporary American society such as *Shattered Lenses,* about a college freshman, caught at intersections of her religious and social identity or *Chrysalis*, a story about a Baltimore drug dealer struggling his Muslim faith and fatherhood. As a storyteller, Dixon is committed to bringing authentic portrayals of Muslim life to the screen:

> There is a huge disparity in representation...honestly people in Hollywood think we (Muslims) come in one package, when, in fact, there are billions of Muslims of various cultures all across the world, so being Muslim does not have a "look," it doesn't have a cultural feel to it that is "Muslim" you can't put it in a box. It is difficult to place a lot of Muslims in films appropriately, I wish there were more Muslims in film and television that were reflective of the diversity of Muslims, such as more African American Muslims. Most of the time in Hollywood when you see a Muslim character, they are Arab or foreign or they speak another language, or they are angry at America over a political problem and that is not necessarily the case because my family has been here in this country ever since this country has been founded. My ancestors helped build this country.[3]

Dixon, like Tucker, credits her faith as the font of her creativity as a screenwriter.

To better understand the experiences of Muslim filmmakers in Hollywood today I also interviewed Libyan filmmaker Abdullah Omeish who is best known for writing, directing, and producing documentary films about the Israeli-Palestinian conflict: *Occupation 101* (2006) and *The War Around Us* (2014). He admits there are certain biases:

> I think being a Muslim in Hollywood is definitely difficult. The industry is brutal as it is. I think being a Muslim, being an Arab, is definitely

> a difficult part in the equation so you have to work 10 times harder and prove yourself 10 times more.

He also spoke of the increasing numbers of Muslims working in film today and views his expertise, linguistic background, and religious background as professional assets, for instance, when HBO need a documentary filmmaker for Libya, Omeish was ready.

> For me, my faith plays a big role because I am constantly asking for guidance in the work that I do, through prayer, through meditation, and trying to find the best way to tell the story that can really resonate with people. I always remind myself that it is coming from my heart, that I am sincere, and all of these things go back to what my faith encourages us to do: to do things with excellence, to do things with sincere intention, to speak the truth...all these go back to my faith, to how I was raised, to being a Muslim.[4]

In sum, there seems to be a new space for filmmakers to include their faith in their films in an organic way.

ROOM FOR IMPROVEMENT AND GROWTH IN RELIGION AND FILM STUDIES

The academic study of religion and film has matured significantly over the past 50 years; however, there are many areas that need development. Perhaps the most fundamental area that requires maturation is general knowledge of the Other. Filmmakers and film scholars need to better understand religion, religionists, and the academic study of religion. Stereotypes of pious effeminate Buddhist monks (*Broken Blossoms*, 1919) or charlatan preachers (*Elmer Gantry*, 1960 or *Leap of Faith*, 1992) might have worked a century ago, but no longer, savvy audiences expect more nuance. Remedying shallow understanding goes both ways: religion scholars who wish to explore film should ground themselves in film history, study film mechanics, and explore critical film theory. Religion and film analysis has moved past a purely theological and narrative approach, but few who approach the topic school themselves in in the basics of film production: production design, cinematography, sound design, etc.

Thankfully both sides are making progress in taking the other seriously, recognizing their lack of knowledge, and striving to learn more.

As with most areas of study in the Global North, the founders of the field were generally heterosexual men of European descent with advanced degrees. Race, class, gender, LGBTQ diversity clearly needs to be sought and supported. As one step in this direction I have made a concerted effort in this book to include films featuring and produced by people of color, women, and those who place themselves on diverse points on the gender spectrum. Although this evolution is occurring naturally as filmmakers themselves diversify and films increasingly explore LGBTQ experiences, we need to seek out and highlight this work. This volume moves away from solely focusing on the work of white men like Ingmar Bergman or Terrence Malick and purposely highlights diverse work from Hollywood pioneer Lois Weber (early 1900s) to the racially provocative work of Jordan Peele to Roger Ross Williams' documentary on the Evangelical campaign against homosexuals in Uganda, Africa.

One of the most exciting and long overdue developments in religion and film is the diversification of religions being featured in films as well as greater interpretation of film from different religious perspectives. The pioneers of Religion and Film Studies were grounded in Christianity. From Herbert Jump in 1909 to Robert K. Johnston in 2020, Christians and Christian theological tropes have dominated the field; however, the past decade has seen compelling and cutting-edge work from Buddhist, Muslim, Jewish, and Hindu perspectives (see suggested reading from Chapter 3 for examples). Smaller faith traditions such neopaganism, indigenous religions, and new religious movements are clearly lacunae that need to be filled. Our profoundly religiously pluralistic world requires a more diversified filmic analysis than has thus far been the case and non-Western religious interpretations are needed as the field matures and grows in the 21st century.

A welcome development is the globalizing of Religion and Film Studies. The first and second waves focused on films from the USA and Europe, and while the USA/Canada and the UK still produce the most films world-wide and generate the most profit by far, the international film market is shifting dramatically in the 21st century and the internationalization of films analyzed has followed. China had the second most profitable market for films in 2020 and India boasts the highest per capita ticket sales. If you are solely considering box office returns, the USA still dominates the billion-dollar film industry. It is also important to note that national boundaries are melting like celluloid when it comes to film production in the 21st century. For example, the highest grossing film thus far in 2021 is *The Last Bogatyr: Root of Evil*, a Russian fantasy comedy film, directed by Dmitry Dyachenko, but produced in collaboration with The Walt Disney Company. Almost half of the box office hits in China today are USA-produced films. Acknowledging this shift and recognizing Asia's significant film industry, the second largest cohort of films in this book are from Asia (8) and West Asia/Middle East (4). *Religion and Film: The Basics*, with its wide variety of films from around the world, models this need to broaden the cinematic canon. As you pursue film and religion, I urge you to consciously seek out films from a region of the world far from your own, as the Laemmle theater chain exhorts us, be a movie lover who is "Not afraid of subtitles." Your viewing choices are powerful and through film, you can become a more informed global citizen. As Tarkovsky taught, "relating a person to the whole world, that is the meaning of cinema" (Tarkovsky, 1986, 66).

Beyond geographic diversification, the growing religion and film canon needs to include more genres. Dramas were considered the primary genre worthy of focus for the first half century of Religion and Film Studies. Documentary film, Noir, Westerns, War, Comedy, Science Fiction, Superhero Adventures films and Horror have all inspired focused studies. More in-depth work needs to be done on experimental film, fantasy, anime, documentary, musicals, romances, and biopics. Genre-merging or genre-hybrid films like *Bladerunner 2049* (apocalyptic-sci-fi-noir, 2017) or *Colossal* (comedy-drama-Kaiju, 2017), or *A Girl Walks Home Alone at Night* (Iranian Vampire-Western-Romance, 2014) are a newer challenge that disrupt our genre viewing expectations and reify them at the same time. Genre blending fosters new interpretive challenges.

Religion and Film Studies has tended to focus on narrative and theological ideas and less on how films affect us. Conversations that include Affect theory (Gilles Deleuze, Brian Massumi, et al.) are beginning to occur, but they need to be pursued further. The phenomenological work of film theorist Vivian Sobchack (*Carnal Thoughts*,

2004) is one fecund place to start thinking about embodied knowledge and cinematic consciousness. Her focus on materiality is one shared by some religious studies scholars who write on film such as S. Brent Plate. Her embodied film analysis is not afraid of metaphysics and echoes assertions of many feminist theologians from Sallie McFague to Ivone Gebara who denounce a mind-body duality and hermeneutic. We need to increasingly incorporate (pun intended) reflection on the materiality of viewing: how are our physical bodies affected, our emotions engaged, how we are changed and inspired after viewing films? Many of us have had the course of our lives altered after viewing a powerful film that affected us deeply. We need to move beyond rational, intellectual reactions and ask questions about how we felt after a screening; for example, how does the exclusive blue and gray palette in Iñárritu's *Biutiful* affect the viewer? The mind-body connection is also developed in the cognitive theory of Tomas Axelson whose "thick-viewing" of films echoes work done by Catherine Bell on ritual. Cross-fertilization between religious studies, philosophy, and film theory should be sought more rigorously in the future. Each group needs to dare to break out of the safety (and biases) of their discipline, humble themselves, and seek to learn from and respectfully engage the other.

Related to this focus on materiality, the field needs to more frequently reference the circuit of culture when discussing film. Cultural Studies asks questions such as: How does film function in people's daily lives? Why do some films, or franchises like *Star Wars* develop into religious myths of their own? How are fan communities functioning as religious communities? Work by Brent S. Plate, Robert K. Johnston, and John C. Lyden have begun to explore these questions, however more work needs to be done in addressing how films influence our lives and shape our spirituality. Asking these functionalist queries related to the power of film raises the issue of how film can be used as political or ethical propaganda. Ideological film theory and critique are another approach that needs greater engagement in future religion and film dialogue and scholarship. Ideological film critique evolved from Marxist roots to now include a variety of disciplines, from Lacanian psychoanalysis to diasporic studies. Ideological analysis considers how society and the economy influence aesthetic film form. I posit engaging more ideological cultural critique would be a fecund and timely development in

Religion and Film Studies. The questions that roil many cultures today, especially questions related to race, politics, economics, power, and difference are found at the center of this critique and those in the field would do well to address their relationship to film. Engaging more of the thought of Fredric Jameson and Slavoj Zizek would challenge and deepen religion and film discussions.

Finally, those of us who are engaged in religion and film need to improve clarifying our working definitions of both. How are we defining religion? How broad is our concept of what qualifies as religion/religious? Lyden uses Geertz' definition in *Film as Religion*, but many avoid defining religion because there is no broadly accepted one-size-fits-all definition. Clearly world religions qualify, but what about zealous atheists or Marxists? If we accept Paul Tillich's suggestion that religion centers on one's ultimate concern, might not *An Inconvenient Truth* (2006) or *Anthropocene* (2018) be considered "religious" films for devout environmentalists or *Food, Inc.* for vegans? In this work, film choice and analysis clarify parameters as to what qualifies as religious.

Similarly, what qualifies as a "film"? Film stock itself has become almost obsolete by 2020 as most "films" are now digital. Should we include streaming film-like miniseries like *Unorthodox*, a three-hour German-American dramatic miniseries (2020) produced by Netflix? The Covid-19 pandemic shuttered movie theaters around the world in 2020 and many cinema chains will not re-open. This pandemic shutdown challenged a struggling theater industry, yet films are more popular than ever. Today "films" are made by streaming giants like Apple, Hulu, and Netflix and created to be watched at home on your TV. What does it mean to live in what some term a "Post-cinema" world? Not only has film media evolved, but the way we experience film is changing dramatically. We are more likely to watch a film in our living rooms today than a theater. The sacred experience of discovering the divine in the dark in movie palaces has been replaced by some who now watch films on their phones while getting their steps on the treadmill…sacrilege! Yet wherever and however we watch, our love of movies is as strong as ever.

Not only has the location of experiencing film shifted, but authorship is evolving as well. Transmedia storytelling that utilizes multiple platforms with multiple creative authors/directors challenges the reverence once reserved for stellar auteurs. How does interactivity change our understanding of artistic control and intention? How might simulation and collective intelligence change the conversation? Religion and Film Studies needs to grapple with these messy boundary issues and dare to include new forms of visual narratives. As media evolves, so must our conversation partners. Religion and Film Studies is enriched by new interdisciplinary conversation partners from Film Studies, Philosophy, Media Studies (including digital, trans and new media), LGBTQ Studies, Cultural Studies, Art History, Visual Culture, Digital and New Media. We need to humble ourselves, be curious, and initiate these conversations and collaborative relationships.

COMMISSIONING OF THE READER

In many ways, the future of religion and film lies in your hands. I hope this book has inspired you to explore the intersection of film and religion on your own. You needn't go to film school or get an advanced degree in Religious Studies to do this well! In our religiously pluralistic contemporary world, films not only depict our existential ideas, hopes, and angst, they can serve as prophetic injunctions and revelations. I trust this introduction has widened your film canon and provided you with tools to respond to films that "plough and harrow" your soul in the words of the late, great filmmaker Andrei Tarkovsky. I leave you with a sentiment I share with director Steven Spielberg who said: "The older I get, the more I look at movies as a moving miracle." Dive into these moving miracles,[5] with eyes to see, ears to hear, an open mind, and a sense of wonder.

NOTES

1 Camille Tucker, interview with author. Los Angeles, California, video recording, June 12, 2014.
2 Lee Isaac Chung, interview, Accessed April 20, 2021, https://www.pluggedin.com/blog/director-lee-isaac-chung-talks-about-faith-family-and-the-award-winning-minari/.
3 Nia Malika Dixon, personal interview with author, June 10, 2014, Van Nuys, CA, audio & video recording.
4 Abdallah Omeish, personal interview with author, June 12, 2014, Los Angeles, CA, audio & video recording.
5 The etymology of "miracle" can be traced back to the Latin *mīrāculum*, "something amazing, marvel," and *mīrārī* "to be surprised, look with wonder at."

APPENDIX A
FILMS ANALYZED IN *RELIGION AND FILM: THE BASICS*

A GLOBAL FILM STUDY

Africa: 2, Asia: 8, Europe: 7, Latin America: 2, USA: 16, West Asia/Middle East: 4.

1: **Discovering the Divine in the Dark: An Introduction to Religion and Film**
   Hypocrites (Lois Weber, USA, 1915).
2: **Dimensions and Bricolage: Methodological Approaches to Religion and Film**
   Breaking the Waves (Lars Von Trier, Denmark/Sweden/Spain/UK/et al., 1996).
3: **Flickering Faith: Exploring World Religions through Film**
   Hinduism: *Jai Santoshi Ma* (Vijay Shwarma, India, 1973) & *OMG* (Umesh Shukla, India, 2012).
   Buddhism: *Departures* (YojiroTakita, Japan, 2009) & *The Big Lebowski* (Joel and Ethan Coen, USA, 1998).
   Judaism: *A Serious Man* (Joel and Ethan Coen, USA, 2009) & *Mountain* (Yaelle Kayam, Israel, 2016).
   Christianity: *Son of Man* (Mark Dornford-May, South Africa, 2006) & *Free in Deed* (Jake Mahaffy, New Zealand-USA, 2015).
   Islam: *Matir Moina* (Tareque Masud, Bangladesh, 2002) & *Malcolm X* (Spike Lee, USA, 1992).
   Interreligious Relations: *Earth* (Deepa Mehta, India, 2004) & *Life of Pi* (Ang Lee, USA/Taiwan/UK, 2012).

4: **Shaking with Fear or Laughter: Exploring Religion and Film through Film Genres Sci-Fi:** *Ex-Machina* (Alex Garland, UK, 2014) & *Arrival* (Denis Villeneuve, USA, 2016).
Horror: *The Wicker Man* (Robin Hardy, UK, 1973) & *Let the Right One In* (Tomas Alfredson, Sweden, 2014).
Comedy: *The Pilgrim* (Charles Chaplin, USA, 1923) & *The Lizard* (Kamal Tabrizi, Iran, 2004).
Pilgrimage/Quest/Road Trip: *The Way* (Emilio Estevez, Spain, 2010) & *Little Miss Sunshine* (Jonathan Dayton and Valerie Faris, USA, 2006).
Drama: *Andrei Rublev* (Andrei Tarkovsky, Russia, 1966) & *Amazing Grace* (Michael Apted, USA, 2007).
Documentary: *5 Broken Cameras* (Emad Burnat, Israel, 2011) & *Jesus Camp* (Heidi Ewing and Rachel Grady, USA, 2008).

5: **Demons, Redeemers, Ghosts and More: Recurrent Tropes in Religion and Film**
Evil and Suffering: *The Exorcism of Emily Rose* (Scott Derrickson, USA, 2005) & *Get Out* (Jordan Peele, USA 2017).
Sex, Gender Roles, and Religion: *Water* (Deepa Mehta, Canada/India, 2005) & *God Loves Uganda* (Roger Ross Williams, USA, 2013).
Religion and Race: *The Other Conquest* (Salvador Carrasco, Mexico, 2000) & *Burden* (Andrew Heckler, USA, 2019).
Redemption, Reconciliation, and Healing: *Central Station* (Walter Salles, Brazil, 1998) & *Magnolia* (Paul Thomas Anderson, USA, 1999).
Karma and Reincarnation: *It's a Wonderful Life* (Frank Capra, USA, 1947) & *Uncle Boonmee Who Can Recall His Past Lives* (Apichatpong Weerasethakul, Thailand, 2010).
Death and Afterlife: *Biutiful* (Alejandro Iñárritu, Spain, 2010) & *From a Whisper* (Wanuri Kahiu, Kenya, 2009).

6: **Before the Credits Roll: A Conclusion**
Minari (Lee Isaac Chung, USA, 2020).

BIBLIOGRAPHY

Abrams, Nathan. *The New Jew in Film: Exploring Jewishness and Judaism in Contemporary Cinema.* Piscataway, NJ: Rutgers UP, 2012.

Anker, Roy M. *Beautiful Light: Religious Meaning in Film.* Grand Rapids, MI: Wm. B. Eerdmans, 2017.

———. *Catching Light: Looking for God in the Movies.* Grand Rapids, MI: Wm. B. Eerdmans, 2004.

Aoki, Shinmon. *Coffinman: The Journal of a Buddhist Mortician.* Translated by Wayne S. Yokoyama. Anaheim, CA: Buddhist Education Center, 2002.

Babington, Bruce and Peter W. Evans. *Biblical Epics: Sacred Narrative in Hollywood Cinema.* Manchester: Manchester University Press, 1993.

Bach, David. Personal email correspondence with Author, May 28, 2020.

Banaji, Shakuntala. *Reading 'Bollywood': The Young Audience and Hindi Films.* New York: Palgrave-Macmillan, 2006.

Barnett, Christopher B. and Clark J. Elliston, eds. *Theology and the Films of Terrence Malick.* London: Routledge, 2016.

Barsotti, Catherine M. and Robert K. Johnston. *God in the Movies: A Guide for Exploring Four Decades of Film.* Grand Rapids, MI: Brazos Press, 2017.

Bazin, André. "Cinema and Theology." In *Bazin at Work: Major Essays and Reviews from the Forties and Fifties,* 61–72. New York: Routledge, 1997.

———. *What Is Cinema?* Berkeley: University of California Press, 2005.

Bell, Jamel S.C. and Ronald L. Jackson, eds. *Interpreting Tyler Perry: Perspectives on Race, Class, Gender, and Sexuality.* London: Taylor & Francis Group, 2013.

Bhrugubanda, Uma M. *Deities and Devotees: Cinema, Religion, and Politics in South India*. New York: Oxford University Press, 2019.

Blake, Richard A. *After Image: The Indelible Catholic Imagination of Six American Filmmakers*. Chicago, IL: Loyola Press, 2000.

Blizik, William L., ed. *The Continuum Companion to Religion and Film*. London: Continuum, 2009.

Booth, Rebecca, Valeska Griffiths, and Erin Thompson, eds. *Scared Sacred: Idolatry, Religion and Worship in the Horror Film*. London: House of Leaves, 2020.

Bridger, Francis. *A Charmed Life: The Spirituality of Potterworld*. New York: Doubleday, 2002.

Bridges, Jeff and Bernie Glassman. *The Dude and the Zen Master*. New York: Blue Rider Press, 2012.

Brode, Douglas and Leah Deyneka, eds. *Sex, Politics, and Religion in Star Wars: An Anthology*. Lanham, MD: Scarecrow Press, 2012.

Butler, Ivan. *Religion in the Cinema*. The International Film Guide Series. New York: A.S. Barnes & Co, 1969.

Callaway, Kutter. *Scoring Transcendence: Contemporary Film Music as Religious Experience*. Waco, TX: Baylor University Press, 2013.

Carr, Steven A. *Hollywood and Anti-Semitism: A Cultural History up to World War II*. New York: Cambridge University Press, 2001.

Casebier, Allan. *Film and Phenomenology: Towards a Realist Theory of Cinematic Representation*. Cambridge: Cambridge University Press, 2009.

Cho, Francisca. *Seeing Like the Buddha: Enlightenment through Film*. Albany: SUNY Press, 2017.

Chong, Kris H.K. *Transcendence and Spirituality in Chinese Cinema: A Theological Exploration*. London: Routledge, 2020.

Coen, Ethan. "Goys, God, Dentistry and 'A Serious Man.'" Interview in http://www.salon.com/2009/10/01/coens/.

Conard, Mark T., ed. *The Philosophy of the Coen Brothers*. Lexington: University Press of Kentucky, 2012.

Costanzo, William V. *World Cinema through Global Genres*. London: Wiley Blackwell, 2014.

Cowan, Douglas E. *Sacred Terror: Religion and Horror on the Silver Screen*. Waco, TX: Baylor University Press, 2008.

Cutrara, Daniel S. *Wicked Cinema: Sex and Religion on Screen*. Austin: University of Texas Press, 2014.

Dalle Vacche, Angela. *Andre Bazin's Film Theory: Art, Science, Religion*. New York: Oxford University Press, 2020.

Davidson, Elijah L. *How to Talk to a Movie: Movie Watching as a Spiritual Exercise*. Eugene, OR: Cascade Books, 2017.

Deacy, Christopher. *Faith in Film: Religious Themes in Contemporary Cinema.* Burlington: Ashgate, 2005.

———. *Screening the Afterlife: Theology, Eschatology and Film.* London: Routledge, 2012.

Deacy, Christopher and Gaye W. Ortiz. *Theology and Film: Challenging the Sacred/Secular Divide.* Oxford: Blackwell Publishing, 2008.

Denson, Shane and Julia Leyda, eds. *Post-Cinema: Theorizing 21st-Century Film.* Falmer: REFRAME Books, 2016.

Derrickson, Scott. "Horror: The Perfect Christian Genre." Interview by Peter T. Chattaway. *Christianity Today,* August 30, 2005.

Derry, Ken and John C. Lyden, eds. *The Myth Awakens: Canon, Conservatism, and Fan Reception of Star Wars.* Eugene, OR: Wipf and Stock, 2018.

Detweiler, Craig. *Into the Dark: Seeing the Sacred in the Top Films of the 21st Century.* Grand Rapids, MI: Baker Academic: 2008.

Dixon, Wheeler W. *A History of Horror.* New Brunswick, NJ: Rutgers University Press, 2010.

Donnelly, Doris. "Divine Folly: Being Religious and the Exercise of Humor." *Theology Today* 48:4 (January 1992), 1–14.

Downing, Crystal. *Salvation from Cinema: The Medium Is the Message.* London: Routledge, 2016.

Dwyer, Rachel. *Filming the Gods: Religion and Indian Cinema.* Abingdon: Routledge, 2006.

Dwyer, Rachel and Divia Patel. *Cinema India: The Visual Culture of Hindi Film.* New Brunswick, NJ: Rutgers University Press, 2002.

Ellison, William. "From the Himalayas to Hollywood: The Legacy of Lost Horizon." *Tricycle Magazine,* December, 1997.

Erlich, Linda C. "Closing the Circle: Why Has the Bodhi Dharma Left for the East?" In *Seoul Searching: Culture and Identity in Contemporary Korean Cinema,* edited by Frances Gateward, 175–188. Albany: State University of New York Press, 2007.

Falsani, Cathleen. *The Dude Abides: The Gospel According to the Coen Brothers.* Grand Rapids, MI: Zondervan, 2009.

Flesher, Paul V.M. and Robert Torry. *Film and Religion: An Introduction.* Nashville, TN: Abingdon Press, 2007.

Flisfeder, Matthew. "Class Struggle and Displacement: Slavoj Žižek and Film Theory." *Cultural Politics* 5:3 (2009), 299–324.

Frankel, David. *The Hidden God: Film and Faith.* New York: The Museum of Modern Art, 2003.

Geertz, Clifford. *The Interpretation of Cultures.* New York: Basic, 1973.

Geivett, Douglas R. and James S. Speigal, eds. *Faith, Film, and Philosophy: Big Ideas on the Big Screen.* Downers Grove, IL: Intervarsity Press Academic, 2007.

Gerstner, David A. and Janet Staiger, eds. *Authorship and Film*. London: Taylor & Francis Group, 2002.

Gilhus, Ingvild S. *Laughing Gods, Weeping Virgins: Laughter in the History of Religion*. London: Routledge, 1997.

Gray, Tim. "How Christopher Nolan's 'Dunkirk' Team Captured the Sounds of Battle." *Variety*. https://variety.com/2017/film/awards/christopher-nolan-dunkirk-sound-war-1202641690/.

Green, Ronald S. *Buddhism Goes to the Movies: An Introduction to Buddhist Thought and Practice*. London: Routledge, 2014.

Hanson, Bradley C. "Christ's Work of Reconciliation." In *Introduction to Christian Theology*, 155–182. Minneapolis, MN: Fortress Press, 1997.

Hubner, Laura. *The Films of Ingmar Bergman: Illusions of Light and Darkness*. New York: Palgrave-Macmillan, 2007.

Iñárritu, Alejandro. Interview with *Deadline.com*. https://deadline.com/2010/12/oscar-alejandro-gonzalez-inarritu-qa-on-biutiful-91880/.

John, Mathew P. *Film as Cultural Artifact: Religious Criticism of World Cinema*. Minneapolis, MN: Fortress Press, 2017.

Johnston, Robert K. *Ecclesiastes through the Lens of Contemporary Film*. Grand Rapids, MI: Baker Academic, 2004.

———. *Reel Spirituality: Theology and Film in Dialogue*. Grand Rapids, MI: Baker Academic, 2000.

Johnston, Robert K., ed. *Reframing Theology and Film: New Focus for an Emerging Discipline*. Grand Rapids, MI: Baker Academic, 2007.

Johnston, Robert K., Craig Detweiler, and Kutter Callaway. *Deep Focus: Film and Theology in Dialogue*. Grand Rapids, MI: Baker Academic, 2019.

Kickasola, Joseph G. *The Films of Krzysztof Kieslowski: The Liminal Image*. Bloomington: Indiana University Press, 2004.

Kickasola, Joseph G. Chapter 5: "Kieslowski's Musique Concrète." In *Music, Sound and Filmmakers: Sonic Style in Cinema*, edited by James Wierzbicki, 61–75, first edition. New York: Routledge, 2012.

King, Mike. *Luminous: The Spiritual Life on Film*. London: Stochastic Press, 2018.

Knauss, Stefanie. *Religion and Film: Representation, Experience, Meaning*. Leiden/Boston, MA: Brill, 2020.

Mitchell, Jolyon and S. Brent Plate, eds. *The Religion and Film Reader*. New York: Routledge, 2007.

Lee, Benjamin. "*Minari* Review-Moving and Modest Coming-of-Age Sundance Hit." *The Guardian*, January 29, 2020.

Leithart, Peter J. *Shining Glory: Theological Reflections on Terrence Malick's Tree of Life*. Eugene, OR: Cascade Books, 2013.

Levy, Gabriel. "Hermeneutics in *A Serious Man*." In *Coen: Framing Religion in Amoral Order*, edited by Elijah Siegler, 217–232. Waco, TX: Baylor University Press, 2016.

Lindvall, Terry. *Sanctuary Cinema: Origins of the Christian Film Industry*. New York: New York University Press, 2007.

———, ed. *The Silents of God: Selected Issues and Documents in Silent American Film and Religion, 1908–1925*. Lanham, MD: Scarecrow Press, 2001.

Lindvall, Terry, J. Dennis Bounds, and Chris Lindvall. *Divine Film Comedies: Biblical Narratives, Film Sub-Genres and the Comic Spirit*. New York: Routledge, 2016.

Lindvall, Terry and Andrew Quick. *Celluloid Sermons: The Emergence of the Christian Film Industry, 1930–1986*. New York: New York University Press, 2011.

Lovecraft, Howard P. *Supernatural Horror in Literature*, Dover ed. New York: Dover Publications, 1973.

Lövheim, Mia. *Media, Religion and Gender*. London: Routledge, 2013.

Lutgendorf, Philip. "Jai Santoshi Ma Revisited." In *Representing Religion in World Cinema*, edited by S. Brent Plate, 19–42. New York: Palgrave, 2007.

Lyden, John, ed. *The Routledge Companion to Religion and Film*. London: Routledge, 2009.

Lyden, John C. *Film as Religion: Myths, Morals, and Rituals*, second ed. New York: New York University Press, 2019 [2003].

May, John R., ed. *New Image of Religious Film*. Kansas City, MO: Sheed & Ward, 1997.

May, John R. and Michael Bird. *Religion in Film*. Knoxville: University of Tennessee Press, 1982.

Miles, Margaret R. *Seeing and Believing: Religion and Values in the Movies*, second ed. Boston, MA: Beacon Press, 1996.

Mitchell, Jolyon and S. Brent Plate. *The Religion and Film Reader*. London: Routledge, 2007.

Monaco, James. *How to Read a Film: Movies, Media, and Beyond*, fourth ed. New York: Oxford University Press, 2009.

Moore, Rachel O. *Savage Theory: Cinema as Modern Magic*. Durham, NC: Duke University Press, 2000.

Nathan, Ian. *The Coen Brothers: The Iconic Filmmakers and Their Work*. London: Aurum Press, 2017.

Neale, Steve. *Genre and Hollywood*. New York: Routledge, 2000.

Nye, Malory. Religion: The Basics. London: Routledge, 2003, 17.

Okuyama, Yoshiko. "Shinto and Buddhist Metaphors in *Departures*." *Journal of Religion and Film* 17 (April 2013), 4–5. http://digital commons.unomaha.edu/jrf.

Petersen, Kristian. *New Approaches to Islam in Film*. London: Routledge, 2021.

Plate, Brent S. *Religion and Film: Cinema and the Re-creation of the World*. London: Wallflower Press, 2008.

———. *Reviewing the Passion: Mel Gibson's Film and Its Critics*. New York: Palgrave-Macmillan, 2004.

———, ed. *Representing Religion in World Cinema: Filmmaking, Mythmaking, Culture Making*. New York: Palgrave Macmillan, 2003.
Polta, Steve. San Francisco Cinemateque. Quoted by Duke Arts Center. https://artscenter.duke.edu/event/nathaniel-dorsky/.
Ramji, Rubina. "Examining the Critical Role American Popular Film Continues to Play in Maintaining the Muslim Terrorist Image, Post 9/11." *Journal of Religion and Film* 20:1 (2016). https://digitalcommons.unomaha.edu/jrf.
Rankin, Phillip. *Film and the Afterlife*. London: Routledge, 2020.
Rindge, Matthew S. *The Bible and Film: The Basics*. London: Routledge, 2021.
Saltzman, Devyani. *Shooting Water*. New York: Newmarket Press, 2006.
Schrader, Paul. *Transcendental Style in Film: Ozu, Bresson, Dreyer*. Berkeley: University of California Press, 1972. Second edition with new introduction published in 2018.
Settle, Zachary and Taylor Worley. *Dreams, Doubt, and Dread: The Spiritual in Film*. Eugene, OR: Cascade Books, 2016.
Shaw, Deborah. *The Three Amigos: The Transnational Filmmaking of Guillermo del Toro, Alejandro González Iñárritu, and Alfonso Cuarón*. Manchester: Manchester University Press, 2013.
Siegler, Elijah, ed. *Coen: Framing Religion in Amoral Order*. Waco, TX: Baylor University Press, 2016.
Sison, Antonio D. *The Sacred Foodways of Film: Theological Servings in 11 Food Films*. Eugene, OR: Pickwick Publications, 2016.
———. *Screening Schillebeeckx: Theology and Third Cinema in Dialogue*. New York: Palgrave Macmillan, 2006.
———. *World Cinema, Theology, and the Human: Humanity in Deep Focus*. New York: Routledge, 2012.
Sobchack, Vivian. *The Address of the Eye: A Phenomenology of Film Experience*. Princeton, NJ: Princeton University Press, 1992.
———. *Carnal Thoughts: Embodiment and Moving Image Culture*, first ed. ACLS Humanities E-book. Berkeley: University of California Press, 2004.
Solano, Jeanette Reedy. "Blessed Broken Bodies: Exploring Redemption in *Central Station* and *Breaking the Waves*." *Journal of Religion & Film* 8:2 (2004), Article 16. https://digitalcommons.unomaha.edu/jrf/vol8/iss2/16.
Stamp, Shelly. *Lois Weber in Early Hollywood*. Oakland: University of California Press, 2015.
Staiger, Janet. *Media Reception Studies*. New York: New York University Press, 2005.
Suen, Eugene. "MINARI, Director and Editor Interview." January 19, 2021. https://www.youtube.com/watch?v=AvoBpaU4wTA.

Suh, Sharon A. *Silver Screen Buddha: Buddhism in Asian and Western Film.* London: Bloomsbury Academic, 2015.

Tarkovsky, Andrei. *Sculpting in Time.* Translated by Kitty Hunter-Blair. Austin: University of Texas Press, 1986.

Tucker, Camille. Interview with author, audio and video tape recording. Los Angeles, California, June 12, 2014.

Ver Straten-McSparran, Rebecca. *Lars von Trier's Cinema: Excess, Evil, and the Prophetic Voice.* London: Routledge, 2021.

Villarejo, Amy. *Film Studies: The Basics*, second ed. London: Routledge, 2013.

Waldron, Dara. *Cinema and Evil: Moral Complexities and the "Dangerous" Film.* Newcastle upon Tyne: Cambridge Scholars Publisher, 2013.

Walsh, Frank. *Sin and Censorship: The Catholic Church and the Motion Picture Industry.* New Haven, CT: Yale University Press, 1996.

Watkins, Gregory J., ed. *Teaching Religion and Film.* New York: Oxford University Press, 2008.

Weerasethakul, Apichatpong. Cannes Film Festival Press Kit. https://cdn-media.festival-cannes.com/film_film/0001/68/500677b471e2d-6f4a386f4e2f30664dab87fa894.pdf.

Weisenfeld, Judith. *Hollywood Be Thy Name: African American Religion in American Film, 1929–1949.* Berkeley: University of California Press, 2007.

Wells, Justin. *How to Film Truth: The Story of Documentary Film as a Spiritual Journey.* Eugene, OR: Cascade Books, 2018.

Whalen-Bridge, John and Gary Storhoff. *Buddhism and American Cinema.* Albany: State University of New York Press, 2014.

Women in TV and Film. "The Celluloid Ceiling Report." https://womenintvfilm.sdsu.edu/wp-content/uploads/2020/01/2019_Celluloid_Ceiling_Report.pdf (Accessed 6–10–2020).

Wright, Melanie J. *Religion and Film: An Introduction.* London: I.B. Taurus, 2007.

Zierler, Wendy. *Movies and Midrash: Popular Film and Jewish Religious Conversation.* Albany: State University Press of New York, 2017.

INDEX

Note: *Italic* page numbers refer to figures.

absolute time 4
affect theory 4, 189
African bishops 149
African Movie Academy Awards 170
A.I. (artificial intelligence-Ex Machina) 97–101
Alfredson, Tomas: *Let the Right One In* 110, 112–114
Amazing Grace 117–119, *119*
American Academy of Religion (AAR) 13, 14
Anderson, Paul Thomas: *Magnolia* 17, 159–163, *161*
Andrei Rublev (Tarkovsky) 47, 114–116
Anker, Roy M.: *Catching Light: Looking for God in the Movies* 22
Annaud, Jean Jacques: *Seven Years in Tibet* 70–71
anti-homosexuality bill 147
Apichatpong Weerasethakul 166, 167, 169
approaches to religion and film: auteur approach 47–49; cultural studies 12, 30, 32–38, 190; film studies 5, 11–16, 18, 29–31, 33, 39–51, 78, 97, 177, 181, 187–192; gendered, racial, political approaches 50–51; philosophical and genre approaches 49–50; religious studies 5, 14, 27, 28–29, 30, 32, 39, 51, 192; theological and biblical 5, 22–28, 40, 51, 104
Aronofsky, Darren 181
Arrival (Villeneuve) 101–102, *102*
Artaud, Antonin 3; "Sorcery and Cinema" 3
Assyrians 23–24
auteurial intention 140–141
auteurs, specialized studies of 179–181
auteur theory 46, 48, 49
Axelson, Tomas 190

Bach, David 43
Bahati, David 147, 148
Bahktin, Mikhail 103
Baily, George 24

von Balthasar, Hans Urs 25
Bangladeshi War of Liberation 83
Barsotti, Catherine 25
Bazín, Andre 3–4, 11
Bell, Catherine 190
Benjamin, Oliver 76; *The Dude De Ching* 77
Bergman, Ingmar 188
Bertolucci, Bernardo: *Little Buddha* (1993) 71, 166
Bhagavad Gita 55, 100, 101, 146
biblical approaches to film 27–28
The Big Lebowski (Coen and Coen) 5, 18, 53, 76
Bird, Michael 12
Biutiful (Iñárritu) 17, 190
black church 153–155
Blake, Richard A.: *After Image: The Indelible Catholic Imagination of Six American Filmmakers* 24
Blizek, William L. 13
Booth, Rebecca: *Scared Sacred: Idolatry, Religion and Worship in the Horror Film* 180
Bosworth Studios 8
Bounds, J. Dennis: *Divine Film Comedies: Biblical Narratives, Film Sub-Genres, and the Comic Spirit* 103–104, 180
Breaking the Waves (Von Trier) 25–27
Bridges, Jeff and Glassman, Bernie: *The Dude and The Zen Master* 179
Broken Blossoms (Griffith) 69, 70, *70*
Buddhism 1, 15, 17, 18, 53, 54, 65, 69–71, 102, 179; *The Big Lebowski* (1998) 5, 18, 53, 76; *Departures* 71–73; fan devotion, religion of Dudeism 76–77; Zen lessons 77–78
Buddhist key concepts: compassionate community (sangha), ego-self, and recognition of other 75–76; death, life, seeing 73–75
Buechner, Frederick 22

Burden (Heckler) 114; cultural context and production of 155–156; KKK and black church 153–155
Burke, Ronald 13
Burke, Thomas: "The Chink and the Child" 69
Burnat, Emad: *5 Broken Cameras* 126, 128–130, *129*

Cage, John 43, 44
Callaway, Kutter: *Scoring Transcendence: Contemporary Film Music as Religious Experience* 45, 181
Cal Philharmonic concert 45
Campbell, Joseph 31
Capra, Frank: *It's a Wonderful Life* (1947) 6, 17–18, 24, 163–165, 167–168; *Lost Horizon* 70
Carrasco, Salvador: *The Other Conquest* (1998) 17, 149–153
Catholic theological approach 24
The Cave of Demons (Méliès) 109
Central Station (Salles) 17, 157–159, *158*
Chaplin, Charlie 16; *Easy Street* 104; *The Pilgrim* (1923) 18, 104–106, *105*
Chesterton, G.K. 104
China 2, 188–189
Cho, Francesca: *Seeing Like the Buddha: Enlightenment through Film* 179
Chocolat (Lasse Halstrom, 1999) 41
Chong, Chris H.K.: *Transcendence and Spirituality in Chinese Cinema: A Theological Exploration* 181
Christian church 147–148
Christianity 54, 78–83, 92, 104, 118, 123, 185–186; diversity in 81–83; *Son of Man* 79–80
Christian redemption 25–27, 156–157
Christian theologians 22
Christian theological analysis 179

Chung, Lee Isaac: *Minari* 184–185
le cinema bruit 3
cinematic theodicy 64–65
cinematography 41
Cinéma Vérité 127
CINESPI Research Group of the Catholic University 182
"Circuit of Culture" approach 34–35
Coen, Ethan 61, 63; *The Big Lebowski* (1998) 5, 18, 53, 76; *A Serious Man* 61–62, 65
Coen, Joel: *The Big Lebowski* (1998) 5, 18, 53, 76; *A Serious Man* 61–62, 65
comedy films 180; comedy genre conventions 103; *The Lizard* (2004) 18, 106–109, *108*; *The Pilgrim* (1923) 18, 104–106, *105*; and religion 103–104
comedy genre conventions 103
consciousness 3, 11, 46, 49, 99, 101, 102, 173, 178, 190
Covid-19 pandemic 15, 191
Cowen, Douglas E.: *Sacred Terror: Religion and Horror on the Silver Screen* 180
Cretton, Destin Daniel 184
critical religious film theory 30
cultural context, role of 140–141
cultural-engagement categories (Tillich) 22
cultural studies approach 32–35; analysis of 143–145; implementation in film 36–38
cultural theory 33
Cutrara, Daniel S.: *Wicked Cinema: Sex and Religion on Screen* 51, 181

Dalai Lama 72
darshan 59–61
death 73–75
death and afterlife 169–175; *Biutiful* 172–175, *175*; *From a Whisper* (2009) 170–172
Delluc, Louis 11

DeMille, Cecil B. 6: *King of Kings* 79; *Noah's Ark* 60; *The Ten Commandments* 60
Departures (Takita) 18, 53, 71–74, *74*
Derrickson, Scott 184; *The Exorcism of Emily Rose* (2005) 17, 136–139
Detweiler, Craig 123, 182, 184; *Into the Dark: Seeing the Sacred in the Top Films of the 21st Century* 13, 25
devotional cinema 4
devotional films 54, 57
Direct Cinema 127
Dixon, Nia Malika 186
documentary film 126–128; *5 Broken Cameras* 128–130, *129*; Insiders and Outsiders in study of religion 128; *Jesus Camp* (2007) 126, 130–133, 149
Dolby Surround Sound 42
Donelly, Doris 104
Doniger, Wendy 31, 32
Dornford-May, Mark: *Son of Man* (2006) 79–80
Dorsky, Nathaniel 4, 5, 28, 29, 40, 41; *Devotional Cinema* 41
The Double Life of Veronique (Kieslowski) 44
dramas 114, 189; *Amazing Grace* 117–119, *119*; *Andrei Rublev* 47–49, 114–116
Drew Ali, Noble 85–86
Drew, Robert 127
Dreyer, Carl Theodor: *The Passion of Joan of Arc* 41, 45
dual redemption 157–159
Dudeism 5, 53, 76–77
Dulac, Germaine 3
Dunkirk 42
DuVernay, Ava 156
Dyachenko, Dmitry: *The Last Bogatyr: Root of Evil* 189

Earth (Mehta) 36, 89, 91, 94, 143
Ebert, Roger 46

ecstatic behavior 130
Edison, Thomas 6
editing 40–42
Eisenstein, Sergei 44
Eliade, Mircea 31, 32
Elijah Muhammad 86, 87
Epstein, Jean 2–3, 11
Erasmus 104
ethnography 36
Ettiger, Bracha Lichtenberg 50
Evangelical Christianity 131
evil and suffering 136–143
Ewing, Heidi 133; *The Boys of Baraka* 130–131; *Jesus Camp* 126, 130–133, 149
Ex Machina (Garland) 98–101
The Exorcism of Emily Rose (Derrickson) 17, 136–139
exorcism 83, 136–139; *Free in Deed* 81, *82*
experimental films 40–41
external evil 136–139

Falsani, Cathleen: *The Dude Abides: The Gospel According to the Coen Brothers* 179
film: biblical approaches to 27–28; criteria for selection of 18; cultural studies approach implementation in 36–38; defining 191; elements, specialized studies of 179–181; emerging stage (1960s–1980s) 11–12; growth in study 187–192; inter-religious relations in 88–94; maturation in 180; methodological maturation and expansion (1990s) 12–13; and religion dynamics 2–6; religious history in 6–7; religious studies approaches to 28–32; in religious themes 1; Roman Catholic scholars in 24; sample theological reading of 25–27; self-critique and methodological innovation 13–14; studies, evolution of 11–14; using sound theory in 43–45

"film-as-text" literary approaches 5, 30
filmmakers, religionists and scholars as 183–187
"film *qua* film" 40
film studies approaches 39–40
Fire (Mehta) 36, 89, 143
Fischer, Becky 130, 133
5 Broken Cameras (Burnat) 126, 128–130, *129*
Flaherty, Robert: *Moana* 126–127
Foley sound effects 42
Frazer, James 31; *The Golden Bough* 111
Free in Deed (Mahaffy) 81–83, *82*
von Freilitzen, Cecelia 38; four ways to relate to media 38
French New Wave 3
Freud 30
functionalism 28–29

Garland, Alex: *Ex Machina* 98–101, 121, 178
Gebara, Ivone 190
Geertz, Clifford 5, 31, 36, 191; "Religion as a Cultural System" 29
Geivett, Douglas: *Faith, Film, and Philosophy: Big Ideas on the Big Screen* 179
gender: in Hinduism 17; roles and religion 143–149
gendered approach 50–51
genre approach 49–50
genre-merging/genre-hybrid films 189
genres 96–97, 178; comedy 103–109; documentary film 126–132; drama 114–119; horror 109–114; pilgrimage/quest/road trip 120–126; science-fiction 97–102
Get Out (Peele) 17, 139–140; auteurial intention and role of cultural context 140–141; white supremacy 141–143, *142*
Giancchino, Michael 45

Gibson, Mel: *The Passion of the Christ* 79
Gilhaus, Ingvild 103
Glassman, Bernie and Bridges, Jeff: *The Dude and The Zen Master* 179
God Loves Uganda (Williams) 147–148
Goizueta, Roberto S. 14
Grady, Rachel 133; *The Boys of Baraka* 130–131; *Jesus Camp* 126, 130–133, 149
Grant, Rev. Dr. Percy Sticky 28
Grek, Feofan 115
Grierson, John 126, 127
Griffith, D.W. 6, 106; *Broken Blossoms* 69, 70, *70*

Hanson, Bradley 26, 156, 162
Hardy, Robin: *The Wicker Man* 110–112, *111*
Haskell, Molly: *From Reverence to Rape: The Treatment of Women in the Movies* 50
Hebrew temple sacrifice 26
Heckler, Andrew: *Burden* 114, 153–156
Heidegger, Martin 46
Hemphill, Ray A. 81
Hindu 36–37, 54, 100
Hinduism 54–55, 61, 145–147, *146*; fan devotion 57–58; *Jai Santoshi Maa* 55, 57–61, *60*; key Hindu concept 55–56, *56*; sex and gender in 17, 145–147; theological message 57; and women's roles 145–147, *146*
Hindu key concepts: *darshan* 59–60; God is everywhere 55–56, *56*
homosexuality 147–149
horror films 109–110; *Let the Right One In* 112–114; pagan horror *The Wicker Man* 110–112, *111*; woke horror-*Get Out* 141, 143;
Hoseyni, Javed 109

Hubner, Lauren: *The Films of Ingmar Bergman: Illusions of Light and Darkness* 24, 180
humor 103–104
Hypocrites (Weber) 7–10, *9*, *10*, 177

Iberian Hispanic Colonial racism 17
ideological film analysis 190
Iñárritu, Alejandro 17, 172; *Biutiful* (2010) 17, 172–175, 190
in-depth auteur study 24
India 2; religious diversity of 36
Indigenous-Spanish relationships 150–153, *151*, *152*
indigenous spirituality 149
international conferences 181–182
The International House of Prayer (IHOP) 147
International Religion and Film Conferences 181
inter-religious relations 88–94; *Life of Pi* (2012) 92–94
"inverted midrash" method 179
Iranian Shiite 106
Islam 54, 83–88, 104; key Islamic ideas 83–84; life in madrasah 84–85; Nation of Islam 85–88
Islamicate films 54
Islamic Revolution in Iran 106
Israeli Orthodox 65–67
Israeli-Palestinian conflict 128–130, 186
It's a Wonderful Life (Capra) 6, 17–18, 24

Jai Santoshi Maa (1975) 57–60, *60*, 61
Jameson, Fredric 191
Jedism 5
Jerusalem 65–67
Jesus 6, 26, 27, 78–80, 82, 83, 104, 112, 117, 118, 123, 132, 139, 156, 157
Jesus Camp (Ewing and Grady) 126, 130–133, 149
Jewish hermeneutics 62–63; gender roles 67, *68*; Israeli Orthodox walls and gender roles 65–67;

Jewish-Muslim friendship in Jerusalem 68–69; problem of evil and innocent suffering 64–65
Jews 54, 60; in Jerusalem 68
Job 58, 61–62, 64, 65
Jodoshinsu (Shin) Pure Land Mayahana Buddhism 72
John, Matthew P. 37; *Film as Cultural Artifact: Religious Criticism of World Cinema* 36–38
Johnson, Richard 34
Johnston, Robert K. 22–25, 188, 190; *Reel Spirituality* 13, 22; *Reframing Theology and Film: New Focus for an Emerging Discipline* 14; *Useless Beauty: Ecclesiastes through the Lens of Contemporary Film* 13, 27
The Journal of Biblical Literature (Reinhartz) 27
The Journal of Religion and Film entry 5, 13, 181
Judaism 60–61, 65, 66
Judeo-Christian ideas 23; tradition 104
Jump, Herbert 11, 188
Jung, Carl 31

Kahiu, Wanuri 17: *From a Whisper* (2009) 170–172
Kaoma, Kapya 147, 148
karma and reincarnation 163–169; *Uncle Boonmee Who Can Recall His Past Lives* (2010) 166–167, *167*; in *It's a Wonderful Life* (1946) 163–165; and memory 168–169
Kayam, Yaelle 66, *68*, 69; *Mountain* 65–69
Kayanja, Robert 147
Keiser, Ellwood 185
Kendrick brothers 183
Khomeni, Grand Ayatollah Ruhollah 106
Kickasola, Joseph 43, 44
Kieslowski, Krzystof 45; *Blue* (1993) 44; *The Double Life of Veronique* (1991) 44
King, Richard 42
Ku Klux Klan (KKK) 106, 114, 150, 153–155

Laemmle, Carl 60
Lambeth global conference of Anglican bishops (1998) 149
Landaker, Gregg 42
Lasky, Jesse 60
Leacock, Richard 127, 128
Lebowski, Jeff 76
Lee, Ang 92
Lee, Christopher 110
Lee, Spike 85, 156; *Malcolm X* 87–88, *88*
Leithart, Peter: *Shining Glory: Theological Reflections on Terrence Malick's Tree of Life* 46
Let the Right One In (Alfredson) 112–114
Levy, Gabriel 65
Lewis, C.S. 14
LGBT civil rights of 148–149; community and experiences 188
Life of Pi (2012) 92–94
Lindsey, Vachel 11
Lindvall, Chris: *Divine Film Comedies: Biblical Narratives, Film Sub-Genres, and the Comic Spirit* 103–104, 180
Little Buddha (Bertolucci) 71, 166
Little Miss Sunshine (Dayton and Faris) 16, 18, 25
The Lizard (Tabrizi) 18, 106–109, *108*
Lord Shaftesbury 104
Lovecraft, H.P. 109
Luce Foundation 14, 22
Lutgendorf, Philip 59
Lyden, John C. 13, 31, 32, 45, 190, 191; *Film as Religion: Myths, Morals, and Rituals* 5, 29; *The Journal of Religion and Film* 5, 13, 181; *Routledge Companion to Religion and Film* 13
Lynch, Gordon 34, 35

madrasah, Islamic life in 84–85
Magnolia (Anderson) 17; regret, law, forgiveness, love and reconciliation 160–163, *161*; wising up and reconciling 159
Mahaffy, Jake: *Free in Deed* 81–83, *82*

Malcolm X 85, 86
Malcolm X (Lee) 87–88, *88*
Malick, Terrence 2, 46, 181, 188; *A Hidden Life* 46; *Tree of Life* 46
Malone, Peter: *Lights Camera, Faith* 24–25
Marsh, Clive 39; *Explorations in Theology and Film* 22
Masud, Catherine 84
Masud, Tareque: *Matir Moina* 83–84
materiality 190
Matir Moina (Masud) 83–84
The Matrix 1
May, John R.: *Religion in Film* 12, 22
McFague, Sallie 190
Mehta, Deepa 37; *Earth* 36, 89–94, 143; *Fire* 36, 89, 143; *Water* 36, 89, 143–147, *146*
Méliès, George: *The Cave of Demons* 109; *The Devil's Manor* 109; *Justice and Vengeance Pursuing Crime* 6; *Le manoir du diable* (1896) 136
memory 168–169
methodological bricolage 21–22, 51, 178
Mexico: racism in 150; views on life and death 172–175
Apted, Michael: *Amazing Grace* 117–119, *119*
Michel, Annaliese 136–139
Miles, Margaret R. 34, 36; *Seeing and Believing: Religion and Values in the Movies* 12, 33
Minari (Chung) 184–185
Mitchell, Jolyon: *The Religion and Film Reader* 13
monomyth 31
Mountain 65–69
mourning 171–172
Muhammed (570–632 CE) 83
Museveni, Yoweri 147
music 80
musical score 45
musique concrète 44
Muslims 85; in Jerusalem 68; in Spain 151; working in film 186–187; *see also* Islam

Myth of Eternal Return 31
mythological films 54, 57
myths 31–32

Naked Truth 8–10, *9*, *10*
National Board of Censorship 10
Nation of Islam 86–88
neocolonialism 50, 147–148
Niebuhr, Reinhold 22
Nolan, Christopher 42
Novelle Théologie movement 3

Obama, Barack 140, 148, 156
Omeish, Abdullah 187; *Occupation 101* (2006) 186; *The War Around Us* (2014) 186
OMG (Shukla) 55–56, *56*
orthodox Judaism 68
Ortiz, Kaye: *Explorations in Theology and Film* 22
The Other Conquest (Carrasco) 17, 149–150; Indigenous-Spanish relationships 150–153, *151*, *152*; racism in Mexico 150
Otto, Rudolph 128

Pacette, Sister Rose: *Lights Camera, Faith* 24–25
Pan African Film Festival 170
The Passion of Joan of Arc (Dreyer) 41, 45
The Passion of the Christ (Gibson) 79
The Passion Play of Oberammergau 6
Peele, Jordan 188; *Get Out* (2017) 17, 139–143, *142*
Pentecostal Christians 81–83, 131–132
Phalke, D.G.: *Raja Harischandra* (1913) 54
philosophical approach 49–50
philosophical themes 180
The Pilgrim (Chaplin) 18, 104–106, *105*
pilgrimage/quest/road trip 120–125; *Little Miss Sunshine* (2006) 16, 18, 25, 122–126, *124*, *125*; *The Way* 120–122
Plate, S. Brent 4, 30–32, 41, 190; *Cinema and the Re-Creation of the*

World (2008) 5, 30; *The Religion and Film Reader* 13
Plato: *The Republic* 2
political approach 50–51
Polta, Steve 40
Priddy, Ed and John 182
Prophetess Libra 81

Rabbi Shlomo Yitzchachaki 61
racial approach 51
racism 17, 139–143, 149–150, 178; *Burden* (2020) 114, 153–156; in Mexico 150; *The Other Conquest* (1998) 150–153
Rahman, A.R. 143
reception studies approach 32–35, 38–39
reconciliation: interpersonal (Magnolia) 17, 141; racial (Burden) 150
redemption 25–27
redemption and healing 156–157; *Central Station* 157–159, *158*; *Magnolia* 159–163, *161*
Reformed Christianity 27
reincarnation 168–169
Reinhartz, Adele: *The Journal of Biblical Literature* 27; *Scripture on the Silver Screen* 27
relative time 4
religion 1; comedy and 103–104; of Dudeism 76–77; and film dynamics 2–6; and film studies, evolution of 11–14; growth in study 187–192; history in film 6–7; maturation in 180; methodological maturation and expansion (1990s) 12–13; and race 149–156; Roman Catholic scholars in 24; sex, gender roles and 143–149; sexual orientation and 51; specialized studies of 179–181; and theology 40
religion and film: diversification of 179, 188, 189; globalization of 188
Religion, Film, and Visual Culture Group (AAR) 13

religionists, as filmmakers 183–187
religious studies approaches: functionalism and ritual theory 28–29; myths 31–32; world building 30–31
rituals 53; and myth 32
ritual theory 28–29
Rizzo, Gary 42, 43
Robards, Jason 159
The Rocky Horror Picture Show (1975) 6, 59
The Room (2003) 6
Rouch, Jean 127
Rublev, Andrei 16

Saint Augustine 136
Salles, Walter: *Central Station* 17, 157–159, *158*
sangha 75–76, 114
Schaffer, Anthony 110
scholars, as filmmakers 183–187
Schrader, Paul 50; *First Reformed* 11; *Transcendental Style in Film: Ozu, Bresson, Dreyer* 11, 49
science-fiction (sci-fi) films 97–98, 178; *Arrival* 101–102, *102*; *Ex Machina* 98–101
score 42–45
Scorsese, Martin 24; *Kundun* (1997) 70; *Taxi Driver* (1976) 11
The Seashell and the Clergyman 3
Senyonjo, Christopher 147, 148
de Sepúlveda, Juan Ginés: *On the Just Causes for War Against the Indians* 152
A Serious Man (Coen brothers) 61–62, 65
sex/sexuality: and the church 149; in Hinduism 17; and religion 51, 143–149
Shiism 106
Shin Buddhism 72
Shinmom, Aoki: *Coffinman: The Journal of a Buddhist Mortician* 71
Shinran Shonin 72
Shoes (Weber) 7
Shukla, Umesh: *OMG* 55–56, *56*

INDEX 211

shunyata 123
Siddhartha Gautama 69, 102
Sidhwa, Bapsi: *Ice Candy Man* 89
Siegler, Elijah: *Coen: Framing Religion in Amoral Order* 180
Sison, Antonio D. 51; *World Cinema, Theology and the Human* 181
Smalley, Phillips 7
Smith, Johnathan Z. 31
Sobchack, Vivian 189–190
social films 54, 57
social scientific research 32–33
Son of Man (Dornford-May) 79–80
"Sorcery and Cinema" (Artaud) 3
sound 42–45
sound theory, using in religion and film 43–45
Sourniau, Etianne 5; levels of film realities 31
Spanish xenophobia 151
Spiegal, James: *Faith, Film, and Philosophy: Big Ideas on the Big Screen* 179
spirituality 185, 190; relationship between cinema and 2
splagchnizomai 123
"spot-the Christ-figure" approaches 5, 30
Sripariyattiweti, Phra: *A Man Who Can Recall His Past Lives* 166
Ssempa, Martin 147, 148
Star Wars 42, 82
Stoller-Lee, Will 182
Straten-Mcsparran, Rebecca Ver: *Lars von Trier's Cinema: Excess, Evil, and the Prophetic* 180
Suh, Sharon A.: *Silver Screen Buddha: Buddhism in Asian and Western Film* 72, 179
Sundance Film Festival 182–183
Sunni Muslim group 86, 88
Sufi Islam 84, 85

Takita, Yojiro: *Departures* (2009) 18, 53, 71–74, *74*
Tarkovsky, Andrei 47–51, 189; *Andrei Rublev* 47–49, 114–116; *Ivan's Childhood* 47; *Mirror* 47; *Nostalgia* 47; *The Sacrifice* 47; *Sculpting in Time* 47–48, 168
The Ten Commandments (Demille) 60
theodicy 60, 64–65, 139
theological-biblical lenses 22–25; *Concussion* (2013) 23
THX 42
Tibetan Buddhism 70, 71, 123
Tillich, Paul 191; *Theology and Film* 22
time 4
toglen 123
Tonantzin 150, 151
topics, specialized studies of 179–181
transmedia storytelling 191
Tucker, Camille 183–184
Turan, Kenneth 133
Tyler, Edward 31

Uncle Boonmee Who Can Recall His Past Lives (2010) 17, 166–167, *167*
Unorthodox 191
USA 188–189; Nation of Islam in 85–88; race in 139–143, 153–156

Vertov, Dziga 127
Villeneuve, Québecois Denis: *Arrival* 98, 101–102, *102*, 178
"Visions and Prophecies in Cinema" 182
visual media 1
Volf, Miroslav 14
Von Trier, Lars: *Breaking the Waves* 25–27, 78
vrat katha 57

Wach, Joachim 128
Water (Mehta) 36, 37, 50, 89; auteur and cultural studies analysis of 143–145; Hinduism and women's roles 145–147, *146*
Watkins, Gregory 14
The Way (Estevez) 120–122
Weber, Lois 6–7, 188; *Hypocrites* 7–10, *9*, *10*, 177; *Shoes* 7

Weerasethakul, Apichatpong: *Uncle Boonmee Who Can Recall His Past Lives* 17, 166–167, *167*
Weisenfeld, Judith: *Hollywood Be Thy Name: African American Religion in American Film 1929–1949* 51, 180–181
Wells, Justin: *How to Film Truth: The Story of Documentary Film as a Spiritual Journey* 126
white supremacy 141–143, *142*
The Wicker Man (Hardy) 110–112, *111*
Wilberforce, William 16; *Amazing Grace* 117–119
Williams, Roger Ross 188; *God Loves Uganda* 147–148
Windrider Forum 182–183

Winter, Ralph 185
women theologians 22
Wright, Melanie J. 51; *Religion and Film: An Introduction* 13, 39

Yeffeth, Glen: *Taking the Red Pill: Science, Philosophy, and the Religion in the Matrix* 179

Zecca, Ferdinand: *Samson and Delilah* 6
Zen fundamental tenets 53; lessons 77–78
Zierler, Wendy I.: *Movies and Midrash: Popular Film and Jewish Religious Conversation* 62, 179
Zimmer, Hans 42
Zizek, Slavoj 191